THE UNHOLY BIBLE

Blake, Jung and the Collective Unconscious

THE UNHOLY BIBLE

Blake, Jung and the Collective Unconscious

JUNE SINGER

Sigo Press
Boston

SIGO PRESS,
Boston, Massachusetts

Publisher and General Editor: Sisa Sternback-Scott

Library of Congress Cataloging-in-Publication Data

Singer, June.
    The unholy Bible.

    Includes facsim. ed. of Blake's The marriage of
Heaven and Hell (24 plates)
    Bibliography: p.
    Includes index.
    1. Blake, William, 1757-1827—Knowledge—Psychology.
2. Psychology in literature.   3. Subconsciousness
in literature.   4. Archetype (Psychology) in literature.
5. Jung, C. G. (Carl Gustav), 1875-1961.   I. Blake,
William, 1757-1827. Marriage of Heaven and Hell. 1985.
II. Title
PR4148.P8S5   1986   821'.7   85-22139

ISBN 0-938434-24-1
ISBN 0-938434-25-X (pbk.)

In loving memory of Judith and Michael

"He who binds to himself a joy
Doth the winged life destroy;
But he who kisses the joy as it flies
Lives in Eternity's sun rise."

Table of Contents

Preface

When I first explored the writings of C. G. Jung, I found that underneath his complex theory of the structure of the psyche lies a basic principle: respect for the gift of Imagination that makes man at once human and godlike. Jung asserts that while mankind lives in the everyday, empirical world, it is not entirely *of* that world, but is connected by the slender filament of the symbol to a world beyond, which he calls the "collective unconscious." Unlike Jung, Blake did not theorize—he shaped myths and symbols to express his world-view. Jung examined the statements of his patients and the symbol-rich literature of the world with an eye to finding out how the individual could become his most creative self. Blake had the temerity to gaze directly into the abyss and call forth its contents, which he then embellished with vivid images for all to see.

The initial impetus for my study of Blake in relation to the psychology of Jung was the need to write a thesis for my analyst's diploma at the C. G. Jung Institute in Zurich. Blake had been my favorite poet ever since my mother read me his poem "Infant Joy," when I couldn't have been more than three years old. Later, in the course of my personal analysis, when I was breaking with the

collective pressures that had limited me in the past, the words of
Blake that had the greatest significance for me were:

> I must create my own system, or be enslaved by another man's
> I will not reason and compare, my business is to create.

Create I did—the gods helping. Blake was on my mind for weeks.
I read everything on him that I could find, though my sources
were limited to what I could find among the somewhat dusty
volumes at the English Library of Zurich. I found every book
fascinating, as each revealed some hidden aspect of the man about
whose personal life so little was known. One night I woke up at
about two o'clock and reached for the yellow lined pad I used to
record my dreams. I wrote and wrote while the clock at Römerhof
struck the quarter hours and then three. The outline of my thesis
slowly took shape under my pen. Exhausted, I finally finished, put
down my pen, and fell back to sleep.

In the morning when I awoke I half expected to find the paper
blank, as if I'd dreamed it all. But miracle of miracles, it was there
in language so clear that all I had to do was type it just as it was!
I presented it as a proposal for my thesis and it was accepted. I
wrote on Blake's long poem, "The Marriage of Heaven and Hell,"
the problem of the contraries and the final resolution of the
problem of opposites being the paper's major focus: "Without contraries there is no progression." This principle has also been a leitmotif throughout the works of Jung. All the time I was writing,
it was as though Blake stood at my right shoulder and Jung at my
left. I was not bound by the strictures of literary criticism, nor
by adherence to historical fact. The guiding figure was Divine
Imagination, and I allowed myself to be led by It through the
Blakean labyrinth.

When I returned to the United States, I revised and expanded
my Zurich thesis to include Blake's later major "prophetic" works.
The Jung Foundation published my book in a small edition, which
quickly went out of print. Blake's genius continued to inspire my
writing, even as I turned to other subject matters. In my next
book, *Boundaries of the Soul,* I attempted to give my reader a picture of some of Jung's more difficult psychological and philosophical concepts, the works of the poet often articulating these more
clearly than I, as psychologist, could have done. For example, in

creating an impression of how archetypes hidden in the collective
unconscious give rise to species-specific behaviors, I called upon
this passage from Blake:

> With what sense is it that the chicken shuns the rav'nous hawk?
> With what sense does the tame pigeon measure out the expanse?
> With what sense does the bee form cells? have not the mouse
>   and frog
> Eyes and ears and sense of touch? yet are their habitations
> And their pursuits as different as their forms and as their joys.
> Ask the wild ass why he refuses burdens, and the meek camel
> Why he loves man: is it because of eye, ear, mouth or skin,
> Or breathing nostrils? No, for these the wolf and tyger have.
> Ask the blind worm the secrets of the grave, and why her spires
> Love to curl round the bones of death; and ask the rav'nous snake
> Where she gets poison, & the wing'd eagle why he loves the sun;
> And then tell me the thoughts of man, that have been hid of old.

Blake's last great work, "Jerusalem," came to mind as I was
pondering questions about the nature of the "masculine" and
"feminine" aspects combined in each individual—questions whose
resolution led me to write my next two books, *Androgyny* and
Energies of Love. Blake use a mythic form, teeming with images
and symbols, to deal with the theme of the separation and alienation of the masculine and feminine principles in the psyche—
"masculine" and "feminine" here referring not to specific sexual
elements, but rather to archetypal characterizations common to
all mythologies: for instance, the "masculine" rational thinking of
Apollo versus the "feminine" emotional spontaneity associated with
Dionysus. For Blake, "Albion" represents England in the throes
of the Industrial Revolution, enslaved by the soulless machine, the
"looms of Locke." "Jerusalem" is Albion's soul, its anima, the
carrier of the feminine principle. Albion has cast Jersualem
aside—this being the metaphor Blake uses for the triumph of
Reason over Feeling, of the Rational Mind over Imagination.
Blake's vivid descriptions of what happens in a world where the
masculine principle is overdeveloped and the feminine principle
is suppressed provide a framework for my own work on gender and
relationships. I have searched for evidence of feminine wisdom-
figures who bring into being what can only be conceived when
male and female energies engage co-equally in dynamic interplay.

I found Shakti and Sophia, and Shekhinah, the Rose of Sharon, and the Queen of Sheba. Each character in her own way represents the Anima Mundi, that feminine principle which, when separated from its masculine counterpart, throws the external world and the worlds within out of balance. Such a figure is Blake's Jerusalem:

> England! awake! awake! awake!
> Jerusalem thy Sister calls!
> Why wilt thou sleep the sleep of death
> And close her from they ancient wall?
>
> Thy hills and valleys felt her feet
> Gently upon their bosoms move:
> Thy gates beheld sweet Zion's ways:
> Then was a time of joy and love.
>
> And now the time returns again:
> Our souls exult, and London's towers
> Receive the Lamb of God to dwell
> In England's green and pleasant bowers.

When, fifteen years ago, *The Unholy Bible* was first published, neither Jung nor the basic concepts of his work were well known or generally understood. Today the work of Jung is widely known and respected, having undergone a critical revival similar to that accorded to the works of Blake himself—yet I do not believe that the souls of these two men are any more appreciated today than they were by those earlier writers who had only their feelings and intuitions to go by, and who lent their pens to the muses, "the Eternals," even as did William Blake. Now, at last, this psychological interpretation of Blake's work is again available, and I believe the time for it is ripe.

Even in the field of physics, over recent years, many people have come to belive that one cannot understand the universe by tearing it apart and analyzing the pieces. A more wholistic view is becoming recognized in which the relationship between interacting forms is being preceived as more important than those between objects or events. We have come to know that reality is not exactly what it appears to be, for the range of our senses and our intellect is limited and cannot give us access to the infinite. Only through dreams and meditation, through intuition and imagination, can we find evidence for an invisible Source behind all that we see. Blake, of course said it better: "What is now prov'd was only once imagin'd."

The prominent theoretical physicist, David Bohm, speaks of an "implicate order" and an "explicate order." He sees the implicate order as the Source of the universe, in which is enfolded all the potentialities of existence. This higher order, so to speak, unfolds into the manifest order, the world in which we have our being, and which Bohm calls the "explicate order." Seen subjectively, it is the unconscious that unfolds, beginning with our birth (or perhaps, as some belive, with conception), expanding as consciousness throughout our lives in this explicate order until, in old age, we begin the process of folding up again. At our death, our consciousness is again enfolded into the implicate order.

For Blake there is an archway dividing this world from that mysterious one, and above the archway is written:

> There is a Void outside of existence, which if enter'd into
> Englobes itself and becomes a Womb . . .

And for Jung:

> Life has always seemed to me like a plant that lives on its
> rhizome. Its true self is invisible, hidden in the rhizome. The
> part that appears above ground lasts only a single summer. Then
> it withers away, an ephemeral apparition. When we think of the
> unending growth and decay of life and civilizations, we cannot
> escape the impression of absolute nullity. Yet I have never lost a
> sense of something that lives and endures underneath the central
> flux. What we see is the blossom, which passes. The rhizome
> remains.

The beauty of Blake's oeuvre derives from the fact that he didn't only *write* about the contents of the collective unconsciousness, he experienced them as well. He conveyed his eidetic images to paper, both in words and picture. He printed "in the infernal method, by corrosives, which in Hell are salutory and medicinal, melting apparent surfaces away, and displaying the infinite which was hid."

This then is the key to the mystery of Blake's "Bible of Hell," which I have called *The Unholy Bible*. Blake's testament avows its purpose: to penetrate the walls of ancient traditions, built with the stones of dogma. It acknowledges one Source behind the universe, giving rise to all the gods in this manifest world who, despite their grandeur and majesty, their angers and their jealousies, are but fragments of the invisible Whole.

Introduction

BLAKE'S WRITINGS HAVE NOT BEEN VERY WELL KNOWN UNTIL recently, with the exception of some of his shorter poems, namely those of the early years of his life. His style is not easily understood and the symbolic figures of his mythology are obscure in meaning. His early work appears deceptively simple, but already the major problem that was to occupy the thoughts of his mature years was expressed in the unforgettable poem:

> Tyger! Tyger! burning bright
> In the forests of the night,
> What immortal hand or eye
> Could frame thy fearful symmetry?

This poem expresses the god-like passion and ruthlessness of the king of the beasts but ends with a question, a question already asked in his poem, "Little Lamb, who made thee?" Here, however, the question takes on a new and deeper significance, foreshadowing the profound problem of good and evil, of submissiveness and aggression, or suppression of desire and its expression that was to occupy Blake all the rest of his life.

When the stars threw down their spears,
And water'd heaven with their tears,
Did he smile his work to see?
Did he who made the Lamb make thee?

Tyger! Tyger! burning bright
In the forests of the night,
What immortal hand or eye
Dare frame thy fearful symmetry?

Evidently Blake was beginning to face the enigma of God in his dual nature—gentle and loving *and* prolific and devouring.

Blake was thirty-three when he expressed his conflict over this dichotomy in *The Marriage of Heaven and Hell,* the book that marks the turning point from simple or seemingly simple lyrics to the later profound prophetic works. In this short book, consisting of twenty-seven engraved plates with text and pictures and decorative marginal designs, Blake portrayed the problem of good and evil and announced his belief that the rule of order, convention and morality expressed in the then current codes of behavior as taught by law and the churches was static, restrictive and deadening, while the free exercise of desire and the energies of the psyche were life-giving. To him, just as to Milton in *Paradise Lost,* the Devil represented the life-giving and creative energy. He was the true hero, bringing redemption to a world grown old and stale.

In her commentary on *The Marriage of Heaven and Hell,* June K. Singer brings this view and its implications concerning the creative process forcibly before us. Especially in the section on "The Proverbs of Hell" does her amplification of the material shed a beam of light on the problem Blake was facing, a problem that is no longer seen only by one or two creative minds, as it was in the eighteenth century. Today it has erupted into the open. For the lid of repression has slipped aside and energy, instinctive energy, is rampant. Excess is the order of the day, at least among the young. In these "Proverbs" the problems we are facing in the twentieth century were already set forth by a creative genius, and a solution or resolution of the problems

involved was suggested. Instead of facing the either-or of the opposites, we are directed to consider the cyclic form of energy expressed in the seasons: "In seed time learn, in harvest teach, in
winter enjoy." The creative process, we are told, follows a
similar law: receptivity at seed time must be followed by productivity and harvest. "Exuberance is beauty." "If the fool
would persist in his folly he would become wise." It is the law
of the enantiodromia as enunciated by Heraclitus and elaborated by Jung in his discussion of the functioning of the
opposites.

These "Proverbs" also describe the fourfold nature of man
as an expression of the divine nature within him. But if this
divine image is to be recognized man, must really live according
to his intrinsic individuality and give voice to his "desire."
This requires that he recognize the individual nature of his
experience, of his perceptions of the object and, even more, of
his subjective reaction to what he perceives. For this is individual and unique; it is indeed one evidence of his relation to
the divine within him.

The fact that Blake calls his aphorisms "Proverbs" suggests
that he considers them to be of ancient origin, the formulation
of wisdom acquired by ages of experience. Indeed they are expressions of *archetypes,* the term Jung uses to express the fundamental energetic patterns underlying psychic functioning. Dr.
Singer sums up her discussion of the Proverbs dealing with the
fourfold nature of man by saying: "We may conclude, therefore,
that the archetypal images produced by Blake in his symbolic
visions have this in common with those produced by the dreams
of modern man. Their meaning is that man is able to have the
experience of the *God within.*" But for Blake this necessarily
includes the acceptance of a man's desire, of energy, even of excess, an attitude which he says marks the man as "of the Devil's
party."

The Song of Liberty is not actually a part of *The Marriage
of Heaven and Hell* but is always published together with it. It
is a universalized expression of the change wrought by revolution. The old king, like the sun, sets in the west. The new
saviour is born as a child of fire; his coming is proclaimed by a
prodigious cry, for his advent will spell destruction of old values

and freedom for those formerly oppressed by the rule of the old order. This *Song* heralds the prophetic work that occupied Blake for the remainder of his life.

The Marriage of Heaven and Hell was followed by a series of six books which Blake called "Prophecies," in which the ideas first mentioned in *The Marriage* are elaborated. These minor prophecies are mostly written in the form of poetic dramas whose protagonists are mythological figures representing psychological functions and whose subject matter is a myth of creation. This myth is carried forward and culminates in *The Four Zoas* where Blake portrays the outcome of his inner conflict in the experience of an inner marriage, the *coniunctio* of the fourfold nature of man. *The Four Zoas* was never engraved and remained during his lifetime as a secret and sacred happening of the poet's inmost heart.

Jerusalem was Blake's final major work, bringing together the ideas enunciated in *The Four Zoas*. The fourfold city in Blake's mythological scheme is the counterpart and opposite of Albion, symbol of fallen man. *Jerusalem* is concerned with the union of the four aspects of man, making this unity a numinous symbol corresponding to the inner image of the divine which has been in man's unconscious since the beginning.

It is not possible in a short introduction to consider the whole range of Blake's work that Dr. Singer unfolds before us. The work brings us a grandiose vision of man in his relation to the dual aspect of God and the struggle he is compelled to undertake with the many contradictory elements in his own experience. The later works of Blake, the "Prophecies," are not an attempt to foretell the future in a historical sense but are rather warnings that we today would consider as referring to psychological events occurring in individual men and more especially, perhaps, in mankind. For example, Blake says, "Every honest man is a Prophet; he utters his opinion both of private and public matters. Thus: If you go on So, the result is So. He never says, such a thing shall happen let you do what you will. A Prophet is a Seer, not an Arbitrary Dictator."

Dr. Singer handles this often abstruse text with remarkable insight and has produced out of seemingly chaotic material a meaningful whole. When properly understood these prophetic books can at last take their place among the literary and psychological masterworks of English literature.

A final chapter on the psychological aspects of the vision brings this study to a close. The book is more than a critique or even an interpretation of Blake. It carries his ideas on into the psychological realm and makes his profound insight accessible to the modern reader, whether his interest is literary or psychological. Dr. Singer has steeped herself in Blake's strange mythological world without losing her own standpoint in the twentieth century, so that she is able to relate, even to translate, his intuitive grasp of the unconscious background of life into terms that are appropriate to the present day and so make them accessible to contemporary man. The result is that we are introduced to a way of thinking about problems that are not only perplexing today but which have also concerned mankind down the ages. They have been couched in language appropriate to each generation, to each cultural stage of development. First, when entirely projected onto a metaphysical world, they appeared as mythology and the affairs of the gods; then, when seen in terms of the rational intellect, they appeared as philosophical speculation and rational enlightenment; now, in our day, they have been rediscovered and voiced in psychological language. If we are to carry forward the quest for consciousness versus the unconscious these problems must be experienced consciously. This is the task and the responsibility of each generation. Release from the compulsion of raw instinct can be found by man, not by repressing but by giving full expression to *all* his desires, not necessarily in overt behavior but rather in inner creative activity. In this way man may become whole. For when he is free to live *what* he is, man shows himself to be motivated by spiritual impulses as well as by blind instincts and when both are given freedom to live they do not cancel each other out but produce a condition moving toward the wholeness of the individual. This is the truth that Blake proclaimed in his "Proverbs of Hell," and it is also the most fundamental insight that psychology has brought us. The process of individuation, as Jung has shown, is based on the antinomy and reunion of the opposites—of the carnal instincts and of spirit. Interestingly enough, while Blake discussed the problems involved in the difficult and fundamental reconciliation of body and spirit under the imagery of a marriage—a marriage of above and below, of Heaven and Hell—we find the same symbolism in Revelations where the culmination of man's lifelong effort and devotion will be found in the marriage consummated in Heaven between the Lamb and Jerusalem. Jung, too, basing himself on his psychological researches into the dreams and fantasies of modern people, writes of this reconciliation under the symbol of a marriage, a strange marriage, the *mysterium coniunctionis,* in which consciousness and the unconscious are united.

These things are not easily understood; they belong to the mystery of man's psychic nature, and Dr. Singer has expressed them in psychological terms without explaining them away. One reads her book with a sense that it is indeed dealing with profound problems of the human psyche and is grateful that the author succeeds in keeping her feet on the ground while at the same time she is able to penetrate the mystery of Blake's vision through her own poetic feeling.

M. Esther Harding
New York, May 1970

"Every man carries heaven and hell with him in this world . . ."

Jacob Boehme

1
Approaching Blake

READ WILLIAM BLAKE's *The Marriage of Heaven and Hell*
with your uninhibited feelings as well as with your intellect, and
you will know why the author tells us that at the end of life
Heaven and Hell are joined. Flames of desire lick at man's heels
as he hurries through his days. At the moment of death they
merge with the fragile visions of the sublime which inspired
him, coloring his ideas and shaping them into graceful images.
In one evanescent moment the Devil, boldly with eyes afire, or
subtly disguised, clasps a shining Angel in his embrace. Opposites which struggled within the spirit of man while he walked
the earth are united now in one vast paroxysm. Contraries are
no longer set one against the other. Differences are resolved into
a cloud that dissipates upward. A small mound of dust remains
upon the ground.

We have few documented facts concerning those days in
Blake's troubled life when Heaven and Hell vied for domi-
nance. His record is his strange unearthly work as poet, painter
and self-styled prophet. Only the ground bears witness to the
day in which he vanished into the anonymity of a pauper's grave
where "within two days of his remains being lowered into the

1

earth those of another were placed above him and on the following day yet another body was placed above that." [1]

Most of what we know about Blake is discovered in the reading of his poetic and prophetic works, at times so obscure as to
baffle the patient literary scholar, at times so brilliant as to have
stirred the creative spirits of such men as Swinburne, Shelley,
D. G. Rossetti and Yeats. A small band of Blake cultists was
quietly gathering adherents from the time of Blake's maturity
until a century later when one of their number, Herbert
Jenkins, devoted several years to searching out the place where
the body of Blake was buried. Jenkins located the unmarked
plot in Bunham Fields which had been used on eight occasions,
three times before and four times after Blake's interment, without even a headstone to mark the place.

Contemporary knowledge of Blake's personal history was
scant: his name was missing from the encyclopedias of his day.
Rare mentions occurred in biographical dictionaries, and those
were sketchy and inaccurate. Yet between his death in 1827 and
the appearance of the first biography in 1863, a body of memo-
rabilia about Blake emerged which was to create for him a
reputation as a unique genius. The material for *The Life of
William Blake* was collected by Alexander Gilchrist out of conversations with many of the people still living who had known
Blake personally.

Gilchrist had begun to cast about, in 1855, for information
for his biography of Blake. An industrious researcher, he was
moved (sometimes in conflicting directions) by a passion for
accuracy and a love for his subject. He contacted many close
friends of Blake: Linnell, Tatham, Palmer, Richmond, and
Crabb Robinson. Reflecting the uncritical opinions of this tiny
group of Blakean enthusiasts, he wrote of the poet's style:

One must almost be born with a sympathy for it. He neither wrote
nor drew for the many, hardly for workaday men at all, rather for
children and angels; himself a 'divine child,' whose playthings were
sun, moon, and stars, the heavens and the earth.[2]

Gilchrist's book abounds with anecdotes ascribing to Blake
a personality that first awes people by its ingenuous reference to
a world beyond the reach of the senses, then warms them with

evidence of his very real contact with that world and his ability
to draw from it tremendous sustenance in the form of psychic
energy. Gilchrist tells of young students and artists who approached Blake for counsel and advice on how to come into
contact with that "other world" in which new concepts arise
and visions have their birth. Although Blake labored at his art
and his handicraft every day of his adult life, he managed to find
time for gentle discourse with those who would carry on his
legend, to speak with them concerning the richness of immediate experience that they might enjoy "if the doors of perception were cleansed." [3]

Recollections of Blake's conversations, notes and letters, annotations scrawled on the pages of books in his library, and
selections from his major works made up the nucleus of material
from which Gilchrist worked. He pieced this material together
with such admiration and fascination that his writing often
took on the quality of the stylistically elaborate Victorian
eulogy. Were this not enough to burden the text, Gilchrist
died before his work was complete. His wife Anne finished it,
adding the weight of her own emotional attachments to the
subject of the work as well as to the writer and assembler of the
"facts." Mrs. Gilchrist is generally credited with having written
at least one-third of the text of the Gilchrist biography. Thus
it is a romanticized collection of memoirs and encomiums that
give us the "definitive" biography of Blake, and it is upon
this work that all later writings dealing with his life are based.
It is no wonder, then, that those who have become seriously
interested in the real Blake have cursorily passed over the
narrative of his personal history and have concerned themselves primarily with the content of his work.

In a recently published annotated bibliography on Blake,[4]
editors Bentley and Nurmi insist that Gilchrist's is still, in many
respects, the best biography, though one reason for its in-
dispensibility is a defect. As Anne Gilchrist said, "Unfortu-
nately it was a tradition in the Gilchrist family to avoid notes,
to recast the text rather than to use them." [5] Alexander and
Anne Gilchrist, and William Michael and Dante Gabriel Rossetti are known to have had close contacts with a large number
of people who had known Blake more or less intimately. The

information which these people supplied was oral, not specified
as to origin by Gilchrist, and is often now not traceable. As
a consequence we are forced to depend entirely upon Gilchrist
for many facts which cannot be verified elsewhere, and we do
not even know who his oral authorities were. But Nurmi and
Bently are able to cite many examples which illustrate how
very careful and responsible Gilchrist and his collaborators
were. The editors feel that the sources were treated with great
respect and accuracy, and we must add that it was not altogether Gilchrist's fault if the friends of Blake were inordinately
affected by the captivating quality of the poet's personality.
Blake has that effect on people.

What we do not know about the interaction between Blake
and his environment is more than compensated for by what we
are told in his writings concerning his relationship with a subjective world which held for him the dazzle of an imagery
against which his everyday experiences showed so dim in comparison that he found them scarcely worth committing to
paper.*

The doctrine of William Blake is concerned with a confused
assemblage of sexual desires and creative impulses arising
within the depths of the individual and their encounters with
the limitations and restraints which seemed to the author to
be imposed by reason, logic and law. Blake preaches a vast
gospel of *liberty of the spirit* to man, whom he sees as a victim
of tyranny in an eternal struggle against his chains.

It is no accident that Blake has become a hero of today's
radical student. Deeply impressed by the tempo of unrestrained
activity in the American and French Revolutions, with all of
their social consequences, Blake applied Revolutionary principles to his reflection upon the dynamic development of the individual. He was willing to upset all "establishments," both
religious and political; his writing exhorted each man to search
out his own moral and spiritual values. He adopted an anarchi-
cal position vis-à-vis the orthodox positions of contemporary
Christianity and the traditional notions of good and evil. Ra-

---

* J. Bronowski says that Blake experienced "eidetic images," that is,
when he thought, his thoughts appeared as images not in his mind
but outside himself.

tional and scientific beliefs which were being enunciated in the Age of Enlightenment were reversed by Blake in his concentration upon inner images which derived from man's deep and essential emotions rather than from his acquired intellectual or technical skills. In this respect Blake anticipated the work of the contemporary depth psychologist who recognizes that every outer event is affected by the person who experiences it and that his emotional as well as his cognitive responses are elemental parts of the phenomenon being observed. Furthermore, the images in many of Blake's books, particularly his later works, shed identity with their time or place and acquire the universal quality of fairy tale motifs and mythologems which recur over and over in widely separated places. Paradoxically, it is just this universality of theme and style that sets Blake apart as the prophet of the individual, for with his emancipation from the stated attitudes of the contemporary English tradition he was thrown upon his own resources to create an independent personal philosophy which would support him in his lonely search for patterns of meaning.

The prodigious quantity of work produced by Blake may be roughly separated into an early period and a later period, with the division between being marked by the composition of *The Marriage of Heaven and Hell,* when Blake was in his middle thirties. Several of the early works were lyrical in nature. A collection, *Poetical Sketches,* was written while Blake was still in his teens. Only two of the early books of poetry, *Songs of Innocence* and *Songs of Experience,* were printed during his lifetime. The *Songs of Innocence* were mostly simple in form with a delicate quality and a deliberate, although not always regular, rhythm. In many of them a charming naiveté veiled a depth of feeling and a sensitivity to symbolism which exalted such homely themes as "The Little Boy Lost," "The Chimney Sweeper." or "The Lamb." But Blake's entire work might have been forgotten in the years after his death were it not for one poem in *Songs of Experience* in which the striking image achieved immediate popularity. Almost every English schoolchild knows it by heart, yet its implications stir the most sophisticated to ponder the mystery of the ultimate creative power.

6

THE UNHOLY BIBLETHE UNHOLY BIBLE

The Tyger

Tyger! Tyger! burning bright
In the forests of the night,
What immortal hand or eye
Could frame thy fearful symmetry?

In what distant deeps or skies
Burnt the fire of thine eyes?
On what wings dare he aspire?
What the hand dare seize the fire?

And what shoulder, & what art,
Could twist the sinews of thy heart?
And when thy heart began to beat,
What dread hand? & what dread feet?

What the hammer? what the chain?
In what furnace was thy brain?
What the anvil? what dread grasp
Dare its deadly terrors clasp?

When the stars threw down their spears,
And water'd heaven with their tears,
Did he smile his work to see?
Did he who made the Lamb make thee?

Tyger! Tyger! burning bright
In the forests of the night,
What immortal hand or eye
Dare frame thy fearful symmetry? [6]

The lasting and overwhelming response to this poem acknowledges the recognition of a central concept in Blake's
work. This is the need to become aware of the other side of
God, the side not accepted either by social agreement or by
orthodox religious practice. Blake says that while he who
made the Lamb is worshipped and praised in all the churches,
he who fashioned the Tyger to pierce the darkness of the

tangled forest with his perceptive eye, he is also God. God of the Lamb is worshipped at prescribed intervals, but God of the Tyger is held in fear by day and night, for none may escape him when he pursues. Blake wrote as though he felt that enough had been said about that symbol of gentleness which is traditionally associated with Jesus. He was more concerned with the fierce and the frightful which threatens innocence and light. And it follows that such a man would address himself boldly also to the darker area of man's life, which is hidden in shadow and must be invaded and explored if man is to approach any degree of self-awareness.

Less notable works of Blake's early period include various poems, some of which incorporate narratives based on the legendary history of England. Others are hymns to Nature in an idealized form. There are some meditative essays which reflect moods more than thoughts, and there is a ribald satire on contemporary philosophy and the arts titled "An Island in the Moon," which was a euphemism for England in the Romantic era. He annotated Lavater's popular *Aphorisms on Man* and Swedenborg's *Divine Love*. He wrote two iconoclastic tracts against Deism, *There is no Natural Religion* and *All Religions are One;* the latter begins with a typically Blakean subtitle: "The voice of one crying in the Wilderness."

The first two of his many long narrative poems belong to this period also. They are allegories and were written around 1789 and named for their leading characters: *Tiriel,* and *The Song of Thel.* Next came *The French Revolution,* the one work of Blake which appears, superficially, to be most related to the problems of his contemporary world. But this work, too, when we begin to examine it, will be seen as less pertinent to its age than to its author.

It was during the period between 1790 and 1793 that Blake's concern with inner development began to take precedence over everything else and compelled him to compose the extremely personal volume which holds the key to his creative life: *The Marriage of Heaven and Hell.*

Around 1793 Blake entered the most prolific period of his career which continued unabatedly for almost thirty years until his death. During this time he managed to earn a meager living

mostly by making engravings on commission for book illustrations. His real devotion and energy, however, was lavished on
the literary works that constituted, in effect, an entire mythology having as its subject the Fall and Generation of Man. There
were three major manuscripts: *Vala, or the Four Zoas; Milton;*
and *Jerusalem.* They are voluminous, elaborate and abstruse.
Images topple over upon each other as in Michelangelo's "Last
Judgment"—the effect is one of splendid tumult, but it has been
planned and executed with passionate painstaking. There is a
mysterious surging energy in these three works, but the dynamism is not apparent to everyone who reads them. The sensitive reader who is attracted to the grandeur of the epic form
can put aside logic and permit the sensuous words to flow over
him like an exhilarating surf. The literary scholar tries to
understand the meaning by deciphering the language of symbolism that Blake has constructed. The analytical psychologist
sees it primarily as a projection of unconscious factors in Blake
upon mythological characters which arise from transpersonal or
archetypal foundations.

The question may well be asked: Why, if the three major
works are so important, do we propose to emphasize this obscure and little known volume before going on to the later
works? *The Marriage of Heaven and Hell* is a small book consisting of twenty-four plates of text and illustration, both
engraved by Blake's own hand. Relatively little attention has
been paid to this book until now, possibly because it has been
so difficult to classify. It is the one book which is undeniably
subjective, and in which Blake writes of mystical experiences of
so private a nature that in approaching them one is often
seized by an acute sense of embarrassment. Yet appearing as it
did, between the youthful period when Blake was primarily
concerned with his impressions of the world of nature and with
social and political problems and the time of maturity when he
was occupied with the underlying forms that determine the
lives of men and nations, *The Marriage of Heaven and Hell*
challenges us to find out whether its pages may contain hidden
clues to the discovery of the ingenerate factors in the spiritual
transformation and creative development of its author.

The very circumstance that the work *is* so personal predisposes it to psychological analysis. Even more important than the fact that Blake is here relating his personal philosophy is his willingness to expose his most improbable fantasies and visions which, like dreams, illuminate the dark and murky regions of the unconscious.

Not that Blake was himself necessarily aware of what he was doing, in the sense of the modern depth psychologist who concerns himself with the relationship between what is conscious and what is unconscious in man. The hypothesis of the unconscious as a real entity which complements the conscious life of man and which can be scientifically investigated and systematically integrated into the conscious ego was first enunciated by Freud. He admitted that the concept of the unconscious was not new to him, that throughout history many persons had been aware of forces which were not and could not be known in their entirety by man. In his lecture on "The Meaning of Symptoms," [7] Freud refers to Pierre Janet who, in the 1880's regarded neurotic symptoms as expressions of *idées inconscientes*. Freud felt that to Janet the unconscious had been nothing more than a manner of speaking, *une façon de parler,* that he had nothing "real" in mind, and that it was his own task to establish beyond doubt the reality of the unconscious through the study of its manifestations in everyday life and in dreams. Thus, before Freud it cannot be said that the unconscious was conceived as a functioning entity.

It remained for Carl G. Jung to delineate this unconscious entity as a reality with which man could consciously and deliberately attempt to carry on a dialectical realtionship. Consciousness and the unconscious flowed in and out of one another in earlier times as now, but in Blake's day they were not differentiated analytically, that is, by using specific techniques to arrive at a position where both might be viewed with some objectivity and their influence upon one another observed and utilized for therapeutic purposes or for the more complete development or reconstruction of the human personality. Without this relative objectivity there could be, nevertheless, a dynamic relationship between the conscious aspect of man and the dark forces so strange and incomprehensible to him. Always there have been those who could experience these forces as tremendous powers

which might threaten to overwhelm them at certain times and
at other times infuse them with a creative urge which would
drive them to produce original ideas, works of art or new
scientific concepts. Blake was fascinated by this extra dimension of psychic life and he was impelled to write of how it
manifested itself in him. Without the detachment of the
modern psychologist, he wrote of his own experience more as a
participant than as an observer and yet the raw material of the
inner drama is all there. From his stance at the end of the
eighteenth century Blake described visions which appeared to
him. The depth psychologist would say they were autonomous
images emerging from the unconscious and he would say that
Blake was not aware of this. In the future men may smile as
they talk about our twentieth century "primitive conceptuali-
zations." Other perspectives give rise to other illusions, and
who is to say which resembles reality more closely? Our position enables us to take a step away from Blake and to consider
his writing as descriptive of the psychological processes that
were going on in him. This is not to imply that those processes
are basically different in kind from those which are going on
in every man. It is only that, acting upon his naive conviction
that what he wrote was dictated by an unseen voice and that
his paintings were no more than reproductions of what the
inner eye had already perceived, Blake threw a brilliant light
into a realm that for most men is sheathed in the darkness of
disbelief.

Whatever it was that happened within Blake during the
writing of *The Marriage of Heaven and Hell,* the work was
followed by a tremendous burst of creative activity. Before
writing this book his production was relatively slight and
sparse. Afterwards he was able to labor with unflagging energy,
to the exclusion of virtually every other interest, even without
pausing in times of illness. It would appear that new sources
of energy became available to him during the composition of
this work and remained with him throughout the rest of his
life. To come to an appreciation of what the ongoing psychological processes may have been, it will be necessary to
examine in detail the work itself.

The slim volume contains traces of all the spiritual contents of Blake's life and writings. But its elements are not ordered; they pour forth in profusion. Poetry declaiming man's expulsion from Eden is followed by a scene at the tomb of Christ which Blake uses to illustrate his doctrine of the dynamic contraries. Then comes a bombastic passage in which Blake rejects and replaces what he sees as the essence of "All Bibles and sacred codes." Next he examines with studied indelicacy the nature of Desire and asks whether it is from Hell or from the Angels. Then he encapsulates himself in the first "Memorable Fancy." There are five of these, each of which leads the reader into a grey half-world of tangled images through which he can scarcely find a path. Between two of these Fancies is a group of about seventy statements, ranging from quiet wonder to shocking blasphemy, which Blake calls the "Proverbs of Hell." They are a series of unconventional reactions to the popular aphorisms of his day. Interspersed through the manuscript are such gems as Blake's summary in a few lines of the entire historical development of man's concept of God and bitingly ironical criticisms of his former teacher Swedenborg, whom he has left far behind, clinging to the coattails of organized religion. The end of the book glimpses the beginning of a rapprochement between the bitter opponents, Angel and Devil, but it is only the barest beginning.

The Marriage of Heaven and Hell raises a number of problems which circumambulate a central theme: *Every phenomenon consciously experienced by man is accompanied by its polar opposite in the unconscious, and the psychological state of man is determined by the kind of relationship which he is able to maintain between these opposites.* Blake did not use this language to formulate his belief; indeed, the phraseology might have been taken directly from the psychological writings of C. G. Jung. It is inevitable that a Jungian analyst, in attempting to understand and interpret the Blakean doctrine, should see in *The Marriage* a pre-form of certain of Jung's essential concepts. Jung himself found pre-forms of his system in the myths and legends of the primitives, in the Tantric Yoga of India, in alchemical studies and many other places. Universal principles describing the psychological constitution of man are expressed in literature and religion and science, where men freely seek to know themselves through experience or experiment rather than through acceptance of the collective projection. Blake looked unashamedly at his own soul—came face to face with the unconscious, if you will—and then enunciated principles which would be empirically tested and affirmed by Jung a century later, to form some of the fundamental postulates of analytical psychology.* The back and forth between a balanced tension and a precarious imbalance in the psyche of Blake was in itself a dynamic out of which creative activity could proceed, in the presence of favorable conditions. This will become apparent through the study of the text of *The Marriage of Heaven and Hell.*

Some of the major problems which concern Blake in this work are: the basic duality of man as expressed in the terms "material and spiritual" or "body and soul" and the nature of the relationship between them; the clash of the forces of freely flowing libidinal energy with the inhibiting forms of reason; the confrontation of conscious personal attitudes with the accepted values of contemporary society; and the relationship of the personal unconscious (corresponding to the Freudian concept of the unconscious, whose contents consist primarily of instincts and discarded or repressed material deriving from individual experience) and a collective unconscious (consisting of typical patterns of human experience and behavior, *i.e.,* of the inherited potentiality of psychic functioning as in the psychology of C. G. Jung) which is shared by all mankind.

These issues tend to dissipate into meaningless phrases if they are dealt with only as abstract concepts. Abstractions lend themselves better to mathematics and the natural sciences where one can deal with measurable data. Many problems of the individual psyche are not measurable in the same way, that is, they cannot be compared with a predetermined standard of measurement, for they are subject to an infinite complexity of variables which serve to color each experience differently. There are more suitable ways in which the unique qualities of individual man can be described and communicated, and

---

* *Analytical psychology* is the Jungian term which corresponds to the Freudian *psychoanalysis.*

Blake, being both poet and painter, found in the language of symbolism the natural expression of his thoughts and feelings. Through the brilliance of the symbol made visible in images he was able to achieve a vital and meaningful encounter with the indescribable forming-elements which are the symbols' matrix. The problems which Blake raises in *The Marriage of Heaven and Hell* are, in part, problems of the book itself, growing out of the implication of the title: marriage—the forming of a union or, at the very least, a supportable relationship between the opposites which man finds within himself. They are also problems of Blake as a man and his problems as a creative person—as a totality. A brief survey of the first thirty-three years of his life, up to the time he began working on *The Marriage,* will indicate some of the important factors in his background, some experiences, relationships and trends of thought, which brought him to the crucial period that largely determined the future course of his creative activity.

2
The First Half of Life

No star heralded the birth of the man whom Gilchrist introduced in the biography as "the most spiritual of all artists." It was a gray 28th day of November in the year 1757, in London, when Catherine Blake bore her second child, William. James, father of the brood which was to number four, was a moderately prosperous clothing merchant in Golden Square at 28 Broad Street. At that time the once fashionable district was still in a highly respectable condition; it had yet to sink into the seedy category. William was christened on the 11th of December—one in a batch of six—from Grinling Gibbons' ornate font in Wren's noble Palladian church of St. James. The name attached to him in the group ceremony was the first in the category of many outward appurtenances that held little significance for him. It was detached at the time of his burial, again in an impersonal setting, a mass grave with no headstone. The names of things were their objective labels, and Blake was primarily concerned with the singular appearance of the object to the subject, as is any true introvert.

> The Sun's Light when he unfolds it
> Depends on the Organ that beholds it.[1]

Conservatism in outlook marked young William's first years,

and the aspirations of his parents for him were limited. James was not a man to insist on any more education for his children than might be necessary for them to be able to secure their own financial independence. Nor did James have any preconceived notions about how this education was to be achieved. When William had grasped the fundamentals of reading and writing and showed no further inclination toward further formal cultivation of the intellect, his father agreed that what he had was sufficient. From then on most of William's knowledge was self-acquired.

Living on the edge of town, Blake spent a great deal of his time sauntering out into the countryside, enjoying the green fields and pleasant villages and groves. He strode the "sweet hill and vale and sylvan wilds" of rural Dulwich. Beyond stretched hilly Sydenham to the south; eastward in the purple distance, Blackheath; or to the Southwest a favorite day's wandering would take him through the ancient rustic town of Croydon which in those days was a compact, clean and cheerful Surrey village near the fertile verdant meadows of Walton upon Thames. The beauty of those scenes in his youth was a lifelong reminiscence. Blake stored his mind with the lovely pastoral images that were to appear over and over again in his poetry and prose.

By this time Blake had discovered that it was possible to disregard the immediate world of practicality in favor of a compellingly attractive playground in the limitless fields of imagination. At the age of eight or nine, as he subsequently related, he experienced his first vision. Sauntering along on Peckham Rye, the boy looked up and saw a tree filled with angels, their bright translucent wings bespangling every branch like stars. He casually related the incident when he returned home, as he was always to speak of his visions in later years, with the most matter-of-fact tones. Only through the gentle intercession of his mother was he spared a beating at the hands of his father for having told a lie.[2]

This is the first time in Blake's life, according to our records, that angel images appear. Another time he sees them on a summer morning disporting themselves among the haymakers. Here the Angel symbolizes the spiritual presence which accompanies man on his worldly experiences, and participates with him if he is able to perceive it. The Angel is to accompany Blake throughout his lifetime, but its symbolic character and meaning will undergo many changes. Later the Angel will act as a mediator between the aspects of man associated with his boundless energies and those which exert controls upon the expression of such energies. But at this time the angels expressed pure joy, leading the boy beyond himself, into a more colorful and more delightful world than that known by his contemporaries.

Gilchrist relates that one day a traveler at the Blake home was recounting some of the wonders he had seen in a foreign city. "Do you call that splendid?" broke in young William. "I should call a city splendid in which the houses were of gold, the pavement of silver, the gates ornamented with precious stones." [3] Such an outburst might have caused the hearer to think that it was uttered by someone more than a little crazed, except that it came from the lips of a child. But the vision never faded and, near the end of Blake's life when he produced his masterpiece, *Jerusalem,* he wrote about such a splendid city which he had experienced as a symbol of profound numinosity:

O lovely mild Jerusalem! O Shiloh of Mount Ephriam!
I see thy Gates of precious stones, thy Walls of gold & silver. [4]

By the time William was nine years old his talent for drawing was evident. Almost from the time his hand could hold a pencil, he had been scrawling rough likenesses of men and animals and making timid copies of pictures. His father, appreciating his interest, allowed him to visit museums and the salesrooms of art dealers, where he could find pictures to copy and often receive free instruction. At ten he was sent to Mr. Pars' drawing school, the preparatory school for juvenile artists then in vogue. Pars was a chaser, a craftsman who embossed designs on metal. This decorative art was becoming less and less popular; consequently its decadence led Pars into the junior art-academy profession. In his school much drawing was done from plaster casts of ruined temples which he had brought home from Greece. Some of Pars' drawings are to be seen today in the Elgin Room of the British Museum, along with the Parthenon marbles from which he worked. There was never any drawing from the living figure at Pars'.

When William was fourteen the practicalities of life asserted themselves and could not be avoided. James Blake, recognizing that his son would never be an asset in his business, agreed to apprentice the boy to an engraver—a suitable trade in line with the boy's talents and requiring less expensive training than that needed by an aspiring painter. William was taken by his father to the studio of one William Wynne Ryland, an artist of considerable talents and even, some said, of genius; but the boy himself raised an unexpected objection and the negotiation failed. "Father," said William after the two had left the studio, "I do not like that man's face: it looks as though he will live to be hanged." Wyland was an accomplished and agreeable man so the statement seemed hardly justified, yet the boy must have intuited from his features and manner the basic dishonesty of character which was later to lead him to financial embarrassments, then to forgery, and eventually to the steps of the gallows.

Blake served an apprenticeship with a man of lesser reputation, James Basire, an engraver of dry, hard, monotonous but painstaking style. Under him Blake learned to copy faithfully whatever was put before him, and he was said to be diligent. This was the youth's first exposure to the restraints of rigorous technical standards. It was the first time that Blake had been forced to conform in his work to pre-established patterns. His work at Mr. Pars' had been not nearly so demanding. Yet without this difficult and exacting training it is doubtful whether Blake would have been able later to convey in any kind of communicable form the experiences of his often chaotic visions.

The first two years of Blake's apprenticeship went smoothly enough so far as is known, but then two new apprentices were added to the establishment and they completely destroyed the harmony. Basire said of Blake, "He was too simple, and they too cunning." Because Blake evidently refused to take his master's part against his fellow-apprentices he was sent off to Westminster Abbey and the various old churches in and near

London to make drawings from the monuments and buildings
that Basire was employed to engrave. This was a circumstance
for which Blake was afterwards extremely grateful, for he
found the solitary study of authentic English history far more
to his taste than the disorderly wrangling of mutinous com-
rades. It was here that the romantic turn of Blake's imagination
was stimulated and his natural attraction toward the spiritual
in art strengthened. He was able to do this work month after
month, year after year, unwatched by his master. He developed
a fervent love for the Gothic which lasted throughout his life
and conditioned him to disregard fashionable modes of art
and contemporary techniques in favor of the severity of the
earlier age and the symbolic language of imaginative art. For
many years the then neglected works of art called Gothic
"monuments" were his daily companions. The warmer months
were devoted to sketching the tombs in the Abbey from every
point of view. The enthusiastic artist would frequently be
found standing on the monuments and viewing the figures
from the top. Careful drawings were made of the regal forms
which for five centuries had lain in mute majesty, once amid
the daily presence of priests and muttered masses and lately
in solitude. Here Blake discovered for himself the important
part formerly played by color in the sculptured building. The
vitality color had added to the once radiant "Temple of God,"
now a bleached, dishonored skeleton, was to be applied to
Blake's own plates individually by his hand, to bring them to
a more vibrant expression of feeling than that inadequately
rendered in black and white.

During the service and in the intervals of visits from
strangers, the vergers of the Abbey often turned their keys on
Blake and he would be shut up alone with these solemn memo-
rials of far-off centuries. Then the spirit of the past would be
his familiar companion. He used to tell of a vision of Christ
and the apostles that appeared to him there and of other
shapes from the past that moved before his dreaming eye.

Consider that this was Blake's existence during the teen
years, when patterns of living and working are being set which
will affect the direction of the mature man. These were years
of excessive withdrawal. We have very little record of any

interpersonal relationships that took place during that time.
What we can piece together comes primarily out of his poetry,
which is highly imaginative in nature. There are poems
glorifying the spirits which infuse each of the changing seasons
with its unique ecstatic beauty. Only winter is exempt from
this, for then Blake fears the chill which threatens to envelop
him:

> He hears me not, but o'er the yawning deep
> Rides heavy; his storms are unchain'd, sheathed
> In ribbed steel; I dare not lift mine eyes,
> For he hath rear'd his sceptre o'er the world.[5]

We know as we read this early work that Blake is not only a
spectator but also an active participant in his observations of
the world about him. His verse throbs with response to the
moods of nature, as though he conceived nature as a most
gracious gift from the beloved Creator who is behind every
creative venture undertaken by man. As Blake understood it
within the framework of his own early efforts to write, the act
of creation was a kind of sacrament. It was to be accepted as a
sacred obligation to be fulfilled. This does not imply a serious
or sanctimonious attitude toward the written word but rather
a real acceptance of the mood that came to him. Sometimes it
is macabre as in narratives that have an abbreviated epic
flavor, for example, *Gwin, King of Norway,* which begins:

> Come, Kings, and listen to my song:
>   When Gwin, the son of Nore,
> Over the nations of the North
>   His cruel sceptre bore,
>
> The Nobles of the land did feed
>   Upon the hungry poor;
> They tear the poor man's lamb, and drive
>   The needy from their door! [6]

One can almost smell the moldy tomb wherein such a fantasy might have had its inception as Blake sketched the sar-

cophagus of some fearsome lord interred within the Abbey.

Sometimes the mood was light-hearted and gay. *Song* begins
thus, and the first two stanzas seem to be in praise of the poet's
childhood pleasures. This poem is said to have been written
when Blake was about sixteen and may also foreshadow the
concern he was beginning to feel for those people who were
enmeshed in social changes which challenged their simple,
rustic way of life. One may ask whether this concern also
reflected a parallel inner problem that Blake was then facing,
the recognition that soon he would no longer be able to enjoy
the innocent and carefree joys of his youth.

Song

How sweet I roam'd from field to field
  And tasted all the summer's pride,
'Till I the prince of love beheld,
  Who in the sunny beams did glide!

He shew'd me lilies for my hair,
  And blushing roses for my brow;
He led me through his gardens fair,
  Where all his golden pleasures grow.

With sweet May dews my wings were wet,
  And Phoebus fir'd my vocal rage;
He caught me in his silken net,
  And shut me in his golden cage.

He loves to sit and hear me sing,
  Then, laughing, sports and plays with me;
Then stretches out my golden wing,
  And mocks my loss of liberty.[7]

Early in Blake's seven apprenticeship years he might have
met unwittingly in the streets of London a placid, venerable,
thin man of eighty-four, of erect bearing and abstracted air,
wearing a full-bottomed wig, a pair of long ruffles and a curious
hilted sword, and carrying a gold-headed cane. This would

have been no vision, but the most celebrated of distinguished visionary seers, Emanuel Swedenborg, who came from Amsterdam to London in August of 1771 and died in March of the following year. This possible encounter is suggested by a Mr. Allingham in a note to his collection of lyrical poems, *Nightingale Valley,* which contains a specimen or two of Blake's early work. Gilchrist comments that the coincidence in time was not a trivial one, for of all modern men the engraver's apprentice was to grow up most like Swedenborg. Indeed, he already was so by constitutional temperament and endowment and in his faculty for "theosophic dreaming," for seeing visions while fully awake and in his matter-of-fact grasp of spiritual things. Swedenborg's theological writings, the first English editions of which appeared during Blake's early manhood, were to have a very great influence upon Blake's religious development.

Blake's apprenticeship years coincided with the beginning of the Industrial Revolution in England. He saw that miners and handworkers were losing their means of support as machines took over their jobs more and more, he observed the rise of prices and taxes and a rapidly growing population of hungry men. Riot became a part of the response to the government by a society whose poor had no vote and no press. Like many idealists Blake looked forward to a new era to come, heralded by the successful American Revolution which was a sign of hope to oppressed people all over the world.

His apprenticeship ended in 1779 and he returned to his father's home. There he continued his studies while supporting himself as a journeyman engraver. Soon he began paying court to a young lady who took his attentions rather lightly. When he complained about her interest in another young man and insisted upon more than a passing notice from her she told him to take his proposals elsewhere. He was desolate.

One evening, a short time later at a friend's house, he was bemoaning his unhappy love experience when a listener, an attractive and generous girl, told him that she understood his suffering. "Do you pity me?" he is reported to have asked. "Yes, I do, most sincerely." "Then I love you for that," he replied with enthusiasm, and a second, more profitable courtship began. Catherine Sophia Boucher was a young woman of extremely humble station. Her family had no position, her education was non-existent, and she had to sign the bridal register with her mark, an X, as the book in the parish still testifies.

It was the kind of marriage which might have been expected of an intensely introverted man. Catherine was a woman who made very few demands upon him, and it was unlikely that she distracted him from his preoccupation with the expression of his own ideas. Her education from the time of her marriage was composed almost entirely of what her husband taught her. Living with such a woman could be extremely gratifying to a man, at least for a time. Catherine's opinions would correspond with his own, and she would listen transfixed when he came to her with the new ideas which followed fast on the heels of everything he read, every conversation he had with a friend and every political event he heard about.

On the practical side, Catherine proved to be a good house-wife in the ever-straightened circumstances which were the lot of the Blakes. Submissive and uncomplaining, she performed the duties necessary to relieve the artist of concern for household matters. She never nagged him about his failure to make more of a living—and it was only when there was no more money in the strong-box and no more food in the pantry that she would place an empty plate before her husband at meal-time to remind him to complete one of his commissions and take it to the waiting customer who would readily pay him in cash for it.

In the estimation of many who wrote about William and Catherine Blake, theirs was an ideal marriage. But one is impelled to wonder what it was about Blake that caused him to be attracted to Catherine, for Blake was not the sort of man to whom subservience and practicality were marks of special virtue. It seems more likely that the earlier love experience, incomplete as it was on the level of reality, evoked in Blake the image of an ideal woman who directed his attention toward a spiritual experience of elation and brought about an influx of psychic energy which became manifested in his desire for her. That his first sweetheart was of a common sort with a great many beaux is beside the point; she must have possessed a quality of natural femininity which Catherine Boucher never approached. What *he* saw in her was the important perception, and it was a subjective one, related more to his inner capacity for seeing than to the object seen in the outer world. Blake's attitude toward longed-for experience of the feminine is expressed in a poem, presumably written about the young woman to whom his attentions had been objectionable.

My feet are wing'd, while o'er the dewy lawn
I meet my maiden, risen like the morn;
Oh bless those holy feet, like angel's feet;
Oh bless those limbs, beaming with heav'nly light!

Like as an angel glitt'ring in the sky
In times of innocence and holy joys;
The joyful shepherd stops his grateful song
To hear the music of an angel's tongue.

So when she speaks, the voice of Heaven I hear:
So when we walk, nothing impure comes near;
Each field seems Eden, and each calm retreat;
Each village seems the haunt of holy feet.

But that sweet village where my black-ey'd maid
Closes her eyes in sleep beneath night's shade,
Whene'er I enter, more than mortal fire
Burns in my soul, and does my song inspire.[8]

Whatever Catherine may have been able to do for her husband, it is unlikely that she was able to inspire him. The feminine figure whose voice was the "voice of Heaven" was the one Blake always sought to contact. In his first romance he was able to maintain the hope that such a being existed outside the realm of his own soul, and his rejection by the love object only served to strengthen this hope. Hurt and grieving from his disappointment, longing for a motherly bosom upon which to rest, he found Catherine, whose words, "I pity you," were perfectly harmonious with his depressed, self-depreciating mood. The man who in his active and productive periods had a fine and delicate feeling for sentiment, now in a passive and inward-

looking frame of mind fell prey to the easy mistress of senti-
mentality.

With time his energy returned in its natural and boundless
measure and he attempted to take up his concept of love as a
free and open expression of emotion, living it out in his marriage. His emotions would rise to great heights of spirituality
and religious consecration and would extend into every physical desire and its satisfaction as well. Blake was an earthy man
who knew his body as a receptacle of the creative force of the
universe and gladly accepted it as such. He was eager to experience the fullness of sexuality like all other pleasures, without
being bound by the limitations of tradition or a contemporary
religiosity. He was, however, married to a woman who believed
that the only justification for sexual intercourse was the desire
to have children. And when after a reasonable time it became
apparent that this was not to occur, Catherine's religious
scruples, or possibly her inability to attain to the expectations
of her husband, were reflected in her withdrawal from the physical relationship. The "perfect wife" role, for which Blake's
biographers, especially Gilchrist, so often praise her, may be
seen as a compensation for her basic lack of appreciation of the
needs, desires or capacities of the man to whom she was married.

At one time early in the marriage William made the unconventional proposal that a young woman be added to their
household who might perform those aspects of the marital
relationship which Catherine felt to be beyond her duty or
capacity—a young woman who might bring Blake the children
he so ardently desired.

The man who wrote these words must have found poetry a
pale substitute for the reality of a child of his own:

> Sweet dreams, form a shade
> O'er my lovely infant's head;
> Sweet dreams of pleasant streams
> By happy, silent moony beams.
>
> Sweet sleep, with soft down
> Weave thy brows an infant crown.
> Sweet sleep, Angel mild,
> Hover o'er my happy child.

Sweet smiles, in the night
Hover o'er my happy child.
Sweet smiles; Mother's smiles,
All the livelong night beguiles.[9]

Yet poems did become a substitute and real babies became for Blake symbols of grace and hope. He was unwilling to bring home a concubine against Catherine's strenuous objections nor would he permit his marriage with her to come to an end. He accepted her as his companion; he undertook to teach her to read and write, and then to assist him in technical details of his work. Her daily devotion to drudgery included everything from cooking and managing household accounts to working at her husband's side laboriously filling in with color the outlines of his engravings as he had instructed her.

The regard which William had for Catherine Blake may be inferred from an incident which occurred while they were living in a *ménage à trois* with Robert, William's beloved younger brother. Catherine, inclined at times to be rather hot-tempered, addressed some sharp words to her brother-in-law. Hearing this, William demanded angrily, "Kneel down and beg Robert's pardon directly or you'll never see my face again." It was a heavy threat, uttered in tones which showed unmistakably that it was meant. Catherine "thought it very hard," as afterward she would tell, to beg his pardon when she was not at fault. But, being a dutiful wife, she did kneel down and meekly murmur, "Robert, I beg your pardon, I am in the wrong." "Young woman, you lie!" he abruptly retorted, "I am in the wrong!" [10]

One might suppose from this that what real feeling William excluded from his relationship with Catherine found some expression, at least, in connection with his brother. The deep and enduring emotion which William felt for Robert, not only during Robert's lifetime but afterwards when Robert was to appear in visions as a spiritual guide,[11] was not what is commonly conceived of as love, meaning a complex and encompassing relationship between two people. For if Robert was beloved during his lifetime, that ineffable spirit which had animated him continued even more as the object of William's love after the living personality had been separated from it.

There is an engraving done by Blake in which the corpse of a
young man in a shroud lies stiff and still upon a marble couch.
Rising from his body is a supple maiden who tenderly bends
over to gaze upon the face of the deceased, her long hair
showering light upon his lifeless form. A window at the left
opens out onto a view of mountains reaching upward into a
radiant sky, the abode of the soul-maiden, the anima, the
feminine component which exists in every man. She is, indeed,
Psyche, beloved of the god Eros. Without her there can be no
enduring relationship. It was she in Robert whom William
loved, and the passion for her was so great that by contrast
ordinary relationships were insignificant. But the anima expressed herself not only in the gentle spirit of Robert. The
witch goddess aspect of the anima has already been seen in the
young sweetheart. She reappears in many guises throughout
Blake's life, to lead him in mysterious paths, and we will see
her more than once in our study of *The Marriage of Heaven
and Hell.*

Early, Blake began to deal with the emerging contents of the
unconscious which appeared as sensual demands, by writing
them out, painting them, or perhaps losing himself in magically
transporting visions. In this way, what seemed to be personal
concerns were transformed into transcendent images that went
far beyond his own experience. So, for example, the concluding
lines of the "Cradle Song" in which the child he so ardently
desired as an extension of his own being, now is transformed
into the Divine Child who becomes flesh to satisfy the yearnings of all men for immortality:

> Sweet babe, in thy face
> Holy image I can trace.
> Sweet babe, once like thee,
> Thy maker lay and wept for me,
>
> Wept for me, for thee, for all,
> When he was an infant small.
> Thou his image ever see,
> Heavenly face that smiles on thee.

Smiles on thee, on me, on all;
Who became an infant small.
Infant smiles are his own smiles;
Heaven and earth to peace beguiles.[12]

During the early years of his marriage Blake, along with his
wife, became an ardent follower of Swedenborg. He had already
left behind the Church of England, which having long ago won
the controversy with Deism, had absorbed its defeated enemy
and become Deist in spirit.[13]

Deism is the dominant system of Error in Blake's poetry.
Blake's Deism and historical Deism are not the same thing, but
we need to know a minimum about the historical phenomenon
if we are to understand Blake's outspoken loathing for his
"Deism."

Deism, or Natural Religion, the fashionable philosophy of
the Age of Reason, attempted to make religion intellectually
respectable by the application of common sense. The Age of
Reason came as a reaction against the fanaticism which had
caused the bloodiest of wars. It was an outgrowth of the rise of
the sciences reflecting the principles of Bacon, Newton and
Locke; the appearances of scholarly historians like Gibbon and
Hume; and the beginnings of higher criticism trumpeted so
defiantly by Thomas Paine. Deism attacked tradition and inspired such scoffers and freethinkers as Voltaire and Rousseau.

It was a religion made by historians, sociologists and econo-
mists, not by the religious, the metaphysicians or the mystics.
Deism was based on the facts of nature, and was not evolved by
logic from metaphysical premises. The great earthquake of
November 1, 1775, which destroyed Lisbon and some fifteen
thousand of its inhabitants, strengthened the position of the
Deists, who took it as proof of their theory that the Creator did
not interfere with the workings of his creation.

The Deists accepted God the Creator; but once his creation
was established according to his principles, there was no reason
for him to interfere in it. Therefore they regarded all miracles
and revelations as delusion and superstition. They held the
conviction that man was created naturally good, and the moral

systems of all religions were derived from his laws of conduct, as found in human nature. They insisted that all religions were basically one, and that a religion based on Reason, like Deism, should as a consequence be universally acceptable.[14]

All his life, Blake fought Deism. He required an escape from skepticism and from the tyranny of nature and reason, and he assigned to imagination the power to create its own order in space and its own consciousness in time.[15] His first illuminated printing, ca. 1788, was *There is No Natural Religion,* where he states his primary objection to Deism:

If it were not for the Poetic or Prophetic character the Philosophic & Experimental would soon be at the ratio of all things, & stand still, unable to do other than repeat the same dull round over again.[16]

Blake rejected the Deist God as remote, impassive and inaccessible. He believed that God exists actively within the individual. He objected to the Deistic nature-worship with its idea that the world is one of three dimensions only, and that everything within it can be explained by the mechanical operation of cause and effect. His position was that the Deists were completely unaware of the deeper life, with its corollary that all effects are the result of spiritual causes. Blake also objected to the Deist ethic, as he denied that man was naturally good, and that ethics derived from man's laws of conduct were necessarily true. He regarded the Deist ethic as only a system of artificial values of Good and Evil and of Justice with its single standard which disregarded the individual and therefore was inhuman. He associated Deism with all pagan moral systems, including Aristotle's, saying that they overlooked and omitted the supreme Christian virtues of humanitarianism, love, and the forgiveness of sins. Finally, he objected to Deistic psychology, which taught that Reason is man's supreme faculty, and he vigorously proclaimed that the creative imagination is the true fount of our being:[17]

I must create my own system or be enslaved by another man's. I will not reason and compare, my business is to create.[18]

Swedenborg's attraction for Blake may have been that he placed no limits on the exercise of imagination. He could be, therefore, a harbor for those who sought a refuge from the literalism that dominated the Anglican Church at that time. Swedenborg welcomed the vision beyond the senses as proof of man's immediate experience of God. His use of imagery in his writings attracted Blake's attention, particularly his graphic descriptions of Heaven and Hell. Swedenborg's concept of Heaven was of a virgin land, spotless and sterile. It was a place of negations: the regions where evil never came to life because desire was never awakened. He taught that man should bend his hopes toward reaching this void on high, that to achieve it he must deny his passion and live a life of restraint and watchful concern for his perishable soul. Against such a Heaven, Swedenborg set a contrasting Hell which was the source of all human emotion, and which opened like a great abyss beneath the feet of man whenever he became too deeply involved in matters of the world.

Enthusiastically, Blake began a study of Swedenborg, annotating the text of *Divine Love*. Through a careful scrutiny of his comments we are able to discern how Blake gradually began to see that man could not deny the passion that gave life itself the force to continue and that was inherent in every creative act. He observed that one might perhaps transpose this energy from one form into another, but he recognized that it would emerge in some phenomenon of experience, however disconnected from the original source of the emotion it might seem to be. To fix one's gaze too firmly upon Heaven was to invite one's foot to stumble into the pit below. Nor did one dare to contemplate that pit too much, for its limitless depths could devour a man. The precarious balance which Blake attempted to maintain created a tension which threatened to tear him apart. His energy was employed largely in the act of holding a relatively static position between the contaries of perfect goodness and contaminating evil. As Blake continued to study Swedenborg's work, he began to recognize that it was only another dogma, a more imaginative one to be sure than that of the Deistic religion current in the England in which Blake had been raised, but nevertheless still a system of restraints and rules which denied the essential nature of man. At last in a mood of revolt, perhaps against the restraints he felt in his own life, Blake left the Swedenborg group, but not without having been strongly influenced by its doctrines. The bitterness arising in Blake out of the realization that he had been seduced by Swedenborg's imaginative language into an unfamiliar but nonetheless structured orthodoxy, was to be verbalized in some of his most damning satire in *The Marriage of Heaven and Hell*.

Blake was approaching a crisis in his entire attitude toward religion, but he was not yet fully aware of this. Anxiety clouded his perception and appeared in the form of projections upon the outer world. His own unrest, brought about by the stirring of instinctual passions which he sternly rejected, was unrecognized by him for what it was. Its mirror image was observed by Blake as the unrest of his time. His own emotional state predisposed him to relate to the blood-lust rising in England and, even more, in France in the years preceding the outbreak of the French Revolution. The "divine right of kings," by which principle the collective concept of God's will could be utilized to subjugate a nation of people, mirrored the Swedenborgian concept of a God whose unmitigated goodness was the essence of his nature. This was the kind of heavenly authority which Blake was to question as he meditated upon his own impulses. In *The Marriage of Heaven and Hell* he elucidates the relationship between his personal conflict and the wider, collective conflicts of his day.

A major influence in the development of Blake's changing religious attitudes was his reading of Jacob Boehme (1575-1624), or Behmen, as Blake referred to him. Boehme, known as "The Teutonic Philosopher," was one of the great mystics of his time. He dealt in his writings directly with some of the problems that were concerning Blake as he wrestled with Swedenborgian concepts of good and evil, and was instrumental in breaking the spell of the new dogma which had replaced the Deistic anathema for Blake.

Born of poor German parents, Boehme was apprenticed to a

shoemaker who discharged him because for a full week he was in a mystical ecstasy. He became an itinerant cobbler and then settled in Gorlitz where he married and had six children. About 1600, a ray reflected from a polished metal dish filled him with the light of God and opened to him the mysteries of the universe. In 1610, a third "flash" unified his insights and inspired him to write. In 1612, his manuscript *Aurora* caused him to be banished; but he left the book unfinished and promised to write no more. Then, about 1618, he was so driven to write that he produced some thirty other books in that and ensuing years.

Blake, in his reading of Boehme, must have become imbued with the idea that the divine inspiration had a function that went beyond that of making possible a sense of oneness with God. It also carried with it an obligation to accept the stimulation of this inspiration and to follow the ideas that came of it until they were captured and committed to permanent form. The same insistent quality of vision that Boehme experienced and wrote about was also to come to Blake when he took up the conflicts that arose out of his clash with Swedenborgian orthodoxy.

It is often overlooked that the work of Boehme affected Blake profoundly because it is such difficult reading. Boehme, in struggling to record his discoveries, used the vocabulary of scripture, astrology, and Paracelsus, thus initiating the school which interpreted alchemy mystically. At times he was even driven to invent terms of his own which he called "The Language of Nature." Blake's interest in Boehme was a major factor in freeing him from the feeling that it was necessary to cast his lot with any accepted tradition, be it orthodox or iconoclastic. The basis for the expression of ideas was to be the intimate experience of them as personal revelations. Blake had written to his friend Flaxman,[19] "Paracelsus and Behmen appear'd to me before the American Revolution," and at that time he already felt that this was a "divinely inspired man." [20]

During these years, Blake was employed as an engraver by Joseph Johnson, a publisher and bookseller and also the friend of enthusiasts for American independence and of those who were hopefully watching the Revolution in France and planning a democratic but bloodless program for England. Johnson gave weekly dinners for his intimates above his shop in St. Paul's Churchyard, and here Blake may have met old Dr. Price, the preacher who provoked Burke's *Reflections on the French Revolution,* the advocate of international peace and religious toleration and the inventor of the doctrine of human perfectibility. Already threatened with a government prosecution for his *Rights of Man,* Thomas Paine came here also to talk about those ideas which had inspired the American struggle for liberty. One evening Paine was recapitulating an inflammatory speech of the night before when Blake told him he was a dead man if he went home, where, in fact, arrest awaited him. Paine was saved from the gallows by that peculiar sense of Blake's, which time and again seemed to know when matters were coming to a climax of tensions that would be able to be endured no longer.

Considering that event from the standpoint of analytical psychology, it would appear that the politically tense situation coincided meaningfully with Blake's inner situation, where the stress was approaching a breaking point. Blake was sensitive to the fact that a dangerous condition existed, but he perceived the danger in the form of an external predicament, *i.e.,* as a threat to Paine's life. By saving Paine, Blake acted to mollify his own demon, but since his act was not brought fully to consciousness, the demon was soon to seek another vehicle of expression.

The shift in attitude, based on Blake's rage against any principle which seemed to inhibit his own freedom, and reinforced by his study of Boehme, was verbalized in his work, *The French Revolution.* It is believed he began it in the latter half of 1789, and planned for it to be composed of six books. Only one is now in existence; the others have been lost, if indeed they were ever written. The work was scheduled for publication in 1791, but was withheld either by Johnson's caution or by Blake himself.

In this book Blake rejected any remnants of the tolerance he might have felt for the threatened nobility who still were claiming to be the representatives of God on earth. When he wrote

about the storming of the Bastille, he did not dwell upon the
relentless fury of the mob, but rather upon the miserable condition of the seven living corpses, six men and one woman, who
were found behind the dungeon walls:

> ... a man
> Pinioned down to the floor, his strong bones scarce covered
>   with sinews; the iron rings
> Were forged smaller as the flesh decayed ...
>   a loathesome sick woman bound down
> To a bed of straw; the seven diseases of earth, like birds of prey,
>   stood on the couch
> And fed on the body ...
>   a strong man sat
> His feet and hands cut off, and his eyes blinded; round his
>   middle a chain and a band
> Fasten'd into the wall; fancy gave him to see an image of
>   despair in his den,
> Eternally rushing round, like a man on his hands and knees, day
>   and night without rest:[21]

In these people Blake saw the terrible fate of victims of a
humanity which had permitted itself to be dominated by "divine" reason. The prisoners were not the ones whose spirits had
been subdued; rather they were the ones who had listened to the
demands of their own natures. What were their crimes? The
woman "refused to be whore to the Minister, and with a knife
smote him." One man was "friend to the favourite." Another
"by conscience urg'd, in the city of Paris rais'd a pulpit. And
taught wonders to darkened souls . . ." while another "was con-
fin'd for a writing prophetic." [22]

If we regard these lines as disguised subjective expressions of
Blake's own problem, it appears that Blake sees the Bastille-
prisoner aspects of his own fiery nature as expressing themselves
and then being punished for that expression. The bitter response of Blake to the agony of the prisoners was an enunciation
of his own agony, and his own is joined with that of all men
who are torn between the inner urge to behave in a manner

consonant with their individual needs and at the same time to exist with as little friction as possible within the postulated laws and order of the collective society.

The Bastille was an enclosed fortress wherein wrongdoers, according to the laws of the State, were confined. Although the State had been restrictive and incognizant of the rising urge toward a freer life under a more moderate government, the overthrowing of the government heralded by the downfall of the Bastille did not result in the more orderly political climate that might have been anticipated. On the contrary, the very breaking of the bars presaged a period of anarchy in which the revolutionaries were bathed in the same blood as their overlords. Were Blake to have realized that his own inner revolution would lead to terrors which would make his descriptions of the fall of the Bastille seem pallid by comparison, one wonders if he would have had the courage to revolt against the spiritual framework in which he had existed, as he did when he addressed himself to the writing of *The Marriage of Heaven and Hell.* In the course of *The French Revolution,* he perceived the coming of a state of confused degradation as a reaction by the revolutionary collective against the breaking of the bands of restraint. A depth psychologist might interpret the phenomenon as an indication of an overwhelming of his own ego position by powerful contents issuing from the unconscious. Both ways of experiencing the situation are implicit in the lines which the Archbishop of Paris addresses to the Monarch of France as he relates the words of an aged, white-robed man who appeared to him and wakened him as he was "sleeping at midnight in my golden tower":

'For the bars of Chaos are burst; her millions prepare their
    fiery way
Thro' the orbed abode of the holy dead, to root up and pull
    down and remove,
And Nobles and Clergy shall fail from before me, and my cloud
    and vision be no more;
The mitre become black, the crown vanish, and the scepter and
    ivory staff
Of the ruler wither among the bones of death; . . .

They shall drop at the plow and faint at the harrow, unre-
deem'd, unconfess'd, unpardon'd;
The priest rot in his surplice by the lawless lover, the holy
beside the accursed,
The King, frowning in purple, beside the grey plowman, and
their worms embrace together.' [23]

Mona Wilson, in her biographical study of Blake,[24] shows her
awareness of the connection of the political events of the day
with the personal spiritual upheaval which Blake was experiencing concurrently with them, when she writes that in the scheme
of *The French Revolution* the author was clearly not content
to be merely a political revolutionary, but was feeling his way
toward a subversive metaphysical doctrine. The suggestion
is made that Blake was in so close a relationship with his personal unconscious and with wider unconscious realms that
his psychic experience merged at some point with the collective
experience—that the collective flowed in and through him and
that in some contexts he was indistinguishable from it. This
seems to be substantiated by those incidents in Blake's life
which demonstrated his ability to sustain visions that were not
only beyond an ordinary man's sensory capacity but were also
beyond the scope of Blake's personal experience.
Blake possessed a mysterious quality of personality which
has been recognizable in certain individuals in all ages, but
which men have been at a loss to identify. Whether it was a
gift of "genius"—a term much used but little understood—is
highly questionable in the case of Blake, for his insight was invariably more highly developed than were his modes of expression. In studying his early work one feels that the poetry and
prose, the sketches and small illustrations, are like the illumination from many candles in the depths of huge winding
caverns. Proceeding to the masses of material which constitute
his later work (he himself declared that he had written more
than Shakespeare and Milton combined [25]), perusing pages
filled with tales of superhuman characters with cryptic names
who are engaged in monumental and rapidly shifting cosmic
dramas, one is struck with wonder at the brilliance of his
vision. The reader who is unshakable in his devotion to the

logical process will be impressed by the limitations of his own capacity to order this plethora of imagery into meaning.

The writing of the book, *The Marriage of Heaven and Hell,* marked a turning point in the creative development of William Blake, as we have already indicated. As a youth he had developed a strong ego, which was reflected in his ability to take a firm position with respect to the social and political streams of his day, to establish himself in a career, and to enter into a way of life which seemed to be happily compatible with his innate capacities. A little poem, which he wrote while still in his teens, discloses his feeling at that time that man was no longer moved by the muses. It suggests that he had begun to grope for the voice of inspiration, which is somewhere beyond the ego, but that he had not yet developed a relationship with it. Aware of a presence beyond the immediate area of consciousness which is the well-spring of creative energy, he lamented man's inability to partake of it.

To the Muses

Whether on Ida's shady brow,
  Or in the chambers of the East,
The chambers of the sun, that now
  From ancient melody have ceas'd;

Whether in Heav'n ye wander fair,
  Or in the green corners of the earth,
Or the blue regions of the air,
  Where the melodious winds have birth;

Whether on crystal rocks ye rove,
  Beneath the bosom of the sea
Wand'ring in many a coral grove,
  Fair Nine, forsaking Poetry!

How have you left the ancient love
  That bards of old enjoy'd in you!
The languid strings do scarcely move!
  The sound is forc'd, the notes are few! [26]

Northrop Frye noted that it has been said that "in this poem the eighteenth century dies to music." He comments that the eighteenth century was a little too healthy to expire in any such trifle, and perhaps it would have been better to say that in *The Marriage of Heaven and Hell* the age of Swift and Sterne and Fielding and Hogarth plunges into a vigorous Beethovenish coda which, though organically related to what has gone before, contains much new material and is big with portents of the movements to follow.[27]

As Blake matured, he focused his attention more and more upon the processes of his inner life. He grew less concerned with the events which were taking place in the world at large, and when he did write about them, he tended to deal with them symbolically as the expressions of underlying forces and more universal movements. He ceased to maintain a firm grip upon objective reality, as in his own thinking the object began to merge with the symbol—which can never be altogether defined or understood.

The symbol presents a visible image with its own meaning, behind which an invisible, profounder meaning is hidden. As Bachofen wrote, "Words make the infinite finite, symbols carry the mind beyond the finite world of becoming into the infinite world of being. They awaken intimations; they are tokens of the ineffable, and like it they are inexhaustible." [28]

As Blake became more and more involved in symbolic writing, his ego became less of a dominating factor in his writing. He was coming to the realization that the creative spirit could not be simply willed into operation, but that it required a petition for help, and a passive receptiveness to its outpourings. This spirit was immanent in the creative person, and yet it lay beyond the threshold of his consciousness most of the time. *The Marriage of Heaven and Hell* is the record of Blake's commitment to this spirit, which corresponds to the ancient concept of the muses. A portion of his ego was offered up as a sacrifice to them, and the rational attitude retreated in the face of the inclination toward the irrational. From this time on his writings were no longer couched in the phrases of ordinary writers, but seemed to come from a source different from the ones he had used in the past, a source beyond conscious control.

Like Jacob Boehme, he was to abandon himself to that other;
and in the future he would begin his works with invocations
such as this one:

> Eternals, I hear your call gladly.
> Dictate swift winged words & fear not
> To unfold your dark visions of torment.[29]

It seems to me that the lost spirit of the muses returned to
Blake as the "Eternals" during the course of his writing of
The Marriage of Heaven and Hell. The Eternals are carriers
of the symbols which put Blake, and through him the reader,
into contact with the mysteries of the unknown. It is difficult
to read *The Marriage* with understanding, because no part of it
can be taken literally. A few critics in recent years have attempted to interpret it, and each has come forth with a variety
of conjectures based on historical background or literary critique. I shall not attempt to use either of these approaches. As
the expression of an inner experience concerned with uniting
opposing forces in the rational and emotional nature of man, I
feel that a psychological study may bring to light insights into
the process whereby symbolic literature is conceived and written, and whereby it may be comprehended on many levels. An
effort will be made to discover how Blake himself conceived
of the sources of his creative energy—that energy which, during
the years that followed the completion of this work, led him
to produce in rapid succession the many volumes comprising
the mysteriously powerful mythology known as his prophetic
writings.

3
The Marriage of Heaven and Hell

The Marriage of Heaven and Hell, FROM BEGINNING TO end, is as pure a product of a single human psyche as is possible to imagine. We cannot speak of the text without considering the illustration, for both were the work of a single mind, a single pen, a single vision. The book was completely Blake's from the first blinding concept that burst into consciousness, through the labor of capturing the ideas in words and the sense impressions in pictures, and the forming of these to blend with one another on a page that would move the eye to excitement and the heart to feeling. The image his mind perceived was committed to the copper plate by his own hand using the engraver's tool—letter by letter and form by form, with all the embellishments of scrolls and leaves and trees and airy sprites and sensuous representations of the human body unashamedly giving expression to man's most secret passions. But Blake's personal participation was not limited to giving verbal and graphic form to the concept. He had developed a unique process through which his text and pictures could be printed in a single operation. Blake, who loathed the soulless ma-

chinery which was then being introduced by the Industrial
Revolution, worked as his own printer in an old-fashioned print
shop which held a meaning for him comparable to that of the
laboratory for the medieval alchemist.[1] Blake, like the alchemist,
was concerned with matter, that is, the world, but not as something essentially different from spirit. He found it necessary to
avoid mechanical methods of production and to involve himself personally in an opus by which he would transform a
copper etching plate into an expression of profound ideas.
Every act of manipulation of the materials at hand was infused
with an awareness of the need for a tangible vehicle to carry
ideas and concepts. The alchemists had done this, too, looking
to matter to yield up to them its secrets. They were able to
probe into it, utilizing chemicals, glass tubes, vessels and fire—
and at the same time to understand that there was a parallel
process taking place in their own minds, a yearning after the
meaning and implications of what they were observing and
carefully noting down. They were looking for the hypothetical
one incorruptible substance which was the synthesis of everything imaginable and which could serve every purpose. Along
with this they sought a spiritual center which was known by
the same name as the material goal: the "treasure hard to
attain." It was the gold—which is not the common gold, but the
philosopher's gold—or it was the philosopher's stone, the lapis,
which once found cannot be destroyed, or the elixir which becomes the panacea. All of these were said to be concealed in
matter, but they could not be brought out easily; it was necessary to go through a series of processes to reveal the mystery,
and often the processes only served to make it more obscure. Yet
the alchemists had their goal constantly before them, as Gerhard Dorn, one of the most famous of their number, wrote:

There is in natural things a certain truth which cannot be seen
with the outward eye, but is perceived by the mind alone. The
philosophers have known it, and they have found that its power is
so great as to work miracles.[2]

The manner in which they were to labor was laid out:

So work even in the laboratory by thyself alone, without collaborators or assistants, in order that God, Zealous, may not wish to with-draw the art from thee, on account of thy assistants, to whom He may not wish to impart it.[3]

Gilchrist, in *The Life of Blake,* relates how Blake came into possession of the "secret method" of printing. His description is more metaphysical than precise. However, the idea that such a scheme for reproduction of a manuscript could manage to convey the individual character, the beauty of tracery, and the luminousity of a medieval manuscript, long tantalized his readers. Anthony Blunt [4] says that the method was clearly invented by Blake for his particular purpose. While the alchemical parallel may not have occurred to three recent investigators, the result was found so curious that S. W. Hayter, Joan Miro and Ruthven Todd* made a series of experiments which led to their being able to reproduce exactly the effects created by Blake.[5]

Gilchrist presents us with a fascinating account of how the peculiarly original method of printing and publishing his work was revealed to Blake through a "supernatural agency":

He had not the wherewithal to publish on his own account; and though he could be his own engraver, he could scarcely be his own compositor. Long and deeply he meditated. How solve this difficulty with his own industrious hands? How be his own printer and publisher? After intently thinking by day and dreaming by night, during long weeks and months, of his cherished object, the image of the vanished pupil and brother at last blended with it. In a vision of the night, the form of Robert stood before him, and revealed the wished-for secret, directing him to the technical mode by which could be produced a facsimile of song and design. . . . This method, to which Blake henceforth consistently adhered for multiplying his works, was quite an original one. It consisted in a species of engraving in relief both words and designs. The verse was written and the designs and marginal embellishments outlined on the copper with an impervious liquid, probably the stopping out varnish of engravers. Then the white parts or lights, the remainder of the plate, that is, were eaten away with *aqua fortis* or other acid, so that the outline of the letter and design was left prominent, as in stereotype. From these plates he

---

* Todd is the editor of the excellent Everyman edition of the Gilchrist biography.

printed off in any tint, yellow, brown, blue, required to be the prevailing or ground color of his facsimilies; red he used for the letter-
press. The page was then coloured up by hand in imitation of the
original drawing, with more or less variety of detail in the local
hues.

He ground and mixed his water colours himself on a piece of
statuary marble, after a method of his own, with common carpenter's glue diluted, which he had found out, as the early Italians had
done before him, to be a good binder. Joseph, the sacred carpenter,
had appeared in a vision and revealed *that* secret to him.[6]

Because of the unique quality of the original editions, each
touched with the magic of Blake's hand, it is difficult to imagine
the effect they must have had upon the limited group who were
privileged to see these works. We can, however, absorb something of the feeling by reading the words of Gilchrist:

The designs are highly finished; Blake had worked upon them so
much, and illuminated them so rightly, that even the letter press
seemed done as if by hand. The ever-fluctuating colour, the spectral
pygmies rolling, flying, leaping among the letters; the ripe bloom of
the quiet corners, the living light and burst of flame, the spires and
tongues of fire vibrating with the full prism, make the page seem to
move and quiver within its boundaries, and you lay the book down
tenderly, as if you had been handling something sentient. A picture
has been said to be midway between a thing and a thought; so in
these books over which Blake had long brooded, with his brooding
of fire, the very paper seems to come to life as you gaze upon it—
not with a mortal life, but with a life indestructible, whether for
good or evil.[7]

PLATE 1

We open the brief manuscript to the title page. On a shim-
mering background are emblazed the words *The Marriage of
Heaven and Hell.* Two different kinds of script are used.
Marriage is composed of gentle flowing letters, each one detached from but related to all the others and all rhythmically
moving with a sweep and a swing that fit the lyrical aspect of
the Blakean vision. The connecting words *of* and *and* also have
the easy movement of script lettering, with its exhuberance of
swirls. The other three words have quite a different quality.
The, Heaven and *Hell* are drawn in classical Roman script, of

the kind one is apt to see on public buildings or on tombstones. There is at once a harmony and a dynamism here. At the beginning, before we have read a word, we are faced with the opposition of the contraries. They do not go together, it does not make sense; but then we see that the design engendered is stimulating to the eye and thought in a way that a single style of lettering could never be. Blake serves notice that in this little book we must expect the unexpected.

Although we are fully aware of the intimacy that existed between the creator of the book and his creation, we sense immediately that the subject matter will extend far beyond the personal experience of Blake. Or, to be more precise, it will extend beyond what we know to have been his experience in the world of the senses, limited as that experience was. But the world of the senses is not the subject matter of *The Marriage of Heaven and Hell*. The world as we are prone to conceive it is sliced through on the very title page and we see a cross section. The surface of the earth appears as a thin layer of dust which terminates in a precipice on the left and is swallowed up in a cloud on the right. It is a pale land lying atop a volcano, and those who stroll its surface each day, man and woman hand in hand, walk with a grace that suggests they have not the faintest idea of what seethes far beneath them. Nor do the fires of the deep concern the pair who drop to their knees in a passionate embrace. They are together, they grow up, they make love and they die surrounded by leafless trees and a dull sky. Earth is like a shelf poised above the abyss. One needs only to step off the edge, Blake shows, to tumble into the depths where Heaven and Hell struggle for possession of the soul. The figures of those who fall are paired, male and female, indissolubly bound together, and some of them are trapped by the licking flames while others veer toward the black clouds of an infernal heaven.

We might ask why there is no man or woman without a mate or partner in this downpour of human bodies. Is it because they are bound that they fall? Or does their union indicate an effort to depict the essential oneness of the human personality, with all its diverse physical (or material) and spiritual or (psychological) aspects? The meaning will emerge and will be clarified as we read the book and meditate upon the pictures. Here is posed the question of the androgyne, the male-female paradox: which is that there are separate and distinct contrasexual aspects within every personality and yet they can never be separated. Man is not allowed to forget that the eternal female lies slumbering in his breast, nor woman that she was once fashioned out of his bone, and both from the same dust.

At the very base of the picture, farthest from the earth's surface, two primordial beings lie clasped in each other's arms. Out of the Hell-fire strains the female form, her body vigorous and strong, her long, golden hair streaming down her back. There is activity in the posture, as though she were swimming up out of the flame, as though she herself were a restless and flickering flame, and threatening to consume. At her right rests the male form on his couch of cloudstuff. There is a calmness about him, almost an appearance of serenity in the relaxed way he stretches out his leg and in the way in which his arms encircle her shoulder. Their lips meet where Heaven and Hell come together. Their heads are surrounded by a golden disk that looks like a halo or a distant sun.

The entire picture can be interpreted as Blake's map of the psyche. The surface of the earth is the area which man knows in his everyday experience. He operates from a standpoint based upon earth, thus the earth may represent the realm of his conscious ego, that region in which he feels he has some control over what occurs. In his scheme Blake gives less space to earth than to the underworld because for him the daily activity of conscious life was the palest part of existence. The figures upon the earth are small and undifferentiated. They are male or female but they are not rendered as flesh and blood, rather are they shadowy figures who move about slowly and passively. They seem to be unaware of anything beyond themselves as they approach precariously close to the rim of the bottomless depth from which individual consciousness emerges and where it reaches its ultimate destination.

The roots of trees are the connection between earth and what lies below. They penetrate the ground, into the subterranean region where the opposites struggle for domination even as they hold each other breathlessly close. In the infertile subsoil the roots must find little nourishment, for the leaves are gone and there is no fruit on the trees. There is no shade or comfort, no nesting place for birds, only dry branches, upon one of which a snake is coiled to strike. The trees connect the earth's surface, which is seen as the parallel to consciousness, to the limitless underground regions below the threshold of consciousness. The strength of the trees comes from a deeper source than the surface of the earth, through roots which cannot be perceived from above. Trees drink up the mysteries of the deep, which is the source of all knowledge and wisdom. The branches are like sheltering arms at times, while at other times, they seem to be grasping and menacing. Thus trees embody characteristics of a dual mother, at once fearsome and loving. Their roots seem to have a special meaning for Blake's psychology. They represent that aspect of the collective maternal image through which one can re-enter the womb of the ages.

When Blake comes to a place in his life where his understandings of the world about him—the problems of nations in their struggle for freedom from tyranny, the travail of the working people of his own England trying to maintain themselves against the incursion of the machine—and the lack of satisfaction in his personal life and especially in his marriage, bring him to a point of despair, he sinks his own roots deeper into a place of quiet darkness where he can hope to find restoration.

His rejection by Catherine, who would no longer allow him any sexual intimacy, was still another source of frustration. It was not his nature to criticize this gentle and obedient woman. He spoke his feelings through his art, but the creative spirit is a demanding mistress who keeps the unconscious in constant turmoil. Thus Blake was to realize that there could be no peace for the man who possesses the gift (or the curse) of being able to move back and forth between the plane of consciousness and the depths of the unknown.

It is as though all the elements of the conscious part of his psyche, those troublesome problems upon which his attention was fixed, were falling deeper and deeper, in the form of the

paired figures, down to the nadir of Heaven-Hell, the archetypal opposites from which they sprang.

The great male figure at the base of the picture must be the
one with whom Blake consciously identifies since, being of the
same sex, he represents Blake's conscious attitude. He is on the
right side, the side of consciousness. The self-image or ego ideal
begins to be formed in early childhood, when the child begins
to become aware of his separateness from his mother and consequently of his relationship to her. The formation of this
image is a lengthy and important developmental process re-
sulting largely from the imposition of maternal and societal
standards upon the primitive instinctive nature of the child.
This is particularly true of psycho-sexual characteristics, which
are not as clearly differentiated at so early an age as are the
physiological sexual characteristics. A little boy, following his
mother about the house, is likely to be imitative in his play
and to take up household chores, dressing and undressing dolls
and helping in the kitchen. This is allowed to go on for a time,
but soon the mother may suggest that the mop and the dolls
should be put away and that other activities are more suitable
for the little boy. How much sadness there must be when the
boy is deprived of the free expression of the feminine side of
his nature, and what strong defenses he must build against it
in order to win approval of his mother! The father, too, plays
an important part. It is he who sets the pattern of how a boy
should behave and what is expected of him. The father's role
in eighteenth century England was that of a patriarch.
Through his authority he not only transmitted society's patterns of conduct but he also had a strong connection with the
so-called spiritual side of life, and was largely responsible for
the boy's training in this area. So it was that society and heaven
were identified with the masculine aspects of the personality,
while all those elements that were repressed came to be associated with the feminine; the softness, the receptiveness, the
ability to listen and to observe without asserting oneself in
immediate action, the primary concern with the establishment
and sustaining of relationships.

Man is supposed to be strong enough, and reasonable
enough, according to the tenets of a masculinely dominated

PLATE 1

The Argument.

Rintrah roars & shakes his fires in the burdend air;
Hungry clouds swag on the deep

Once meek, and in a perilous path,
The just man kept his course along
The vale of death.
Roses are planted where thorns grow,
And on the barren heath
Sing the honey bees.

Then the perilous path was planted:
And a river, and a spring
On every cliff and tomb;
And on the bleached bones
Red clay brought forth,

Till the villain left the paths of ease,
To walk in perilous paths, and drive
The just man into barren climes.

Now the sneaking serpent walks
In mild humility.
And the just man rages in the wilds
Where lions roam.

Rintrah roars & shakes his fires in the
burdend air;
Hungry clouds swag on the deep.

PLATE 2

As a new heaven is begun, and it is now thirty-three years since its advent: the Eternal Hell revives. And lo! Swedenborg is the Angel sitting at the tomb; his writings are the linen clothes folded up. Now is the dominion of Edom, & the return of Adam into Paradise; see Isaiah XXXIV & XXXV Chap:

Without Contraries is no progression. Attraction and Repulsion, Reason and Energy, Love and Hate, are necessary to Human existence.

From these contraries spring what the religious call Good & Evil. Good is the passive that obeys Reason. Evil is the active springing from Energy.

Good is Heaven. Evil is Hell.

PLATE 3

The voice of the
Devil

All Bibles or sacred codes. have been
the causes of the following Errors.
1. That Man has two real existing principles Viz: a Body & a Soul.
2. That Energy. calld Evil. is alone from the
Body. & that Reason. calld Good. is alone from
the Soul
3. That God will torment Man in Eternity
for following his Energies.
But the following Contraries to these are True
1. Man has no Body distinct from his Soul
for that calld Body is a portion of Soul discernd
by the five Senses. the chief inlets of Soul in this
age
2. Energy is the only life and is from the Body
and Reason is the bound or outward circumference
of Energy.
3. Energy is Eternal Delight

PLATE 4

Those who restrain desire, do so because theirs
is weak enough to be restrained; and the restrainer or
Reason usurps its place & governs the unwilling.
    And being restraind it by degrees becomes passive
till it is only the shadow of desire.
    The history of this is written in Paradise Lost. & the
Governor or Reason is call'd Messiah.
    And the original Archangel or possessor of the com-
mand of the heavenly host. is call'd the Devil or Satan
and his children are call'd Sin & Death
    But in the Book of Job Miltons Messiah is call'd
Satan.
    For this history has been adopted by both parties
    It indeed appeard to Reason as if Desire was
cast out. but the Devils account is. that the Messi-

PLATE 5

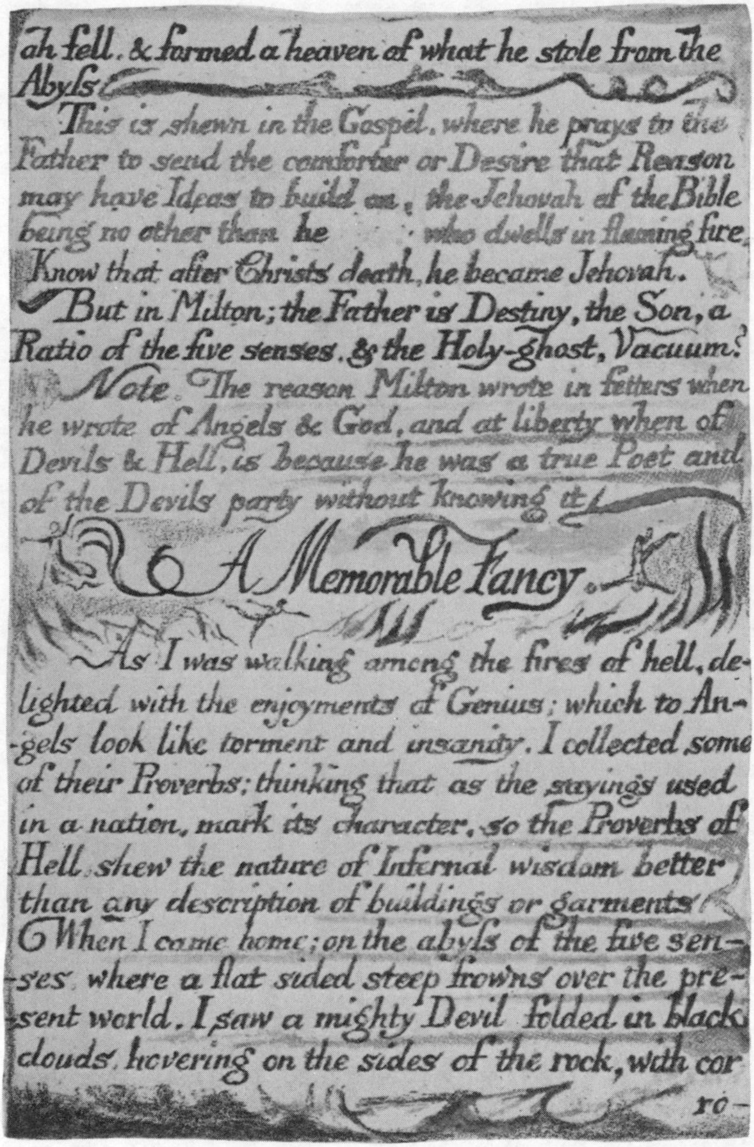

ah fell. & formed a heaven of what he stole from the Abyss.

This is shewn in the Gospel, where he prays to the Father to send the comforter or Desire that Reason may have Ideas to build on, the Jehovah of the Bible being no other than he who dwells in flaming fire. Know that after Christs death, he became Jehovah.

But in Milton; the Father is Destiny, the Son, a Ratio of the five senses, & the Holy-ghost, Vacuum!

Note. The reason Milton wrote in fetters when he wrote of Angels & God, and at liberty when of Devils & Hell, is because he was a true Poet and of the Devils party without knowing it

A Memorable Fancy.

As I was walking among the fires of hell, delighted with the enjoyments of Genius; which to Angels look like torment and insanity. I collected some of their Proverbs; thinking that as the sayings used in a nation, mark its character, so the Proverbs of Hell, shew the nature of Infernal wisdom better than any description of buildings or garments

When I came home; on the abyss of the five senses, where a flat sided steep frowns over the present world. I saw a mighty Devil folded in black clouds, hovering on the sides of the rock, with cor-ro-

PLATE 6

roding fires he wrote the following sentence now percieved by the minds of men, & read by them on earth.

How do you know but ev'ry Bird that cuts the airy way,
Is an immense world of delight, clos'd by your senses five?

Proverbs of Hell

In seed time learn, in harvest teach, in winter enjoy,
Drive your cart and your plow over the bones of the dead.
The road of excess leads to the palace of wisdom.
Prudence is a rich ugly old maid courted by Incapacity.
He who desires but acts not, breeds pestilence.
The cut worm forgives the plow.
Dip him in the river who loves water.
A fool sees not the same tree that a wise man sees.
He whose face gives no light, shall never become a star.
Eternity is in love with the productions of time.
The busy bee has no time for sorrow.
The hours of folly are measur'd by the clock, but of wis-
dom: no clock can measure.
All wholsom food is caught without a net or a trap.
Bring out number weight & measure in a year of dearth.
No bird soars too high, if he soars with his own wings.
A dead body, revenges not injuries.
The most sublime act is to set another before you.
If the fool would persist in his folly he would become
wise
Folly is the cloke of knavery.
Shame is Prides cloke.

PLATE 7

Proverbs of Hell

The fox provides for himself, but God provides for the Lion
Think in the morning, Act in the noon, Eat in the even-
    -ing, Sleep in the night.
He who has sufferd you to impose on him knows you.
As the plow follows words, so God rewards prayers.
The tygers of wrath are wiser than the horses of in-
Expect poison from the standing water.   (-struction
You never know what is enough unless you know what is
    more than enough.
Listen to the fools reproach! it is a kingly title!
The eyes of fire, the nostrils of air, the mouth of water,
    the beard of earth.
The weak in courage is strong in cunning.
The apple tree never asks the beech how he shall grow,
    nor the lion, the horse; how he shall take his prey.
The thankful reciever bears a plentiful harvest
If others had not been foolish, we should be so.
The soul of sweet delight, can never be defild,
When thou seest an Eagle, thou seest a portion of Ge-
    -nius, lift up thy head!
As the catterpiller chooses the fairest leaves to lay
    her eggs on, so the priest lays his curse on
    the fairest joys.
To create a little flower is the labour of ages.
Damn, braces: Bless relaxes.
The best wine is the oldest, the best water the newest
Prayers plow not! Praises reap not!
Joys laugh not! Sorrows weep not!
    The

PLATE 8

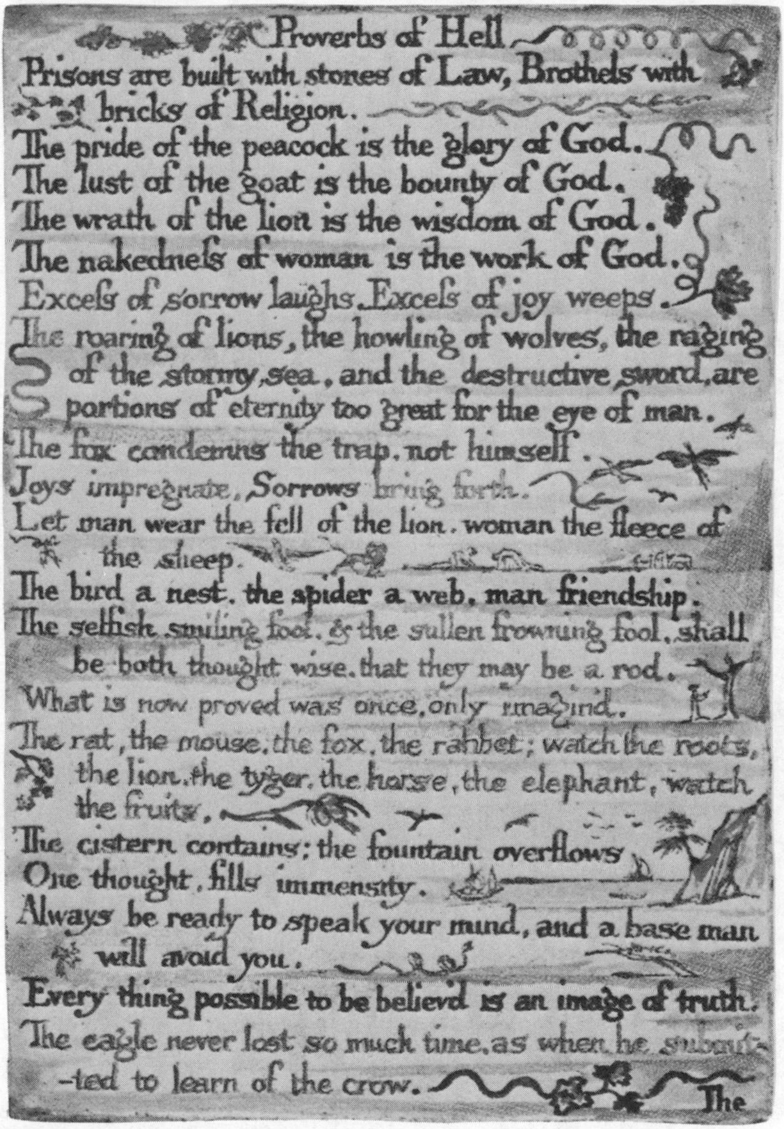

Proverbs of Hell

Prisons are built with stones of Law, Brothels with bricks of Religion.

The pride of the peacock is the glory of God.

The lust of the goat is the bounty of God.

The wrath of the lion is the wisdom of God.

The nakedness of woman is the work of God.

Excess of sorrow laughs. Excess of joy weeps.

The roaring of lions, the howling of wolves, the raging of the stormy sea, and the destructive sword, are portions of eternity too great for the eye of man.

The fox condemns the trap, not himself.

Joys impregnate. Sorrows bring forth.

Let man wear the fell of the lion. woman the fleece of the sheep.

The bird a nest, the spider a web, man friendship.

The selfish smiling fool, & the sullen frowning fool, shall be both thought wise, that they may be a rod.

What is now proved was once, only imagin'd.

The rat, the mouse, the fox, the rabbet; watch the roots, the lion, the tyger, the horse, the elephant, watch the fruits.

The cistern contains: the fountain overflows

One thought, fills immensity.

Always be ready to speak your mind, and a base man will avoid you.

Every thing possible to be believ'd is an image of truth.

The eagle never lost so much time, as when he submit-ted to learn of the crow.

The

PLATE 9

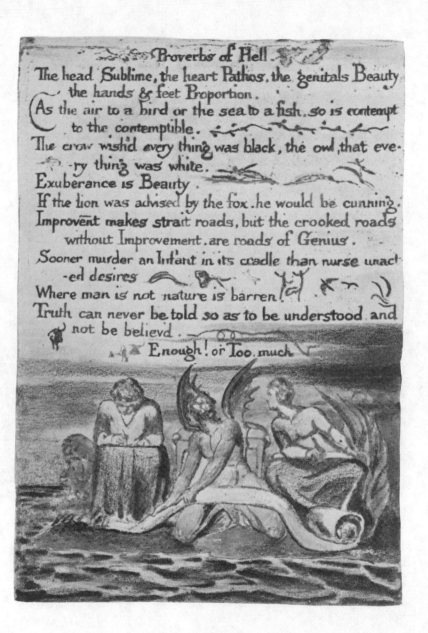

Proverbs of Hell.

The head Sublime, the heart Pathos, the genitals Beauty
the hands & feet Proportion.

As the air to a bird or the sea to a fish, so is contempt
to the contemptible.

The crow wish'd every thing was black, the owl, that every thing was white.

Exuberance is Beauty.

If the lion was advised by the fox. he would be cunning.

Improvement makes strait roads, but the crooked roads
without Improvement. are roads of Genius.

Sooner murder an Infant in its cradle than nurse unacted desires

Where man is not nature is barren.

Truth can never be told so as to be understood. and
not be believ'd.

Enough! or Too much

PLATE 10

The ancient Poets animated all sensible objects
with Gods or Geniuses. calling them by the names and
adorning them with the properties of woods, rivers
mountains. lakes, cities, nations, and whatever their
enlarged & numerous senses could percieve.

And particularly they studied the genius of each
city & country. placing it under its mental deity.

Till a system was formed, which some took advantage of & enslav'd the vulgar by attempting to
realize or abstract the mental deities from their
objects: thus began Priesthood.

Choosing forms of worship from poetic tales.

And at length they pronounced that the Gods
had orderd such things.

Thus men forgot that All deities reside
in the human breast.

PLATE 11

A Memorable Fancy,

The Prophets Isaiah and Ezekiel dined with
me, and I asked them how they dared so roundly to
assert. that God spoke to them; and whether they
did not think at the time, that they would be mis-
-understood, & so be the cause of imposition

Isaiah answer'd. I saw no God. nor heard
any. in a finite organical perception: but my sen-
-ses discover'd the infinite in every thing, and as I
was then perswaded. & remain confirm'd; that the
voice of honest indignation is the voice of God. I
cared not for consequences but wrote

Then I asked: does a firm perswasion that a
thing is so, make it so?

He replied. All poets believe that it does. &
in ages of imagination this firm perswasion removed mountains; but many are not capable of a
firm perswasion of any thing

Then Ezekiel said. The philosophy of the east
taught the first principles of human perception
some nations held one principle for the origin &
some another, we of Israel taught that the Poetic
Genius (as you now call it) was the first principle
and all the others merely derivative. which was the
cause of our despising the Priests & Philosophers
of other countries, and prophecying that all Gods
would

PLATE 12

would at last be proved to originate in ours & to be the tributaries of the Poetic Genius, it was this. that our great poet King David desired so fervently & invokes so patheticly, saying by this he conquers enemies & governs kingdoms; and we so loved our God, that we cursed in his name all the deities of surrounding nations, and asserted that they had rebelled; from these opinions the vulgar came to think that all nations would at last be subject to the jews.

This said he, like all firm perswasions, is come to pass, for all nations believe the jews code and worship the jews god, and what greater subjection can be

I heard this with some wonder, & must confess my own conviction. After dinner I ask'd Isaiah to favour the world with his last works, he said none of equal value was lost. Ezekiel said the same of his.

I also asked Isaiah what made him go naked and barefoot three years? he answerd, the same that made our friend Diogenes the Grecian.

I then asked Ezekiel. why he eat dung, & lay so long on his right & left side? he answerd, the desire of raising other men into a perception of the infinite this the North American tribes practise. & is he honest who resists his genius or conscience. only for the sake of present ease or gratification?

PLATE 13

The ancient tradition that the world will be con-
-sumed in fire at the end of six thousand years
is true, as I have heard from Hell.

For the cherub with his flaming sword is
hereby commanded to leave his guard at tree of
life, and when he does, the whole creation will
be consumed, and appear infinite and holy
whereas it now appears finite & corrupt.

This will come to pass by an improvement of
sensual enjoyment.

But first the notion that man has a body
distinct from his soul, is to be expunged; this
I shall do by printing in the infernal method, by
corrosives, which in Hell are salutary and medicinal, melting apparent surfaces away, and
displaying the infinite which was hid.

If the doors of perception were cleansed
every thing would appear to man as it is: Infinite.

For man has closed himself up, till he sees
all things thro' narrow chinks of his cavern.

PLATE 14

A Memorable Fancy

I was in a Printing house in Hell & saw the method in which knowledge is transmitted from generation to generation

In the first chamber was a Dragon-Man, clearing away the rubbish from a caves mouth; within, a number of Dragons were hollowing the cave.

In the second chamber was a Viper folding round the rock & the cave, and others adorning it with gold silver and precious stones

In the third chamber was an Eagle with wings and feathers of air, he caused the inside of the cave to be infinite, around were numbers of Eagle like men, who built palaces in the immense cliffs.

In the fourth chamber were Lions of flaming fire raging around & melting the metals into living fluids.

In the fifth chamber were Unnamd forms, which cast the metals into the expanse.

There they were reciev'd by Men who occupied the sixth chamber, and took the forms of books & were arranged in libraries.

PLATE 15

The Giants who formed this world into its
sensual existence and now seem to live in it
in chains; are in truth, the causes of its life
& the sources of all activity, but the chains
are, the cunning of weak and tame minds which
have power to resist energy. according to the pro-
-verb, the weak in courage is strong in cunning

Thus one portion of being, is the Prolific. the
other, the Devouring: to the devourer it seems as
if the producer was in his chains. but it is not so;
he only takes portions of existence and fancies
that the whole. ——

But the Prolific would cease to be Prolific
unless the Devourer as a sea recieved the excess
of his delights. ——

Some will say, Is not God alone the Prolific
I answer. God only Acts & Is. in existing beings
or Men. ——

These two classes of men are always upon
earth. & they should be enemies; whoever tries
to

PLATE 16

to reconcile them seeks to destroy existence.

Religion is an endeavour to reconcile the two.

Note. Jesus Christ did not wish to unite
but to seperate them, as in the Parable of sheep and
goats! & he says I came not to send Peace but a
Sword.

Mesiah or Satan or Tempter was formerly
thought to be one of the Antediluvians who are our
Energies.

A Memorable Fancy

An Angel came to me and said. O pitiable foolish
young man! O horrible! O dreadful state! consider
the hot burning dungeon thou art preparing for thyself
to all eternity, to which thou art going in such career.

I said. perhaps you will be willing to shew me
my eternal lot & we will contemplate together upon it
and see whether your lot or mine is most desirable
So he took me thro' a stable & thro' a church
& down into the church vault at the end of which
was a mill: thro' the mill we went, and came to a
cave. down the winding cavern we groped our tedi-
-ous way till a void boundless as a nether sky ap-
-peard beneath us & we held by the roots of trees
and hung over this immensity: but I said, if you
please we will commit ourselves to this void, and
see whether providence is here also, if you will not
I will? but he answerd, do not presume O young-
man but as we here remain behold thy lot which
will soon appear when the darkness passes away
So I remaind with him sitting in the twisted
root

PLATE 17

root of an oak, he was suspended in a fungus
which hung with the head downward into the deep:
   By degrees we beheld the infinite Abyss, fiery
as the smoke of a burning city; beneath us at an
immense distance was the sun, black but shining
round it were fiery tracks on which revolv'd vast
spiders, crawling after their prey; which flew or
rather swum in the infinite deep, in the most ter-
-rific shapes of animals sprung from corruption.
& the air was full of them, & seemd composed
of them; these are Devils, and are called Powers
of the air, I now asked my companion which was my
eternal lot? he said, between the black & white spiders
     But now, from between the black & white spiders
a cloud and fire burst and rolled thro the deep
blackning all beneath, so that the nether deep grew
black as a sea & rolled with a terrible noise: be-
-neath us was nothing now to be seen but a black
tempest, till looking east between the clouds & the
waves, we saw a cataract of blood mixed with fire
and not many stones throw from us appeard and
sunk again the scaly fold of a monstrous serpent
at last to the east, distant about three degrees appeard a fiery crest above the waves slowly it rear
ed like a ridge of golden rocks till we discoverd
two globes of crimson fire, from which the sea
fled away in clouds of smoke, and now we saw, it
was the head of Leviathan, his forehead was divided into streaks of green & purple like those on
a tygers forehead: soon we saw his mouth & red
gills hang just above the raging foam tinging the
black deep with beams of blood, advancing toward
us

PLATE 18

us with all the fury of a spiritual existence.

~My friend the Angel climb'd up from his station into the mill; I remaind alone. & then this appearance was no more, but I found myself sitting on a pleasant bank beside a river by moon light hearing a harper who sung to the harp. & his theme was, The man who never alters his opinion is like standing water, & breeds reptiles of the mind.

But I arose. and sought for the mill & there I found my Angel, who surprised asked me, how I escaped?

I answerd. All that we saw was owing to your metaphysics: for when you ran away, I found myself on a bank by moonlight hearing a harper, But now we have seen my eternal lot. shall I shew you yours? he laughd at my proposal: but I by force suddenly caught him in my arms, & flew westerly thro' the night, till we were elevated above the earths shadow: then I flung myself with him directly into the body of the sun, here I clothed myself in white, & taking in my hand Swedenborgs volumes sunk from the glorious clime, and passed all the planets till we came to saturn, here I staid to rest & then leapd into the void. between saturn & the fixed stars.

Here said I! is your lot, in this space, if space it may be calld. Soon we saw the stable and the church, & I took him to the altar and opend the Bible, and lo! it was a deep pit, into which I descended driving the Angel before me. soon we saw seven houses of brick, one we enterd; in it were a
num

PLATE 19

number of monkeys. baboons & all of that species chaind by the middle. grinning and snatching at one another. but witheld by the shortness of their chains: however I saw that they sometimes grew numerous, and then the weak were caught by the strong and with a grinning aspect, first coupled with & then devourd, by plucking off first one limb and then another till the body was left a helpless trunk. this after grinning & kissing it with seeming fondness they devourd too: and here & there I saw one savourily picking the flesh off of his own tail; as the stench terribly annoyd us both we went into the mill, & I in my hand brought the skeleton of a body, which in the mill was Aristotles Analytics.

So the Angel said: thy phantasy has imposed upon me & thou oughtest to be ashamed.

I answerd: we impose on one another. & it is but lost time to converse with you whose works are only Analytics

PLATE 20

I have always found that Angels have the vanity to speak of themselves as the only wise; this they
do with a confident insolence sprouting from systematic reasoning:

Thus Swedenborg boasts that what he writes is
new; tho' it is only the Contents or Index of already
publish'd books

A man carried a monkey about for a shew, & because he was a little wiser than the monkey, grew
vain, and concievd himself as much wiser than seven men. It is so with Swedenborg; he shews the
folly of churches & exposes hypocrites, till he im
agines that all are religious, & himself the single
one

PLATE 21

one on earth that ever broke a net.

Now hear a plain fact. Swedenborg has not writ-ten one new truth. Now hear another: he has written all the old falshoods.

And now hear the reason. He conversed with Angels who are all religious. & conversed not with Devils who all hate religion for he was incapable thro' his conceited notions.

Thus Swedenborgs writings are a recapitulation of all superficial opinions, and an analysis of the more sublime, but no further.

Have now another plain fact: Any man of mechanic -al talents may from the writings of Paracelsus or Ja -cob Behmen, produce ten thousand volumes of equal value with Swedenborgs, and from those of Dante or Shakespear, an infinite number.

But when he has done this, let him not say that he knows better than his master, for he only holds a can-dle in sunshine.

A Memorable Fancy

Once I saw a Devil in a flame of fire, who arose be-fore an Angel that sat on a cloud, and the Devil ut--terd these words.

The worship of God is. Honouring his gifts in other men each according to his genius, and loving the

great

greatest men best, those who envy or calumniate great men hate God, for there is no other God.

The Angel hearing this became almost blue but mastering himself he grew yellow, & at last white pink & smiling. and then replied, Thou Idolater. is not God One? & is not he visible in Jesus Christ? and has not Jesus Christ given his sanction to the law of ten commandments and are not all other men fools sinners & nothings?

The Devil answer'd; bray a fool in a morter with wheat yet shall not his folly be beaten out of him if Jesus Christ is the greatest man, you ought to love him in the greatest degree; now hear how he has given his sanction to the law of ten command-ments; did he not mock at the sabbath, and so mock the sabbaths God? murder those who were murderd because of him? turn away the law from the woman taken in adultery? steal the labor of others to support him? bear false witness when he omitted making a defence before Pilate? covet when he prayd for his disciples, and when he bid them shake off the dust of their feet against such as refused to lodge them? I tell you, no virtue can exist without breaking these ten command-ments; Jesus was all virtue, and acted from im-pulse

PLATE 23

pulse: not from rules.

  When he had so spoken: I beheld the Angel who
stretched out his arms embracing the flame of fire
& he was consumed and arose as Elijah

  Note This Angel, who is now become a Devil, is
my particular friend: we often read the Bible together in its infernal or diabolical sense which
the world shall have if they behave well

  I have also: The Bible of Hell: which the world
shall have whether they will or no.

One Law for the Lion & Ox is Oppression

PLATE 24

society, to manage on his own with little psychological dependence upon woman. At least this is the typical image for
the ego ideal as built up in the course of the developmental
process of the male. He is inclined to subordinate the female,
then, and to accord her the role of helpmate to enable him to
carry out the duties and responsibilities of his manhood. The
aspects of the feminine which could be positive tend to become more and more ambivalent under repression as time
goes on. This is particularly true when there is an unsatis-
factory marital relationship and the female aspect within the
man fails to find full expression in the verbal and non-verbal
communication of an affectionate relationship with a wife.
It is then that the man's sensitivity to the feminine acquires
a particularly numinous quality; that is, his repressed femininity acquires an inexplicable power over his male side, leading him into an exercise of his irrational functions. He may
experience this in any of a number of forms, from a particular
kind of obstinacy which precludes action all the way to a
surging current which promises to infuse all that he does

This, then, is the archetypal base of the female figure who
is seen in the left side of the plate, the left symbolizing the
sinister, dark or hidden part of the personality. She is seductive, appealing, and she holds her counterpart in an embrace
which is at once strong and tender. She contacts him with her
arms, but the embrace does not involve their bodies. Their
mating is in the area of the head only, which signifies a
spiritual relationship. She is the personalization of the "soul,"
the feminine aspect of man which came to be called "anima"
in Jung's psychological schema. She represents the side opposed to collective consciousness. She is invisible to society, but
clearly evident to Blake. She holds him so that he cannot escape,
if indeed he should desire to do so. If she does not lend him the
warmth of her own flesh, there is the heat of the flame all
about her. From this the masculine must distance himself
enough so that he is not destroyed by it. To embrace her fully
would be to invite the disaster that befell all those characters
of myth and legend who approached too close to the sun-god.

This is an embrace which is in reality a confrontation between the ego and the "other," between the male who sees

himself as a rational being able to perform successfully in the
manner prescribed by the social order and the female afire
with energy which knows no bound or limitation. He is
Blake as the world sees him, and she is his soul, whom only
he knows intimately, but whose light shines through his eyes.
Reason and Energy are seen as the two contraries which
struggle within Blake, and whose interaction so deeply concerns him in this work.

The picture is one of turmoil—the effect is disturbing, yet
there is within it a promise of wholeness. The trinity of Earth,
Heaven and Hell suggests the dynamic quality associated with
the number three. But the fourth is also present, and we see
it as a disk of gold shining behind the heads of the two major
figures. As a perfect circle with no beginning or end, as a
sphere which suggests the whole earth or the sun, it is both
center and circumference. It is the place where the opposites
meet, and also it is the luminous occurrence at the spot of the
miraculous union. It may be thought of as a *mandala,* the
word is Sanskrit meaning "circle." This is the Indian term for
the circles drawn in religious rituals and used as the foci for
meditation. The goal of contemplating the processes having
to do with the *mandala* is that the yogi should become inwardly aware of the deity. "Through contemplation he recognizes himself as God again, and thus returns from the illusion
of individual existence into the universal totality of the
divine state," says Jung.[1] There are innumerable variants of
the *mandala* motif, Jung goes on to explain. "Their basic
motif is the premonition of a centre of personality, a kind of
central point within the psyche, to which everything is . . . arranged, and which is in itself a source of energy. The energy
of the central point is manifested in the almost irresistible
compulsion and urge to *become what one is,* just as every
organism is driven to assume the form that is characteristic of
its nature, no matter what the circumstances. This centre is
not felt or thought of as the ego, but if one may so express
it, as the *self.* Although the centre is represented by an inner-
most point, it is surrounded by a periphery containing everything that belongs to the self—the paired opposites that make
up the total personality."[2]

In the radiant light of the *mandala* circle which forms the halo for the two figures in Blake's picture, the union of the primal pair is symbolized by the meeting of their lips. *The Marriage of Heaven and Hell* suggests by its title that the intrapsychic opposites were joined in Blake through the *operatio* of the creative work but this is far from being the whole story. The theme of the confrontation of the opposites was constellated in this book, and in the course of writing it Blake deals with various aspects of this all-encompassing problem. Yet it will be seen as we examine the text that *The Marriage of Heaven and Hell* illuminated only the *inception* of a relationship. It was a Marriage that took place as a moment in time, a ritual which in itself was impressive and moving but nevertheless a limited experience. What it implied and what was to follow later had to do with Marriage as a condition, an ongoing state of relationship. That relationship was to follow a stormy course without surcease, expressing itself in volume after volume of poetic mythology which was to occupy Blake almost to the end of his life.

PLATE 2

The Argument

Rintrah roars & shakes his fires in the burden'd air;
Hungry clouds swag on the deep.

Once meek, and in a perilous path,
The just man kept his course along
The vale of death.
Roses are planted where thorns grow,
And on the barren heath
Sing the honey bees.

Then the perilous path was planted,
And a river and a spring
On every cliff and tomb,
And on the bleached bones
Red clay brought forth;

> Till the villain left the paths of ease,
> To walk in perilous paths, and drive
> The just man into barren climes
>
> Now the sneaking serpent walks
> In mild humility,
> And the just man rages in the wilds
> Where lions roam.
>
> Rintrah roars & shakes his fires in the burden'd air;
> Hungry clouds swag on the deep.

The book begins with violent emotion. Rintrah is the personification of rage against the status quo, both in the inner life of Blake and in the outer situation. He is Blake's "Own Angry Man," a John the Baptist or Elijah figure, the spirit of prophecy driven out into the wilderness.[1]

There is to be a change which begins a new era, a revolutionary period which overturns the easy complacent segment of society and places it under chains such as it had itself inflicted on those who were meek and subservient before. For those who lived in the comfortable paradise of unconsciousness with respect to the needs and desires of the laboring classes, life would never be the same, for they were to be displaced and forced to deal with the anger of the unruly rebel mob. A similar situation had existed within the psyche of Blake. He had held within him until now the tension of the opposites. Clasped together, as we saw in the frontispiece, they did not present a serious threat, but it was like the moment before creation, before birth—the movement could not be contained. He wrote of this primordial state later in *The Four Zoas*, but we read it here to visualize the moment before Rintrah's arrival on the scene, the pre-dawn of consciousness:

The earth spread forth her table wide: the night a silver cup
Fill'd with the wine of anguish, waited at the golden feast.
But the bright Sun was not as yet; he filling all the expanse
Slept as a bird in the blue shell that soon shall burst away.[2]

"Rintrah roars" must be interpreted as the breaking up of the world's original unity and the splitting apart into contraries, the opposites. These are one in the beginning and one in the end, as they are viewed through the blind trust of the newborn or the fading vision of the dying man. But between birth and death, man is engaged upon the developmental process of differentiation, and through his finite perception he sees the parts of his nature and of human nature in the world at large as isolated elements, rather than as aspects of a totality. Rintrah, a figure who is to recur throughout Blake's work, is introduced in this poem. He is to become an important character in the mythology, which at this time probably was beginning to be formulated in Blake's mind. He is also connected with world events: the outcry and fires of Rintrah are in the burdened clouds, that heavily sink upon the deeps that separate France from England.[3] If we can accept that to Blake France had the inner meaning of the uncontrolled energy of violent rebellion and England was seen as the sanity of man who is menaced by the effect of the turbulent state of his emotions, we can see the manner in which symbolic thinking brings one closer to the inner unconscious meaning of the holocaust brought about by Rintrah. Swinburne observes the image from within and turns it outward: "Rintrah, the spirit presiding over this period, is a spirit of fire and storm; darkness and famine, wrath and want, dividing the kingdom of the world."[4] S. Foster Damon says it metaphorically: "So wrath (Rintrah) materializing as the storm of Revolution, hangs heavily over the world."[5]

Thomas Wright takes a more subjective view of the significance of Rintrah, viewing him as Blake's own spirit of energy which is furious because the just or imaginative man has to walk not in a pleasant garden as before but in deserts.[6] And still another commentator, Emily Hamblen, in her book *On the Minor Prophecies of William Blake* says: "Rintrah is the lion spirit of egoism, the imperious demands of personality to make itself felt. This energy may be employed in the service of enlightenment; Rintrah here stands for it in the arrogant aspect of the rational mind."[7]

However we look at Rintrah, it seems clear that he is the symbol for violence that precipitates change. He appears upon a scene where passivity is the mood. The meek, just man has been measuring his course in that perilous path of life that is always shadowed by death. For his subservience and obedience to God, he was rewarded with the gift of immortality: because man avoided life, he preserved himself from death; he was in a state of innocence, that state into which we all are born, from which sooner or later we separate. In the world man learns that the rose and the thorn grow together. The rose is a symbol of perfection in nature, but the thorn does much to make man take notice of it. The bee with his stinging tail, the rose with its thorn each possesses negative and positive aspects as must be present in anything that lives outside of the primordial paradise.

Rintrah's roar against complacency and insensitivity in paradise frightens the dormant man into 'wakening. In the real world into which he emerges at the beginning of the differentiation process, he no longer avoids the "perilous path" or the forbidden way. That path is planted now, and the water of life begins to flow over the graves of innocence—over "every cliff and tomb" and even over red clay from which the earth-mother brings forth bleached bones. This is the beginning of consciousness. Man, thrust into a world of struggle, arrives not as one, but as two: the villain and the just man. He is Adam and the serpent, Jacob and Esau, he is sneaking hypocrisy displacing outraged honesty. The times are portentous, for man's dual nature is at war with itself. The just man whom we might have imagined in the beginning as the personification of that idea of collective morality sanctioned by Reason, the man represented in the title page illustration, has changed in character. In the first place he seemed to be identified with the side of Heaven—resting as he did on the pillow of cloud. But he is quiet no longer.

Now he rages in the wild where lions roam—he has been incited by the roar of Rintrah and is angered by his expulsion from the paths of ease. He is Adam and Esau displaced from their birthrights and he is the imaginative man also. Now he

will become active, and, as we shall see, will come to be identified with another aspect of the masculine, the far more
dynamic image of the Devil. As to the serpent, who used to
be identified with the Devil, he now begins to sneak about
in "mild humility." Because of his demeanor he has become
the accepted one with respect to the social order. He is also
Jacob and he is now associated with the Angel's party, which
takes on the negative aspect assigned by Blake to the hypocrite. This is the initial transformation, setting the stage for
the complete overturn and reassessment of values within the
personality in the light of the recognition of the contraries
inherent in every human response.

The illustration which accompanies this text depicts Blake's
vision of the lost paradise. Along the right-hand side of the
page, which may be identified with consciousness, are drawn
two lovely maidens, half dryad, half human. One plays high
in a tree. Her swirling garments expose a strong and sensuous
leg. She is warm-blooded and lively looking, and she stands
far above the ground, her foot firmly planted in the crotch of
a branch. She reaches out a hand to the other maiden as
though she could help her climb up into the tree. But this
maiden's feet are planted firmly in the earth and while she
encircles the tree trunk with one arm it seems clear that she
will never free herself from earth, which might here be
thought of as her own rationalistic standpoint.

These two feminine figures recall the wish that Blake once
expressed to bring another woman into his household.
Catherine had refused to admit that lovely young creature,
and Blake was forced to repress his desire for her. She became
incorporated into the archetypal images of the feminine
within his psyche. As an aspect of the unconscious, she was to
make herself manifest through the mechanism of projection.
His unexpressed feelings would arise as visible feminine
images in myriad forms in his writings and his engravings.
They would comfort him with sweetness as in this plate, or
they would plague him with restlessness, or break forth in
such an intensity of heat as to give rise to the picture of the
mistress of the flames whom we see on the next plate.

PLATE 3

We turn the page and she appears from the left side which holds the deeper mysteries. The flames which envelop her signify her immortal and transpersonal nature—she is afire and yet she is not consumed. She is the embodiment of Blake's instinctual energy, which has rarely been expressed in natural sexual terms because of his marital difficulties, his early religious training and his general acceptance of the conventional moral standards of his times. Here the teachings of Swedenborg still have their hold upon Blake, but his satirical motif in *The Marriage* betrays a simultaneous desire to expose him at the same time. The contrast between the text and the picture is part of the piece: while Swedenborg sits calmly at the tomb, obviously having outlived his usefulness, the eternal flame is burning below, supplying energy for the new age, for the new creativity.

In deriding Swedenborg, Blake is also proving that his former mentor was accurate enough in his prophecy that this is the time of the millennium—and that at this point the opposition of the just man and the hypocrite is philosophically and even politically correct. As Schorer [1] points out, Blake enunciates the revolutionary principle of thesis and antithesis toward which the ideas not less than the arrangement of the negations was to point—the conflict of contrary interests and the tension between them that is the precondition of the development of any ideas. He does this in such terms as were available to him, a mixture of theological doctrine and metaphysical abstraction.

The text continues:

As a new heaven is begun, and it is now thirty-three years since its advent, the Eternal Hell revives. And lo! Swedenborg is the Angel sitting at the tomb: his writings are the linen clothes folded up. Now is the dominion of Edom & the return of Adam into Paradise. See Isaiah xxxiv & xxxv Chap.

The old paradise is gone and "a new heaven is begun" but along with it "the Eternal Hell revives." Here is stated clearly the duality that Blake proclaims in the outer world, and senses, if only vaguely, in his own nature. But this clarity dissolves in the next few lines and one must somehow grasp the feeling which inspired the poet through his selection of words rather than through their meaning. For Blake has abstracted emotion and expressed it not in the ordinary prosaic method of association with familiar ideas, but rather as chords that evoke response through symbolic connections. Thus when Blake says, "As a new heaven is begun, and it is now thirty-three years since its advent," "heaven" and "thirty-three" call up the period of Christ's life on earth. Also, we cannot overlook that Blake was born in 1757, and that the writing of *The Marriage of Heaven and Hell* was begun in 1790. Blake, then, at the moment of writing, was also thirty-three years old. Thirty-three, as the age of crucifixion, evokes the image of the cross. Here is the symbol par excellence of the *coniunctio oppositorum*, the meeting of the opposites in a state of tension, which effects a transformation. Jesus incarnate becomes again Jesus united with the eternal God. The question is raised as to whether consciously or, more probably, unconsciously Blake identifies with the God-man and regards the first half of his life as this heaven which has come to an end in a kind of death preceding a rebirth of the spirit which corresponds to the symbolic resurrection of Christ.

C. G. Jung discusses at length the changes which take place in the psychic realm of the individual as he enters upon the second half of life, in his essay, "The Stages of Life." [2] "Man's values," he writes, "and even his body, do tend to change into their opposites . . . . We cannot live in the afternoon of life according to the programme of life's morning; for what was great in the morning will be little at evening, and what in the morning was true will at evening have become a lie." [3]

The first thirty-three years for Blake were years turned outward toward the world. His concern with the French Revolution and the British reaction to it paralleled the psychological changes in Blake which were not yet evident to him. Yet even with its political revolution and its economic upheavals, Britain was still a relative "vale of peace" for Blake when compared with the inner experience in which he was soon to become involved. It was in the early years that he wrote his love poems, his nature poems, his songs of adventure and most of his politically inspired works. But after his descent into the personal—yet far more than personal—Hell with which *The Marriage* deals, and out of the holy union that came to pass there, a new Blake of the libertarian spirit was born, as a resurrected being. In psychological terms one might say that during the course of the writing of this book a transformation took place in Blake whereby he was able to come into a working relationship with the personal unconscious and the collective unconscious. But the numinosity of the experience comes through more clearly when we mingle in our own imagination, as Blake did, the vision of the tomb of Christ and the copper plate upon which Blake etched his design. Thus we come to sense the spirit of the design, made visible through the hand and eye of the artist, and we hear God speak to man through the voice of the muse.

Blake knew of Swedenborg's prophecy announcing a new spiritual dispensation beginning in 1757.

> It has been granted to me to see with my own eyes, that the Last Judgment is now accomplished; that the evil are cast into the hells and the good elevated into heaven, and thus that all things are reduced into order, the spiritual equilibrium between good and evil, or between heaven and hell, being thence restored. . . . It was granted to me to see all these things with my own eyes, in order that I might be able to testify of them. This Last Judgment was commenced in the beginning of the year 1757, and was fully accomplished at the end of that year.[4]

This was the year of Blake's birth and he may have applied the prophecy to his own divine mission. In Blake's account of the resurrection of man, Swedenborg is left behind in his own eschatology.

According to A. C. Swinburne, writing in *William Blake*,[5] Blake's estimate of Swedenborg was that his inspiration was limited and timid, superficial and derivative; that he was content with leaves and husks, and had not the courage to examine the root and kernel of things; that he clove to heaven and shrank from the hell of other men. These comments refer to Blake's attitude toward Swedenborg while he was writing *The Marriage of Heaven and Hell*. Onto Swedenborg, the

"Angel sitting at the tomb," Blake projects the heaven-oriented virtues of logical reasonableness and restraint of instinctual impulse—both of which seem to him to be binding chains which have too long inhibited the free flow of his creative expression. Likewise, Swedenborg's "writings. . . . the linen clothes folded up," may be a symbolic expression for the way in which Blake evaluated his own earlier works, *e.g., The Songs of Innocence* which were written while he was still very much under the influence of the "heavenly" aspect of the collective consciousness. Those clothes were the superficial appurtenances required by Jesus as he walked the earth, but now that he is the risen Christ, his free spirit neither needs nor tolerates them. The division between flesh and spirit is reflected in the separation of Edom from Paradise. The references to Isaiah xxxiv and xxxv deal respectively with the Lord's laying waste to Edom, and making the desert once more fruitful for Zion.

The balance of the text of Plate 3 follows:

Without Contraries is no progression. Attraction and Repulsion, Reason and Energy, Love and Hate, are necessary to Human existence.
From these contraries spring what the religious call Good & Evil. Good is the passive that obeys Reason. Evil is the active springing from Energy.
Good is Heaven. Evil is Hell.

Here Blake clearly states his theory of the opposites, implying the conviction that progression or dynamic development is possible only if the tension between the poles is maintained. What, exactly, is polarity? Alan Watts takes up this pertinent question in a study of the myths of polarity, *The Two Hands of God*. He writes:

Polarity is something more than simple duality or opposition. For to say that opposites are *polar* is to say much more than that they are far apart: It is to say that they are related and joined—that they are terms, ends, or extremities of a single whole. Polar opposites are therefore inseparable opposites like the poles of the earth or of a magnet or the ends of a stick or the faces of a coin. Though what lies between the poles is more substantial than the poles themselves

—since they are the abstract "terms" rather than the concrete body—
nevertheless man thinks in terms and therefore divides in thought
what is undivided in nature. To think is to categorize, to sort experience into classes and intellectual pigeonholes. It is thus that, from
the standpoint of thought, the all-important question is ever, "Is it
this, or is it that?" Is the experience inside this class or is it outside?
By answering such questions we describe and explain the world; we
make it explicit. But implicitly, in nature herself, there are no
classes. We drop these intellectual nets and boxes upon the world
as we weave the imaginary lines of latitude and longitude upon the
face of the earth, and the likewise imaginary firmament of the stars.
It is thus the imaginary, abstract, and conceptual character of these
divisions which renders them polar. The importance of a box for
thoughts is that the inside is different from the outside. But in
nature the walls of a box are what the inside and outside have in
common.[6]

The picture at the bottom of Plate 3 deals in a less abstract
way than does the text with the problem of the polarity or, as
Blake calls it, the contraries. Sexual intercourse is the unifying
substantial reality that exists between the masculine and
feminine opposites and, out of this overriding union, human
existence is able to come into being. Blake illustrates this
principle in his drawing of the process of birth with the howling infant flailing his arms against the sky as he becomes
separate from his mother. The arrival of a new child is the
supreme victory of creation, and it happens only because man
and woman are distinct entities in the abstract sense, but in
the perspective of existence they are able to function as a
totality.

As Blake considers the contraries, it is clear that he is rebel-
ling against Swedenborg's one-sided view of concern only with
the good, with the side of heaven. Blake does not assign
values to attraction and repulsion, reason and energy, love
and hate—he only observes how "the religious" (meaning those
who adhere to the religious orthodoxy current in late
eighteenth century England) evaluate their effect on society.
The passive obedience of a man to his government, to the
ethic of his milieu, to the doctrine of his church, is "reasonable," and a religious collective accepts this as "Good." That
which disturbs the status quo by a flow of energy which acti-

vates opposing forces is considered "Evil" by that same collective. "Good" they assign to heaven, "Evil," to hell.

Swinburne put it well when he said, "To Blake, in whom 'a new heaven is begun,' the one does not seem terrible, nor the other desirable. To him the flaming fire wherein dwells a God whom men call devil seems a purer element of life than the cloudy space wherein dwells a devil whom men call God." [7]

In this section on the *contraries,* and in the one which will follow, *The voice of the Devil,* we can see the influence upon Blake of Boehme's analysis of the psyche and the interaction of its parts. The three worlds which Boehme saw correspond closely with the images comprising the illustration for the title page of *The Marriage of Heaven and Hell.* First of all is Boehme's *Dark Fire-World,* which he also called Hell and which critic S. Foster Damon[8] calls the subconscious. It contains the basic impulses—all the deadly sins. Boehme asserted that these were the sources of life itself. Above is the *Light World* (Heaven). As the evil instincts rise, a certain divine spark transmutes them from evil to good. The sins become the virtues: selfishness becomes generosity and lust becomes love.

Boehme's position came closer to that which Blake was to take when he wrote that these two worlds, Hell and Heaven, are essential to each other; that they exist simultaneously in God. He found that the opposition of the contraries exists in God himself, without which there could be neither light nor darkness. This would not mean an abstract God, but rather the divine immanence in man, as Boehme also wrote "every man carries Heaven and Hell with him in this world." The "subconscious" Hell, and the supra-conscious or "superego" Heaven of Boehme, may be opposite in their appearance but since both are outside of the objective world which is perceived by the five senses, both must be said to belong to the unconscious—which has its way of knowing without sensing.

The third world of Boehme's analysis of the psyche was the *Outer World of Nature.* He regarded this as a mere "outbirth" of the others, a projection, as Damon says, of Man.[9] Boehme had much to say about this "astral" world with its starry wheels, which placed man under the rule of physical laws. He asserted that these laws of cause and effect were actually an expression of the spiritual realities underlying them. The human body is part of nature; and it is the soul within which gives it form.

Boehme helped Blake to resolve the problem of salvation, which had troubled him so greatly in his reading of Swedenborg. Swedenborg, it will be recalled, was felt to be in error by Blake, in that he did not understand the real nature of evil and therefore accepted conventional morality. In Boehme's work, the problem of salvation is that of keeping a harmonious balance of the parts, so that the *Dark World* is kept where the *Light World* can irradiate and temper it. The Fall occurred from lack of balance, specifically the ambition of Lucifer to dominate. Then all the fires of the *Dark World* broke loose, and all the disasters followed. Blake echoed this when he wrote:

> Rintrah roars & shakes his fires in the burden'd air;
> Hungry clouds swag on the deep.

The concept of Boehme's *Three Worlds* answered for Blake the question of how a God of Love could create a place of everlasting punishment for his children. God is good; all things that proceed from him are good in essence, and that essence can never be corrupted. Therefore Hell, which is of God, must be good; and the life force proceeding from it (the libido, or Blake's "Energy") cannot be evil, and far from being everlasting pain, is "Eternal Delight."

In *The Marriage of Heaven and Hell,* Blake puts aside any moral meanings Boehme had attached to the terms "Heaven" and "Hell" and "Good" and "Evil." For Blake they are terms which may be variously interpreted. He feels that Boehme's *Dark World* is indeed the source of life and that only to the short-sighted Angels do its flames appear to be "torment and insanity." He regards the *Light World* as the restraining force identified with reason, which is not creative and, if not itself restrained, is easily capable of tyrannizing over the *Outer World of Nature.*

Boehme's *Three Worlds* correspond to those of Milton and

Swedenborg, but Milton and Swedenborg overlooked the dynamic relationship between them which Boehme had pointed out and Blake had made the basis of his exposition of the sources of creative energy in *The Marriage of Heaven and Hell*.[10]

PLATE 4

The voice of the Devil

All Bibles or sacred codes have been the causes of the following Errors:

    1. That Man has two real existing principles: Viz: a Body & a Soul.

    2. That Energy, call'd Evil, is alone from the Body; & that Reason, call'd Good, is alone from the Soul.

    3. That God will torment Man in Eternity for following his Energies.

    But the following Contraries to these are True:

    1. Man has no Body distinct from his Soul; for that call'd Body is a portion of the Soul discern'd by the five Senses, the chief inlets of Soul in this age.

    2. Energy is the only life, and is from the Body; and Reason is the bound or outward circumference of Energy.

    3. Energy is Eternal Delight.

In the illustration below the text we see the effects of the concepts which Blake had denounced as dualistic. The young child seen here is the newborn infant of Plate 3. He is Imagination, the treasured possession of the feminine spirit of energy. The anima, mistress of the soul, holds fast to her love-child, and keeps him out of reach of the masculine figure who represents Reason. He is in chains, but the female fears him none the less. She is frightened because she has lost her relationship with Reason. Though she may seem to be adrift, the picture shows that she *can* walk on water. Thus she becomes, again, an image of the unconscious, with potentialities that do not seem capable of being realized. Through her energy she is able to save this child from fire, water and from the father, but at the same time she knows that the child is not only hers but also his father's. He has been born of the water and the fire, but also of Reason enchained. The child is the substantial reality between the poles, the paradox of the existence of the contraries.

As we read this section, the title of which credits the energic source upon which Blake draws for his concept, we are able to see what has been happening to Blake's attitude toward the organized religion of his day. His intuitive awareness of God's nearness to him led him at first to seek a broader basis for his own feelings within the Anglican church. When its confines appeared to leave him little room for his personal experience of a God beyond any approach through reason, he sought out the apocalyptic visions in Swedenborg's writings to illuminate his own mystical experience. In his studies he immersed himself in religious outlooks which were basically an expression of one collective or another. Upon close analysis he realized that it mattered little whether that collective was the established church of the land or a splinter group which expressed similar beliefs in the language of visionary revelation. Both reflected the collective consciousness in which Body was set in opposition to Soul and the church was seen as a positive force arrayed on the side of Soul to combat the drives unleashed by Body which would otherwise be uncontrollable.

It is in the individualistic spirit of Boehme that Blake refers to "All Bibles or sacred codes." It must be assumed that he refers to the sacred literature of the Judeo-Christian culture, because studies of his works indicate that his religious background is almost entirely limited to this tradition. Within this tradition, he observes, Energy is associated with the physical nature of man; the instincts and drives originate in man's biological constitution. This is in contrast to Reason which is a separate function, more acquired than innate, belonging to man's spiritual nature. The term "Energy," as Blake understands the popular use of it, refers to that which makes man behave in an active and dynamic way without being especially aware of why he does so. It is for Reason, in this view, to bring order into man's activity, and it does so by opening man's eyes to the meaning of what he does. Energy is that dark and primal force which needs to be restrained, limited and modified by Reason before it is acceptable to God; and God stands outside the apparent duality of man, as a stern

Judge who condemns man for being what his polar nature demands him to be.

Blake, in his own experience, had tried to suppress the free-flowing energy that drove him to explore the nature of the collective religious experience as expressed in the Deism of his day. That very search was instigated by the oppressive pressure of Reason: Reason telling him that he must abide by the standards of collective morality in his marital life, Reason telling him that he must find a berth in some church doctrine, Reason telling him that his beloved England must never become embroiled in such senseless blood-letting as characterized the French Revolution. Reason is the conscious thinking process. It is based on logic and bound by the laws of cause and effect. It is the law of Man, for a man can understand it—but paradoxically it is attributed to God.

At this time when Blake was concentrating his conscious attitude on social necessity, which was the collective canon of his day, compensatory irrational attitudes were repressed to the unconscious. These attitudes belonged not only to the personal unconscious of Blake but they were closely related to the unconscious contents of the collective—for man interacts constantly with his environment even as the environment is affected by the condition of the individual man.

In this situation where rigid morality held sway, with Reason exalted to the position of a goddess of the soul and a handmaiden of God, the scene was ripe for a breaking through of some of the repressed and consequently unconscious material. The dialectical law of Heraclitus, the law of *enantiodromia*, according to which any given position is always superseded by its negation, is based on the psychological fact that a too one-sided conscious attitude has been secured at the cost of repressing the attitudes which tend to threaten the stability of the conscious attitude.[1] The one-sidedness then results in a failure to adapt to the fullness of life and this may be expressed, as it was in Blake's case, in a violent outcry against "All Bibles or sacred codes." [2] Or is Blake here secretly laughing at Swedenborg and the other orthodoxies?

Rejection of the conventional morality, "the game" as it has come to be called, may be at the base of all sorts of functional disturbances with which every psychotherapist is familiar. Whether these are to develop into psychological problems which isolate the individual from society or threaten his ability to relate to his own inner needs, depends upon the channel into which this energy flows when it has surged upward from the unconscious depths. The artist is one who finds a way to order this energy; the genius orders it with great skill to reveal universal meaning; and the madman becomes overwhelmed by it. But the line of division between these three kinds of people is not always clearly marked—each may have something of the other two as aspects of himself.

Blake enumerates three errors which follow from the teachings of Bibles and codes, and sets forth his own contrary notions:

1. His response to the dualistic concept of Body and Soul at war with one another is one of vehement opposition. S. Foster Damon comments on Blake's polemic against the concept of Body and Soul as two real existing principals: "The idea that the body is not a separate thing from the soul is not at all new, and dates back to Xenophanes. Blake had already hinted at it in Principle 1 of *All Religions are One*: 'The Poetic Genius of the True Man, and the Body or Outward Form of Man is derived from the Poetic Genius.'" Damon continues: "This may seem to involve a contradiction in Blake's philosophy. Aristotelian in his belief in the unity of soul and body, he also believed, with the Platonists, in pre-existence. We may well ask how a soul can descend into a body if the two are really one and cannot exist as separate entities. The answer is unexpectedly, perhaps deceptively, simple: Blake believed that the material body was an illusion or error —a part of the soul, but not an essential part." [3]

Blake, who a short time before had demanded a concubine to share his ménage with him and his wife, now suddenly cannot conceive of Body at all, except as one aspect of the wholeness which includes all the perceptual and conceptual capacities of man. He enlarges upon the "Christian idea of the Soul as that entity which stands between Body and Spirit partaking of both, but not identical with either." [4] He would include Body within his Soul concept, and it seems to follow that if the purely physical is included in Soul then also that spiritual nature which is in man at the opposite pole from his instinct is also part of the Soul.

Soul, in Blake's view, approaches what the analytical psychologist conceives of as the "totality of the psyche." In an approach not alien to our psychology, Blake states freely that *matter can be experienced only by the psyche,* when he says: "that call'd Body is a portion of the Soul discern'd by the five Senses, the chief inlets of Soul . . ." The senses or inlets are windows through which Blake experiences life, and it is implicit to him that the senses belong to the corporeal aspect of man. Blake sees not *with,* but *through* his senses, by means of the inner, or subjective, eye. Thus what he sees has not only a materially discernable form, but also a less obvious symbolic meaning. In this respect he may be regarded as an example of the inwardly directed or psychologically oriented man, an anomaly in a time in which Western man was concentrating on expanding his outer horizons in the flurry of social and economic development which was the Industrial Revolution.

2. Contrary to the commonly held view, Blake conceived of Energy as the force from within man's very depths, springing from a Body which is embraced by the Soul, instead of existing in a Body which is at war with the Soul. The Soul has at its core a dynamic which can be expressed only through its biological mechanisms, as the painter's inspiration can only be expressed in the concurrence of brush and canvas, and as weight can only be expressed as the specific gravity of matter. Paradoxically, essential to this energic force is the polar but complementary concept of Reason. That which flows demands a container, and that which radiates outward demands a circumference.

3. The statement that "Energy is Eternal Delight" is a poetic expression that indicates the attitude of Blake toward an aspect of the unconscious which he characterizes as the "Voice of the Devil." It is only when the individual has become aware of the necessity of accepting the devilish *and* the angelic sides of his nature as belonging to him in equal measure, when he is able to recognize the opposites and know that there must be interaction between them, that he has the possibility of

maintaining a state of psychological equilibrium. But Blake fails to acknowledge the necessity of enduring the tension of the opposites. Consequently he falls into a state which delights in the energetic activity of the unconscious while discrediting the governing role of reason. Here we can perceive the *enantiodromia* in action. That Blake is still caught in the net of Swedenborgian reason is seen in the vehemence of his opposition to the views then currently accepted. In permitting himself to adopt a new one-sided attitude, he invites disaster in the form of an overwhelming by unconscious material. He becomes "caught" by the idea of Heaven and Hell, and he must explore their very depths before he can again relate to the real world of which he has his conscious day by day experience.

PLATES 5-6

Those who restrain desire, do so because theirs is weak enough to be restrained; and the restrainer or reason usurps its place & governs the unwilling.

And being restrain'd, it by degrees becomes passive, till it is only the shadow of desire.

The history of this is written in Paradise Lost, & the Governor or Reason is call'd Messiah.

And the original Archangel, or possessor of the command of the heavenly host, is call'd the Devil or Satan, and his children are call'd Sin & Death.

But in the Book of Job, Milton's Messiah is call'd Satan.

For this history has been adopted by both parties.

It indeed appear'd to Reason as if Desire was cast out; but the Devil's account is, that the Messiah fell, & formed a heaven of what he stole from the Abyss.

This is shewn in the Gospel, where he prays to the Father to send the comforter, or Desire, that Reason may have Ideas to build on; the Jehovah of the Bible being no other than he who dwells in flaming fire.

Know that after Christ's death, he became Jehovah.

But in Milton, the Father is Destiny, the Son a Ratio of the five senses, & the Holy-ghost Vacuum!

Note: The reason Milton wrote in fetters when he wrote of Angels & God, and at liberty when of Devils & Hell, is because he was a true Poet and of the Devil's party without knowing it.

When Blake began to listen to the "Voice of the Devil," and to commit himself to the principle that "Energy is Eternal Delight," he fell into a state in which reason was relatively undervalued, as we have seen. Desire, springing from energy, assumed for him a kind of sacred character, sacred to the "Devil's party" rather than to the Angels'. As such, desire could be restrained only when it was weak. Weakening of desire was a consequence of the individual's efforts to meet the demands of collective morality as expressed in orthodox religion. This morality was seen by Blake as a force restraining the individual's natural tendency to express himself spontaneously and in freedom, without respect to practical consequences. He has, in effect, projected onto the generally accepted idea of a judgmental God those qualities which he now opposes—while he ranges on the side of the Devil those qualities which he ardently admires. Thus, it is the present of unlimited desire, brought into being by the availability of energy freeflowing from unlimited sources, which Blake sees as an essential precondition for the emergence of the creative impulse.

Paradise Lost, as read by Blake, is written out of Milton's despair of his earlier apocalyptic hopes, and is a "Song of Experience," a poem that accepts the fallen world's restraint of human desire. According to the Blakean scholar, Harold Bloom, Milton stands for a willingness to restrain the desires of Satan and Eve or to see them punished for not accepting such restraints, because his own desires for knowledge and for the complete fulfillment of his imaginative potential have become weak enough to be restrained. Reason takes precedence over imagination and desire, and governs Milton's visionary powers, though they are unwilling to be so governed. By degrees, Milton's exuberance of invention becomes passive until it is only the shadow of the power that creates the opening books of *Paradise Lost* and the past prophetic glory of *Areopagitica.* This error Blake means to set aright.

Blake sees in *Paradise Lost* the inner history of the psychic process of repression. Satan as fate symbolizes the progressively insidious course of inhibition, which comes about in the shadow of degradation cast by his fall. He turns from active rebellion, which is creativity, to reactive plotting against the restraints of Reason. Blake projects the metamorphosis onto Milton. He sees Milton as being like Swedenborg in that he aged from a Devil into an Angel. It appeared to Milton, the theologian, that Satan, or Desire, was cast into Hell. But in Blake's readings of Milton and of the Bible in their "diabolical" sense, he finds that the true poet, or Devil, was working away within Milton and the authors of the Bible, and indeed within himself.[1]

Blake's identification with Milton has some basis in objective reality, as well as a subjective basis—we refer to his notion of his equivalence with Milton by reason of each one's independent recognition of "eternal truth." That a certain similarity between the two men's concepts of the God-Satan relationship did exist is substantiated by Shelley's description of Milton's espousal of the devil's cause, in his essay "The Defense of Poetry":

Milton's devil as a moral being is far superior to his God, as one who perseveres in some purpose which he has assumed to be excellent in spite of adversity and torture is to one who in the cold security of undoubted triumph inflicts the most horrible revenge upon his enemy, not from any mistaken notion of inducing him to repent of a perseverance in enmity, but with the alleged design of exasperating him to deserve new torments. Milton has so far violated the popular creed . . . as to have alleged no superiority of moral virtue to his God over his Devil.[2]

Blake went even further, for he remarked that the same spiritual attitude which Milton called "the Messiah" is recognized in the book of Job as Satan, the Accuser.

"Here Blake is at his most subtle," Bloom points out.

Milton's Messiah drives Satan out of Heaven with fire, and Eternal wrath burnt after them to the bottomless pit. Hell is thus created by an act of the Messiah. In the Book of Job a hell of external torment is created for Job by Satan, who serves as God's Accuser of sins, going to and fro in the earth to impute sin to the righteous. This crucial resemblance between Milton's Christ and Job's Satan— that each creates a world of punishment . . . inspires Blake's blandest irony: 'For this history has been adopted by both parties. The two parties are Devils—or true poets who write to correct orthodoxy, and

Angels—or ruined poets and theologians who write to uphold moral and religious conventions.[3]

The illustration depicts the confusion that results in the fall of Satan from Heaven to Hell and the corollary splitting apart of the opposites in man's nature. We see the effects of the subjugation by Reason as a futile attempt to deal with the resultant chaos. From the boiling clouds of heaven the Angel falls into the upward-leaping flames which represent the source of true energy born of rebellion. The form which is the archetypal image of the human who is yet to be placed upon the earth, is accompanied by the horse and by part of a chariot with a broken wheel. The myth of Phaeton is called to mind, where again the obstreperous child of the sun-god challenges his father's brilliance and his potency. He is given his head, told to take the reins of the chariot into his own hand; but without the wisdom and experience of Reason, he cannot keep it within bounds. The horse, with all his instinctual drive, is suddenly helpless when he is not controlled; the chariot can no longer carry the rebel in safety, and all tumble into the flames. That sword which also accompanies the Satanic form in its plunge, presages the one which will be used to bar the gates of Paradise against the reentry of man when Satan has had his way.

The picture illustrates the state into which Blake has himself fallen, a condition in which the ordering processes of reason are no longer effective. He has abandoned himself to the chaos in which all possibilities exist, and he proposes to extract from this chaos those darker and less acceptable thoughts, emotions and perceptions which had been suppressed by him for half of his life, especially while he was writing his *Songs of Innocence* and *Annotations to Swedenborg's Divine Love*. It is as though he were now determined to join forces with all the ideas he had rejected in the past. These consisted not only of his personal beliefs which he now found to be unacceptable; they include the instinctual urges and the drives for power which had been rejected by the society in which he lived and worked, or at least insofar as that society publicly declared itself. The collective undertones that play in every age as a discordant

accompaniment to the theme of collective morality were con-
signed to what the religious called "hell," and what may be
compared to an aspect of the concept of the collective unconscious in the psychology of C. G. Jung. Jung's description of
the process by which a man becomes entangled in the collective
unconscious appears to be particularly applicable to Blake's
psychic situation during the composition of *The Marriage of
Heaven and Hell.*

A collapse of the conscious attitude is no small matter. It always
feels like the end of the world, as though everything had tumbled
back into original chaos. One feels delivered up, disoriented, like a
rudderless ship that is abandoned to the moods of the elements. So
at least it seems. In reality, however, one has fallen back upon the
collective unconscious, which now takes over leadership.[4]

Blake's final reference to Milton in the text indicates that he
thinks of Milton and of himself not primarily as individuals
but rather as Poets, who since the time of Homer have been
symbols of creative man exercising his loftiest capacities.
Blake's close identification with Milton, the significance of
which he was probably unaware, is seen in his appraisal of Milton's theological approach which, says Blake, fettered him. As
theologian, Milton had taken Energy for the Devil and Reason
for the Messiah. This was the way Blake interpreted in retro-
spect his own early reaction to Swedenborg's writing. But when
Milton wrote poetry, his highest achievement in Blake's eyes,
he wrote with the freedom of Energy, or his Devil. Jung reminds us that Satan

was exalted to a cosmic figure of first rank in Milton, even emanci-
pating himself from his subordinate role as the left hand of God.
. . . Milton goes even further . . . and apostrophizes the devil as the
true *principium individuationis.* . . . In Milton's time these ideas
were very much in the air, forming a part of the general stock of
culture . . . . The Satan-Prometheus parallel shows clearly enough
that Milton's devil stands for the essence of human individuation.
. . . With the coming of the Enlightenment, metaphysics as a whole
began to decline, and the rift which then opened out between
knowledge and faith could no longer be repaired.[5]

Blake now proposes to follow Milton's Devil, that is, to pay attention to his own desire and permit the impersonal voice of that Devil to speak through him. With this commitment he enters upon the hero's quest, the night sea journey, the dark night of the soul, the voyage which has been called by many names but which all must travel if they are driven toward the goal of realizing their creative potentialities. It is the way of travail and hardship, where the traveler is exposed to the attacks and seductions of worldly and spiritual pleasures because he is open to everything that he may perceive, to sights and voices and all the impressions of the senses, and even to extrasensory impressions. It is an archetypal journey, connected with the principle of human development around a central balancing motif which becomes the essence of the personality. This has been called by Jung the "individuation process." There must be a guide, a psychopomp, and he may appear in anything but a helpful form. He must stimulate and prod, warn and advise, and above all lead away the traveler from the comforts offered by the world to the man who accepts the condition of abiding uncritically by the values of the collective. The *principium individuationis* is hypostasized in the form of Devil. He stirs up desire, and Blake, as any one who follows this path, must pay attention. He must be prepared to walk through Hell, for it is through passion, through subjection to the crucible, that transformation takes place. There is where the ego learns of its own littleness, and where it feels impotent and weak. And there it becomes fused with a greater power than it had ever conceived of, and begins to draw for strength upon that, rather than believing himelf to be the source of any real capacity.

This section in *The Marriage* is a crucial one, for it comments upon the change of attitude which marks the creative man's departure from tradition and from the limiting bounds of Reason. To walk with Satan and his children, called Sin and Death, takes courage and an overwhelming necessity of desire. Those whose desire is weak enough to be restrained will never experience either the tortures or the beatific visions which alternately appear to the traveler on the way of individuation.

PLATES 6-7

Blake was one of those relatively rare individuals who was able to utilize a capacity for meditation to experience in visual form a meaningful relationship with aspects of his own nature which are not usually accessible to consciousness. His "Memorable Fancies," as recorded in *The Marriage of Heaven and Hell,* are descriptions of his ventures into the inner life, where ideas are born. The fanciful characters who people his visions take up his feelings and his reactions and express them according to their apparent nature. That nature is, of course, a projection of one or another side of Blake, as will be evident when we consider the content of his visions.

The visions were not spontaneous, as is a dream. Rather, they were brought about by intense concentration upon the background of consciousness until something would appear out of the nothingness; and this would be captured later in words or graphic art forms. But first it was necessary to experience the nothingness, the void. Blake was able to detach himself from the logical thought processes which are based largely upon perceptions of the outer world, and to turn inward.

There is a threshold that has to be passed over to enter into a different level of consciousness. Focusing the attention upon one object or one idea often helps to avoid intrusion from the objective world. Blake utilized a technique which has long been known to practitioners of yoga, but for different reasons. The yogi's objective is to arrive at a state where loss of ego is as complete as it can possibly be. The ultimate goal is a state of passivity with the loss of all desire. However, with Blake the purpose of the meditation was to achieve a more active rather than less active state of consciousness, but a state in which the ego was not the dominating and directing force. The activity of the unconscious was to serve as stimulus to the ego.

The ego needs to be stimulated to function as the *agent* of the unconscious, because the ego is the means whereby the material of the visionary experience may be transmitted and communicated. Thus the prophet as poet has to step aside from the ego position, as has been indicated, but the observing ego must remain close at hand to record the sights and sounds that come up out of the unconscious once the barriers are removed. Where Blake and other Westerners—Jung included—differ from the Eastern approach to meditation is in their demand that when the contents from the unconscious are brought into view, the ego as an active agent of the personality be present to receive and confront them.

A modern application of this technique is described in Jung's essay, "The Transcendent Function." [1] The technique, known as "active imagination," may take the form of a dialogue between the conscious ego and aspects of the unconscious which are personified. Active imagination is essentially the same process as what takes place in those "Memorable Fancies," where Blake confronts devils, angels, all manner of beasts, as well as Biblical personages and creatures of fable. Concerning active imagination, Jung has written:

The confrontation with the unconscious must be a many-sided one . . . it is a total and integral event in which all aspects are, or should be, included. . . . In coming to terms with the unconscious, not only is the standpoint of the ego justified, but the unconscious is granted the same authority. [2]

Blake was able to focus the wisdom and capacity of the unrealized aspect of his personality upon his own agonizing questions through an ongoing process, the functioning of which is clearly seen in the work under discussion. This technique raised to consciousness in Blake many problems which he will continue to consider and deal with in his succeeding works. Out of the questions voiced here, responses will arise in the years which follow and will combine with Blake's vision to form a complex mythological system. We are interested primarily in the origins of that mythological system, or rather, in the sources from which Blake drew the energy to create it. We must, therefore, turn to the consideration of the place to which Blake's vision led him, to his fiery Hell.

PLATES 6-7

A Memorable Fancy [3]

As I was walking among the fires of hell, delighted with the enjoyments of Genius, which to Angels look like torment and insanity, I collected some of their Proverbs thinking that as the sayings used in a nation mark its character, so the Proverbs of Hell show the nature of Infernal wisdom better than any description of buildings or garments.

When I came home: on the abyss of the five senses, where a flat sided steep frowns over the present world, I saw a mighty Devil folded in black clouds, hovering on the sides of the rock: with corroding fires he wrote the following sentence now perceived by the minds of men, & read by them on earth:

How do you know but ev'ry Bird that cuts the airy way, Is an immense world of delight, clos'd by your senses five?

This first "Memorable Fancy" serves to introduce the "Proverbs of Hell," a series of aphorisms in the popular style of the day—except that in content they are an expression of a natural, spontaneous man, rather than of a religiously acculturated one. He is in fact saying, "I laugh at your pious word games: listen to something fresh for a change." Blake proposes to display through the Proverbs the infernal wisdom that is much more a part of man's essential nature than the creeds to which he offers lip service. What he does bring to light is not so much the Devil's wisdom as a distillation of his own experience. He confronts the precepts by which society pretends to be governed with a lower and more intrinsic wisdom. In doing so Blake alienates himself from the collective—he becomes Satan falling from heaven, the prototype of man forfeiting the protection of the God who specializes in Reason.

"Walking among the fires of hell" refers to fire in the sense of an energic substance making possible an act of artistic creativity. The god of artistry, master of craftsmanship in ancient Greece, Hephaestus, was also master of the fire. He was, like Milton's Mulciber,

Thrown by angry Jove
Sheer o'er the crystal battlements; from morn
To noon he fell, from noon to dewy eve,
A summer's day, and with the setting sun
Dropt from the zenith like a falling star.[4]

The god of fire is eventually restored to Olympus, where he is honored as the workman of the immortals, their armorer and smith. In his workshop he is said to have handmaidens he has forged out of gold, who can move about and help him with his work. The fire is the necessary transforming agent in the creative process.

Blake's creative tool is the word, and this, too, has had an age-old symbolic connection with fire. The two most important discoveries which distinguish man from all other living beings, speech and the use of fire, have a common psychic background. Both are products of psychic energy. There is a Sanskrit word which expresses the situation of subjective intensity in which psychic energy flows most freely, the situation which Blake suggests when he talks about "walking among the fires of hell." The word is *tejas*. According to a Sanskrit dictionary it combines the following meanings: Sharpness, cutting edge; fire, brightness, light, ardor, heat; healthy appearance, beauty; the fiery and color-producing faculty of the human organism (located in the bile); strength, energy, vital force; passion; spiritual and magical power; influence, position, dignity; semen.[5]

Fire is also the messenger of the gods in the Avesta and in the Vedas. And in the Bible, in the book of Daniel (3:24f) the miracle takes place within the fiery furnace:

Then Nebuchadnezzar the king was astonished, and rose up in haste. He said to his counselors, "Did we not cast three men bound into the fire?"
They answered the king, "True, O king."
He answered, "but I see four men loose, walking in the midst of the fire, and they are not hurt; and the appearance of the fourth is like a son of the gods." [6]

The fire is ever changing, and whatever comes into contact with it must be transformed. That is its magic and its power. The Nebuchadnezzar legend of the three men in the furnace is interpreted in the Biblia Pauperum (1471) to refer to a magical procedure by which a "fourth" is produced. Thus the fiery furnace may be seen as a mother symbol, like the fiery tripod in *Faust*. From the tripod come Paris and Helen, the royal pair in alchemy, as Jung has pointed out.[7] The alchemical melting pot signifies the body; the Hermetic vessel represents the uterus. The "fourth" in the fiery furnace appears like a son of God made visible in the fire. And the alchemist, in reading this story, regarded the fourth as the *filius philosophorum*, the final goal which is sought at the end of the long process which involves many transformations.

It is, therefore, appropriate to Blake's theme of opening up the dark caverns and bringing light into them and of transforming thought and experience into art, that he should step into the fires of hell and undergo the personal sacrifice which this means. For who can expect to walk in fire and yet live, unless he is willing to take a new view of life, an eternal rather than a limited view? And is it not essential before anything novel can be created that the dross of what was before must be burned away so that the essential nature of the new may be preceived? That is the mood of Blake's entrance into Hell: a commitment to exposing himself to ideas in a totally different way. It is not that he entirely discards the precepts which govern the society in which he lives. He reexamines them and perhaps is even able to laugh with the Devil about them, recognizing that commandments need to be stated forcefully and restated only because they are so contrary to human nature that man must be constantly reminded of them. And, in working against his own nature, much psychic energy is dissipated. This is what Blake objects to, and this is what he seems to be trying to restore through walking in Hell and coming once again into contact with that mysterious source of energy which manifests itself in flames.

"The enjoyments of Genius" are, for Blake, the creative productions of those who express themselves in liberty, in accordance with his doctrine that inspiration comes only where there is perfect freedom. He was later to confirm his concept of Genius in verses like the following:

The Bard replied: "I am inspired! I know it is Truth! for I sing
According to the inspiration of the Poetic Genius
Who is the eternal all-protecting Divine Humanity
To whom be Glory & Power & Dominion Evermore. Amen.[8]

The enjoyments of Genius, which often express themselves with more emotion than clarity, "to Angels look like torment and insanity." This statement anticipates the charge of madness which was later to become so serious to Blake. Thomas Wright took up this charge when one critic pointed out that at the time Blake produced many of his works he was in an abnormal mental condition. Wright remarks:

That is so; but it must also be remembered that all great imaginative works of the world have been produced in moments of acute mental excitement—and frequently it is at the Hermetic moment that the Eagle of Genius descends upon man. Then it is that he is truly inspired—possessed. Every man at the moment he is producing work that will live is, in a sense, off his balance.[9]

Blake's "torment" consisted in part in the struggle to remain in contact with the flowing stream of creative energy yet to resist being drawn into whirlpools from which the individual may never be able to emerge. One senses, as he reads Blake, that there alternate in this man the downward pull into senseless spinning of uncontrolled fantasy and the upward thrust of an inner demand for order. First one takes precedence, then the other, and we may see these opposites reflected in the major occupations of Blake's life—first the preposterous vision; then the delicate and painstaking transcription with the engraver's tool, making visible and tangible every letter and every ornamental scroll and every figure and shape. This is one way in which psychic balance may be restored; it is the way Blake managed to preserve his sanity.

"When I came home" suggests that he has now grasped and contained the product of his imagination to the point where he can write about it. But, just as he prepares to speak in the language of the five senses, the language which communicates to other people because it uses terms of the perceptual experiences common to everyone, the mighty Devil suddenly appears again and writes a warning sentence in lines of "corroding fires." To better understand the meaning of writing in fire in this context, we may turn to the words of that other, earlier mystic, Jacob Boehme, upon whom the charge of madness was also levelled. He spoke of his own writing:

I could have written in a more accurate, fair and plain manner, yet the reason I did not was this, that the burning fire often forced forward with speed, and the hand and pen must hasten directly after it; for that fire comes and goes as a sudden shower.[10]

Blake comes home, to "the abyss of the five senses." He attempts to regain his equilibrium, after his experience in the existence beyond the ordinary senses. He can do this to the degree that he can observe that other Blake, the one who is dictated to by the Devil himself, and he can record the words through the objectifying ability of his own conscious ego. He "sees" through a sense which is not seeing in the ordinary meaning of the word, but in the sense of "I see," connoting "I understand"—he sees the Devil write the sentence now read by men on earth:

How do you know but every bird that cuts the airy way
Is an immense world of delight, clos'd by your senses five?

It is as though the Devil sends a bird to fly across his line of vision so that he becomes aware as the wings flash by, that what man writes is bound to earth by his humanness. Man is caged by the perceptions of his senses, by his habits of reasoning and his acquisition of the methods of logic. Tradition bolts the door and neurosis intimidates and finally kills the desire to escape. But this bird, the bird of imagination, symbolizes the poetic spirit in man which is freed by the Devil. He is able to cut the airy way, to soar above the earth to which the ordinary man is bound, and fly alone. He experiences the joy of wings, which enable him to enter the world of pure spirit. The senses are left behind, and the "world of delight" is ahead. This is Heaven and, paradoxically enough, Heaven only becomes available to the man who has dared to venture into Hell.

In attempting a justification of the existence of so excruciating a hell in the same universe that contains the beatific vision of love itself, we must remind ourselves of the inevitable conclusion that heaven and hell are polar, and thus mutually self-sustaining. Blake has said that without the Contraries there is no progression. Alan Watts carries the idea forward when he states that:

The *sine qua non* of absolute goodness is absolute evil. . . . There is not the least doubt that Hell is unqualified, absolute, and unimaginable evil. But if Heaven and Hell, and thus also the Lord and the Devil, are polar, the reality of the two is the unity which lies implicitly between them. In this light the War in Heaven begins to look like a conspiracy, an immense cosmic drama, an ultimate 'big act' whereby the universe scares itself stiff for the thrill of it. For it is as if in the far-off beginnings, behind the scenes, before the world drama began, the Lord and the Devil had *agreed* to have a battle, like Tweedledum and Tweedledee—their agreement being in their inexpressible, unmanifest, and their ineffable unity.[11]

"The Proverbs of Hell," which come out of Blake's excursion below and also his vision following the bird above, would read very much like the script of the "cosmic drama" that Watts describes. Here Blake, having observed this magnificent game of opposites has caught the devilish repartee, and presented it to us in epigrammatic form.

PLATES 7-10

Proverbs of Hell

PLATE 7

In seed time learn, in harvest teach, in winter enjoy.
Drive your cart and your plow over the bones of the dead.
The road of excess leads to the palace of wisdom.
Prudence is a rich, ugly old maid, courted by Incapacity.
He who desires but acts not, breeds pestilence.
The cut worm forgives the plow.
Dip him in the river who loves water.
A fool sees not the same tree that a wise man sees.
He whose face gives no light, shall never become a star.
Eternity is in love with the productions of time.
The busy bee has no time for sorrow.
The hours of folly are measur'd by the clock; but of wisdom,
    no clock can measure.
All wholesome food is caught without a net or a trap.
Bring out number, weight & measure in a year of dearth.
No bird soars too high, if he soars with his own wings.
A dead body revenges not injuries.
The most sublime act is to set another before you.
If the fool would persist in his folly he would become wise.
Folly is the cloke of knavery.
Shame is Pride's cloke.

PLATE 8

Prisons are built with stones of Law, Brothels with bricks of
   Religion.
The pride of the peacock is the glory of God.
The lust of the goat is the bounty of God.
The wrath of the lion is the wisdom of God.
The nakedness of woman is the work of God.
Excess of sorrow laughs. Excess of joy weeps.
The roaring of lions, the howling of wolves, the raging of the
   stormy sea, and the destructive sword, are portions of eter-
   nity, too great for the eye of man.
The fox condemns the trap, not himself.
Joys impregnate. Sorrows bring forth.
Let man wear the fell of the lion, woman the fleece of the
   sheep.
The bird a nest, the spider a web, man friendship.
The selfish, smiling fool, & the sullen, frowning fool shall be
   both thought wise, that they may be a rod.
What is now proved was once only imagin'd.
The rat, the mouse, the fox, the rabbet watch the roots; the
   lion, the tyger, the horse, the elephant watch the fruits.
The cistern contains: the fountain overflows.
One thought fills immensity.
Always be ready to speak your mind, and a base man will
   avoid you.
Every thing possible to be believ'd is an image of truth.
The eagle never lost so much time as when he submitted to
   learn of the crow.

PLATE 9

The fox provides for himself, but God provides for the lion.

Think in the morning. Act in the noon. Eat in the evening. Sleep in the night.

He who has suffer'd you to impose on him, knows you.

As the plow follows words, so God rewards prayers.

The tygers of wrath are wiser than the horses of instruction.

Expect poison from the standing water.

You never know what is enough unless you know what is more than enough.

Listen to the fool's reproach! it is a kingly title!

The eyes of fire, the nostrils of air, the mouth of water, the beard of earth.

The weak in courage is strong in cunning.

The apple tree never asks the beech how he shall grow; nor the lion, the horse, how he shall take his prey.

The thankful reciever bears a plentiful harvest.

If others had not been foolish, we shculd be so.

The soul of sweet delight can never be defil'd.

When thou seest an Eagle, thou seest a portion of Genius; lift up thy head!

As the catterpiller chooses the fairest leaves to lay her eggs on, so the priest lays his curse on the fairest joys.

To create a little flower is the labour of ages.

Damn braces. Bless relaxes.

The best wine is the oldest, the best water the newest.

Prayers plow not! Praises reap not!

Joys laugh not! Sorrows weep not!

PLATE 10

The head Sublime, the heart Pathos, the genitals Beauty, the
hands & feet Proportion.

As the air to a bird or the sea to a fish, so is contempt to the
contemptible.

The crow wish'd every thing was black, the owl that every
thing was white.

Exuberance is Beauty.

If the lion was advised by the fox, he would be cunning.

Improvement makes strait roads; but the crooked roads with
out Improvement are roads of Genius.

Sooner murder an infant in its cradle than nurse unacted
desires.

Where man is not, nature is barren.

Truth can never be told so as to be understood, and not be
believ'd.

Enough! or Too much.

Most of Blake's Proverbs were inspired by a popular book by Lavater, *Aphorisms on Man*. Blake had annotated it about 1788, and wryly took issue with Lavater on many points. The vogue for aphorisms in the last days of the eighteenth century implied that the individual did not need to think out his own morality. As might be expected Blake took this attitude as a challenge, and acted upon it with vigor. Other well-read works of the day were the sayings of Fuseli, Ben Franklin's *Poor Richard's Almanac,* and Bishop Hall's *Meditations.* Blake read all of these, and the "Proverbs of Hell" reflect his reactions. The key to his satire in his use of the very word "proverbs," a word which denotes the imprimatur of time. Insolently Blake's new ideas are called "proverbs," for he writes with the Devil's authority which, it could be argued, has been accepted in certain circles for quite a number of centuries.

Blake scoffs at the currently fashionable insistence upon the virtues of moderation, humility and self denial. He does not stoop to question these values—he destroys them categorically with short, biting sentences, and in their place leaves a charge to the individual to pursue the path which is uniquely his.

Blake does not present an ordered plan for the differentiation of the various aspects which are present in the individual man. Yet, in his spontaneous and impulsive way, he indicates a method of arranging the chaos that is hidden in the dim regions beyond man's conscious awareness. To comprehend Blake's intention it is helpful to find the several threads of meaning which connect the Proverbs with one another. These threads then can be rewoven into the "stuff," the material, of the creative process. The language is imagery, pregnant with the mystery of the symbol, calling up far more emotional response than may be dealt with here. However, it is hoped that by identifying some of the major themes in the "Proverbs of Hell" clues may be found regarding the way in which Blake understood man's connection with the sources of energy available for creative activity. Among the basic ordering themes that seem to be suggested by the Proverbs are:

The fourfold nature of man and his relationship to
  the divine.

The recognition that man must follow his inner need,
as expressed in the desire that he feels.

The meaning and intrinsic value of each man's
individuality.

The essential subjectivity of perception through the
five senses, plus the non-sensory dimension of
perception which is imagination.

The necessity of knowing excess in order to approach
balance.

The establishment in life of an orderly system
alternating between purposive activity and
restorative passivity, that is, between progression
and regression.

The fourfold nature of man and his relationship to the divine.

Blake, with his constant awareness of the divine essence
which is unlimited by time or space, was constantly seeking to
comprehend man's relationship to that Other. He knew that
the source of his own ideas came from beyond his consciousness,
whether within or without his own personality is not altogether
clearly expressed. More than likely it was not a matter of ex-
cluding the immanent Divinity in favor of the trancendent
One, but rather of admitting both the one and the other as
microcosmic and macrocosmic aspects of the Divine, aspects
which are separate and yet belong to a basic Unity. Blake's
whole mythology is filled with numinous pluralisms, which
grow out of man's imagination and embrace his perception.
In order to find his place in this cosmology, man must know
his own nature, and therefore within the structure of the
"Proverbs of Hell" Blake explores his concept of the human
being's consciousness of himself.

The fourfold nature of man, which is the theme of several
of the Proverbs, reflects the age-old and presumably prehistoric
quaternity symbol associated with the world-creating deity.

Nevertheless, it is rarely understood as such when it occurs among people today in dream symbolism or in the eruptions of the unconscious that manifest themselves in artistic or literary work. Jung had much interest in how his patients, if left to their own devices and not informed about the history of the symbol of quaternity would interpret it to themselves. He was careful, therefore, not to disturb them with his own opinions, and as a rule he discovered that they took it to symbolize *themselves* rather than *something in themselves*. They felt it belonged intimately to them as a sort of a creative background, a life-producing sun in the depths of the unconscious. For example, when certain mandala drawings appeared that were almost exact reproductions of Ezekiel's vision, it very seldom happened that people recognized the analogy even when they knew the vision. He found that what one could almost call a systematic blindness is simply the effect of the prejudice that God is *outside* man. Although this prejudice is not exclusively Christian, Jung says that there are certain religions that do not share it at all. On the contrary, they insist on the essential identity of God and man, as do certain Christian mystics, artistic geniuses and others whose relationships to God are experienced as being directly inspired by the Divine Word.[1]

Through the study of comparative religions, Jung has come to the conclusion that the quaternity is a more or less direct representation of the God who is manifest in his creation.[2] We may therefore conclude that the archetypal images produced by Blake in his symbolic visions have this in common with those produced by the dreams of modern man: their meaning is that man is able to have the experience of *the God within*.

Jung warns that it would be a regrettable mistake if anybody should take his observations as a kind of proof of the existence of God. He asserts that they prove only the existence of an archetypal God-image, which he feels is the most we can hypothesize about God psychologically. The structure of the archetypal concept of God in Christian symbolism is a Trinity, but the formula presented by the unconscious is a quaternity. This difference occurs because the orthodox formula is not quite complete—it contains only those aspects of God which are acceptable to the collective consciousness. The dogmatic aspect of the principle of evil is absent from this conscious doctrine, and leads a more or less awkward existence on its own as the Devil. Nevertheless, it does not seem that the Church excludes the possibility of an inner relationship between the Devil and the Trinity. Jung cites a Catholic authority on this question:

"The existence of Satan, however, can only be understood in relation to the Trinity. Any theological treatment of the devil that is not related to God's trinitarian consciousness is a falsification of the actual position." [3]

"According to this view," says Jung, "the devil possesses personality and absolute freedom. That is why he can be the true, personal counterpart of Christ. " [4] This explains the relationship or even the affinity of the Devil with the Trinity.

Jung discovered the inclusion of the Devil in the quaternity through his reading of the sixteenth century natural philosopher and physician Gerhard Dorn's detailed discussion of the symbols of the Trinity and the quaternity. [5] Dorn's work was familiar to Blake as well, since it was Dorn who translated from German into Latin the work of Paracelsus, to whom Blake frequently refers. The meaning of the quaternity symbol when it is produced by the modern psyche is the same as it has been historically, and that is that it represents the paradox of the God within the Trinity existing alongside a fourth element, a God with whom man identifies himself. This fourth element is nature, the other three elements being of the spirit. Another symbolic expression of the same idea is the representation of the Trinity by the natural philosophers of antiquity as the three "spirits," also called "volatilia," namely water, air and fire. The fourth constituent, then, would be the earth or the body. In a theology where the principle of evil cannot be mentioned, the latter is symbolized by the Virgin. The feminine element then produces the quaternity, she is the matrix from which the quaternity issues. So the fourth can be symbolized in many ways, as devil, or evil, as earth or nature or woman. There is one quality that all these symbols have in common: they are able to join the imperfectable human character of man with the ineffable spiritual character of the Trinity. Three is a firmly-braced triangle but four is a cross with two sticks, each bearing the tension of their opposite poles and straining against one another.

It is this tension of the opposites that forms the psychological basis for Blake's first quaternity of man in the "Proverbs of Hell":

> The head Sublime, the heart Pathos, the genitals
> Beauty, the hands & feet Proportion.

The head is associated traditionally with the idea, or concept-forming capacity, and in psychological terms with the thinking function. It is the seat of *logos,* and *logos* to the man is "sublime," for it is the *logos* which orders the contents of consciousness so that meaning can be derived from them.

The heart, Pathos, is carrier of the feeling function, and it is opposed to the head, as Jung suggests:

The unconscious is commonly regarded as a sort of incapsulated fragment of our most personal and intimate life—something like what the Bible calls the "heart" and considers the source of all evil thoughts. In the chambers of the heart dwell the wicked blood-spirits, swift anger and sensual weakness. This is how the unconscious looks when seen from the conscious side.[6]

The genitals are the creative aspects of consciousness, yet their creative activity is not that of thinking—they are, rather, the dynamic activity that springs over the hurdles of *logos*; nor are they Pathos, for their function refuses to become dissolved in the morass of sensuality. The genitals symbolize, rather, that intuitive connection between that which is felt as experience and that which is not yet conceived; and from that connection is born Beauty, the possibility of a new creation.

The fourth and completing aspect of consciousness brings about proportion and balance among all the functions. It is made vivid by the metaphor of hands and feet. Hands touch and feel, form and shape—they are the very essence of active sensation. More than that, hands are the means of accomplishing what head perceives, what the heart feels and what the genitals conceive. The function of feet is to contact the earth and to provide man with a base upon which to stand—they are his basis in reality. Feet make it possible for the whole of man to exist in a state of balance, with each function related to the others, yet with each operating in its own way. One function may be dominant in one person, another in someone else, but all are omnipresent.

As every person is fourfold physically as expressed by head, heart, genitals, hands and feet, so is he fourfold in his non-physical aspects, to which Blake inevitably assigns the more essential reality. For Blake the body is the tangible, temporal expression of the immortal soul—the body exists only to embrace the undying spirit for a moment in time.

There is another fourfold nature of man, but this is not ordinarily recognized in consciousness. Blake raises to the level of the holy those aspects of man which are not ordinarily considered as "morally acceptable."

> The pride of the peacock is the glory of God.
> The lust of the goat is the bounty of God.
> The wrath of the lion is the wisdom of God.
> The nakedness of woman is the work of God.

If we were to consider these lines from a psychological viewpoint, we might say that pride, lust, wrath and nakedness are often repressed into the unconscious, avoided, not talked about. When these attributes are not acknowledged to be aspects of the total individual, they may be seen in their projected form as animals. This has been going on from time immemorial, taking shape in myth, in astrology, and in many other areas of human experience. In contrast, the fable deals with the specific attribute of a man that resembles an animal's characteristic in a quite open and naive way. There is no projection here, the metaphor is used to demonstrate a point, and is effective. But there is no symbol either, because the symbol implies the connection of that which is known through experience, as the pride of the peacock, with that which is wrapped in mystery—the glory of God. Blake brings these energy-infused aspects of man to consciousness and finds them acceptable, not unlike his ancient ancestors, who saw by means of these same animal symbols precisely the characteristics that Blake sees.

The peacock is synonymous with the phoenix [7] who, in the Egyptian religion, was the embodiment of the sun god. The bird was fabled to live 500 years, to be consumed in fire by its own act, and to rise again in youthful freshness from its ashes. Hence it is often an emblem of immortality. The peacock was also "an early Christian symbol of the redeemer . . . second cousin to the phoenix, a symbol of Christ." [8]

Opposed to the peacock with its spiritual connotation is the goat. While commonly taken as a reference to the lecherous man, he also serves to remind man of his close relationship with nature and with his instincts. Neglecting these, man lives in a one-sided way and cannot achieve the wholeness which includes the aspects of man which are animal as well as those which are pure spirit.

In ancient Egypt the lion was connected with the whole complicated mystery of life and death, and is a symbol of death and resurrection. Supporting the marble embalming tables which have been discovered in Egyptian tombs, lions with their heads looking in opposite directions are frequently used, indicating that the lion was the guardian of the subterranean processes which transform death into life again. From medieval up to modern times, lions are often seen carved on the underparts of thrones—and here they represent the power principle, the shadow of the king. [9] Further, the lion represents the quality of righteous rage, which is how Blake sees him. This animal aspect has to be tamed and subdued, and not merely disregarded. He is in every sense masculine, aggressive and dominant. Regal in his massive mane, he is fearsome to approach.

The nakedness of woman is the fourth aspect of his nature which man must accept again into consciousness. Here Blake cannot mean the objective woman, any more than pride, lust or wrath are to be found outside the individual in any sense, except possibly as a projection of inner contents upon the outer world. Man must acknowledge and come to terms with the feminine principle within himself, he must know her in her nakedness for what she is—an integral part of his own psyche. Only then can the pairs of opposites be united, and a quaternity be called into being.

In a third Proverb we see the fourfold aspect of man in yet

another light: "The eyes of fire, the nostrils of air, the mouth of water, the beard of earth." Here we have four features of man's face which, taken together, give him his individual appearance. Paradoxically, this unique configuration of features is equated by Blake with that which is common to all men and to every living being, that is, the four elements: fire, air, water, earth. Again the spiritual Trinity comprising the first three elements is made whole, that is, a quaternity, by the addition of earth. Blake shows that within this all-inclusive totality of man, the individual and the collective, the conscious and the unconscious, which Jung has called the Self, everything possible exists. That totality was the secret goal of the alchemists' quest for the philosophers' stone: "*Lapis noster est ex quatuor elementis*" (Our stone is from the four elements.) [10] "According to the alchemist Hortulanus, the stone emerges from a *massa confusa* containing in itself all the elements. Just as the world came forth from a *chaos confusum,* so does the stone." [11] Blake sees man, too, as arising out of the *chaos confusum,* and though man be differentiated to a high degree, he remains essentially the four elements. Through this recognition man is able to open himself to the creative potential of the collective unconscious: he finds that he cannot separate himself from it nor it from himself. Its resources flow into him, and his work becomes that of shaping what passes across the threshold of his awareness—but he can do this only in a limited way during the short span of his life. The dynamic processes of the macrocosm are forever beyond his understanding, yet he is not alienated from them; indeed, his life is a reflection of that which he can never wholly know, but which guides him nevertheless. Thus in the Proverbs of Hell:

> The roaring of lions, the howling of wolves,
> the raging of the stormy sea, and the destructive
> sword, are portions of eternity, too great for the
> eye of man.

This is a restatement of Blake's question which he had asked earlier about the Tyger: "Did he who made the Lamb make thee?" Even toward the end of his life he seems to have left the question as definitely unsolvable, when, over the fifteenth illustration to the *Book of Job* he inscribed: "Can anyone understand the spreadings of the Clouds, the noise of his tabernacle?"

Side by side with his great awe of the Eternal was a sense of intimate communion with it, and the word "communion" is used here in the religious sense of tasting that which is hypostasized and yet unites man with the incomprehensible mystery of which it remains a symbol. Blake projects this paradoxical relationship of awe and intimacy upon the Godhead, and the projection is expressed in the words: "Eternity is in love with the productions of time."

It is Blake's conviction that as man is concerned with that which extends outward from the rim of consciousness, so the Master of the Infinite is concerned with time-bound man. Blake feels the active interrelationship and describes its nature in more of the Proverbs: "As the plow follows words, so God rewards prayers." And, "Prayers plow not! Praises reap not!" Blake scoffs at those who intellectualize religious feeling through words, *i.e.*, through prayers or praises, that presume to promote a relationship between man and God. He demands the devotion of the whole person in his daily experience of living and working. Even so, Blake asserts, grace is not automatic for everyone, nor does it follow any effort of will. Rather: "The fox provides for himself, but God provides for the lion." or "When thou seest an Eagle, thou seest a portion of Genius; lift up thy head!" Again, the nature of man is transposed into the symbols of the animal world, where man loses his individuality and becomes abstracted into characteristics which illuminate the essence of his nature. The lion occurs again and again in Blake: "the wrath of the lion," "the roaring of lions." He is the powerful sun-animal at the sound of whose coming the lesser animals are paralyzed with fear. He leaps upon his prey and the victim is his by reason of his greater endowment rather than because he has developed a particular skill or technique. He is a symbol of might in being, might which stems from the source of light itself. The fox, on the other hand, is clever at scheming and at evading real difficulties. He is dependent upon his will and his ability to implement his will through trickery. He lives by his own efforts.

Fox and lion are bound to earth, they are extreme polar aspects of the ordinary man. The eagle is of a different sort altogether. He is reputed to gaze unblinded on the sun. Throughout Blake's works the eagle is portrayed as the supramundane symbol of genius. Ever and again he soars above the earth, finding his resting places high in wild craggy rocks between the lofty reaches of the mountains and the lower stretches of sky. There he builds his nest, safe from the eye of lesser animals, and there in isolation from all but the rider of the sun chariot, he rears his young to be as he is—splendid and brave, keen of perception, swift of movement, and able to go where no other creature may set its foot. As the sacred bird of Zeus, it is the eagle who carries to Olympus the young Trojan prince Ganymede to serve as cupbearer to the gods.[12] And it is again the eagle who helps Psyche perform her third task, which is to capture and contain in a vessel the precious water of life as it rushes and boils over the rocky mountain cliffs. Of this torrent, Erich Neumann says:

> . . . we may assume that the secret lies not in the quality of the water but in the specific difficulty of obtaining it. The essential feature of this spring is that it unites the highest and the lowest; it is the uroboric circular stream that feeds the depths of the underworld and rises up again to issue from the highest crags. . . . The problem is to capture . . . the water of this spring symbolizing the stream of vital energy. . . . Aphrodite regards the task as hopeless, because to her mind the stream of life defies capture, it is eternal movement, eternal change, generation, birth, death.[13]

While Aphrodite regards the essential quality of the stream as being precisely that it cannot be contained, the eagle does manage to carry the urn in his beak, caught to his body, as Apuleius related:

> . . . then poised on the vast expanse of his beating pinions, swiftly he oared his way among the fierce jaws of teeth and the forked tongues of dragons that flickered to left and right. The waters denied his access and bade him depart ere he took some hurt, but he feigned that he sought them at Venus' bidding and was her servant. Whereupon they suffered him to approach . . . so he took of the water.[14]

Thus we can understand something of the numinous quality of this mighty bird which Blake felt as he observed the eagle circling overhead. The eagle is genius, it is that which is able to capture a portion of the endless energy of life, and give it to mankind in a form in which he can receive it. He also serves the gods. Blake describes this function in poetic language: "The eagle returns from nightly prey and lifts his golden beak to the pure east, shaking the dust from his immortal pinions to awake the sun that sleeps too long." [15] The genius, then, mediates between the divine and man, by virtue of his unique eagle-nature.

In a second theme of the Proverbs, Blake smashes to bits another idol of collective morality. He insists on *recognition that man must follow his inner need as expressed in the desire that he feels.*

We began to see, in Plate 5, how the freely flowing energy in the unconscious became to Blake a property of the "Devil's party," and how it crossed the threshold of consciousness by assuming the guise of "desire." In the Proverbs of Hell, Blake carries this theme even further by insisting that it is the infernal obligation of man to act upon this desire. This is an inescapable challenge to the creative person to bypass the values of his society in favor of what appears to him to be the demand from within himself. As a man comes to know the power which animates him as an indwelling entity of his own soul—then desire takes on a new meaning: it becomes a "sacred" charge which must not be denied. Or can the word "sacred" apply to the works of Hell?

Although superficially it may appear that Blake's comments on the traditions of his milieu are not so much at variance in content from what some of his contemporaries were saying, an example will indicate how radically different they are in feeling and attitude. Even when Lavater allowed himself to make such a moral overstatement as "An insult offered to a respectable character were often less pardonable than precipitate murder," Blake surpasses this rather surprising statement with a note of gentle satire: "Sooner murder an infant in its cradle than nurse unacted desires." Gilchrist hastily assures us that one is fully aware that the gentle Blake would no more commit infanticide than would the writer Lavater—who was described as "ardent, pious, but illogical, full of amiability, candour and high aspirations" [16]—be guilty of precipitate murder. Blake was an independent thinker, Lavater was not. Therefore Blake smilingly cast the shadow of weakness over all of Lavater's moral virtues, offering in their stead protests against both spiritual and physical oppression, and exhortations to the most complete self-expression. The inhibition of self-expression that results in the murder of the child is also a symbolic act. As we know, the expression of the instinctual side of Blake was inhibited in his outer life, but the writer cannot speak of that guilt for it is too deeply repressed. Instead, he reverses the situation, and compensates for it by seeking free expression in his inner life. This process he regards altogether subjectively. Supreme introvert that he is, Blake is speaking of the killing of the infant within, that is, not letting the Divine Child of inspiration grow to maturity. That is the infant in Blake's cradle, and he must be freed to go forth like the mythic infant Hermes, who stole the cattle of Apollo when he was four days old.

Of forces which would restrain desire, Blake writes: "As the catterpiller chooses the fairest leaves to lay her eggs on, so the priest lays his curse on the fairest joys," and "Prisons are built with stones of Law, Brothels with bricks of Religion." "He who desires but acts not, breeds pestilence."

The man who is able to feel the urgings of his inner nature bears a grave responsibility if he is unwilling to accept their demands. It is as when the Lord came to Jonah and told him that he should arise and go to Nineveh and cry out against that great city, and Jonah rose to flee from the presence of the Lord, and boarded a ship to Tarshish. "And there was a mighty tempest in the sea so that the ship was like to be broken." [17] Then the sailors cast lots to know upon whose account the evil had befallen, and the lot fell upon Jonah.

Then they said unto him, What shall we do unto thee, that the sea may be calm unto us? for the sea was wrought and was tempestuous.

And he said unto them, Take me up, and cast me forth into the sea, so shall the sea be calm unto you: for I know that for my sake this great tempest is upon you.[18]

The man who fails to fulfill the demands of his own nature, Blake finds, is torn by an inner tempest, a spiritual pestilence, that not only destroys him as an individual, but brings a part of his world down with him.

A century after Blake, Francis Thompson wrote in the same spirit of the inescapable necessity of obeying the incessant demand of the Divine in the creative man. Pursued by the "Hound of Heaven," his majestic suffering inspired these words:

> I fled Him, down the nights and down the days;
>   I fled Him, down the arches of the years;
> I fled Him, down the labyrinthine ways
>   Out of my own mind; and in the midst of tears
> I hid from Him, and under running laughter.
>   Up vistaed hopes I sped;
>   And shot, precipitated,
> Adown Titanic glooms of chasm'd fears,
>   From those strong Feet that followed,
>   followed after.
>   But with unhurrying chase,
> And unperturbed pace,
> Deliberate speed, majestic instancy,
>   They beat—and a Voice beat
>   More instant than the Feet—
> "All things betray thee, who betrayest Me." [19]

At times, purity and genuineness of expression may overflow in bitterness and anger and, when it does, the "tygers of wrath are wiser than the horses of instruction." For wrath is the inward suppressed energy seeking for expression appropriate to the creative intention within a man. The horses of instruction are the vital powers, high spirited, yet not too intelligent to submit to guidance and control.

At other times purity and genuineness of expression speak the language of a feminine companion, invisibly present. whispering in a man's ear the words of love without which he must remain incomplete in his maleness: "The soul of sweet delight can never be defil'd." However it comes to him, as the voice in the whirlwind, the roar of the tiger, or the seductive whisper of the feminine, Blake would alert man to heed the imperious summoning of man's divine essence, manifested in desire.

This Divine essence of man is an archetypal concept, that is to say, it has shaped man's philosophical thinking in every age and in every civilization. Its visible form or doctrine has an infinite number of varieties, but it is recognizable wherever it appears by its characteristic of centrality. Jung has given this archetype the name of *Self*, but it has many other names and images. Since we are considering Blake's proverbs in the light of their psychological rather than their theological or metaphysical meanings, it will be helpful to think of the "desire" by which Blake so often seems possessed and by which Francis Thompson was pursued, as a manifestation of what Jung would call the Self. This Self is not really definable because it transcends the ego, which is the vehicle for verbalizing the definition. The word "comprehend" would be better than "define" in this instance, because it is a word with obvious limitations. Comprehension is the act of grasping with the intellect, of understanding fully. And how can one grasp that which is larger than the hand which reaches out, how can one understand fully that which has created it and given it life? If we will let go of our rational function and go with the "Bird that cuts the airy way" we may begin to comprehend what Jung meant by the Self.

The psyche is defined in analytical psychology as the totality of what exists in consciousness for an individual, and what is unconscious. That which is available to consciousness as thoughts and ideas circling about the periphery of attention, is in the pre-conscious or threshold area. So too, with that which has been recently forgotten but can be easily recalled. One may think of the unconscious as supporting consciousness and extending downwards as the bulk of a mountain supports the peak. Below the pre-conscious or border area lies the personal unconscious or that part of the unconscious which is the repository of all that has been repressed and discarded from consciousness by the individual. This would include infantile traumas and the residue of all subsequent experience. Further down exist a man's resources and capacities, his entire potential for creating thoughts and attitudes and ideas. This is the stuff of his innate personal psychic structure. Now, at the base, where mountain merges with earth, the unconscious loses its personal qualities, and embraces the qualities and characteristics which are common to the nation, the various races and eventually to all mankind. This is the area which Jung calls the collective unconscious. And underlying all this, as Jung conceived the structure of the psyche, are the basic formative elements which he designated as archetypes, and which are experienced only through their manifestations in the images they produce.

The individual psyche, then, represents the totality of all that belongs to the non-physical aspect of the human personality, conscious and unconscious. The conscious part of the psyche is subject to the direction of the function known as "ego," the carrier of the will and the expediter of action. Ego development begins as the infant first learns to differentiate himself from his mother, and continues as an ongoing process of further differentiation and growth through successive stages to maturity and beyond. This is a well known aspect of psychology, and is only mentioned here to provide a frame of reference for the more difficult concept, which is that of the archetype of Self. If ego is the center, so to speak, of the conscious personality, then Self is the center of the psychic totality, conscious and unconscious. If ego is largely conscious, then Self is largely, but not altogether, unconscious. If ego is called upon to express desire when it emerges into consciousness, then it is Self which thrusts out the desire from the dark realm of the unknown and pushes it across the threshold of consciousness, where it assumes the disguise of pursuer, or "the voice of the Eternals" or "inspiration" or "impulse." Self is personal insofar as it is experienced as an image of the *Divine in man*. But insofar as Self expresses the all-embracing Divine which is the cosmic creative force, it is impersonal. Here is where the concept of Self finds for itself the religious image or symbol such as Buddha, Christ or Jehovah. Or it is an abstraction which by form or association carries the implication of wholeness: the circle, the sphere, the golden apple, the lapis or philosopher's stone, the diamond, the incorruptible substance, the panacea, the treasure hard to attain, Jerusalem—the heavenly city, the Divine Child. All or any of these and many more may be symbols of the Self, the archetype of centrality.

We cannot say that a man embarks upon a search for the Self, although the quest for the religious experience and the commitment to the psychological process of individuation may appear as a seeking after the basic truth or significance of one's being. It is rather, as Jung and Blake both had to discover, that it is a charge placed upon one's shoulder's, without his consent, and if he is chosen for this burden he has no choice but to take it up. This is what Blake means by saying that "He who desires and acts not, breeds pestilence." He makes a sickness which falls upon the whole world.

If we have gone thus far with Blake and Jung along the path toward the Self inspired by divine desire, we are led to consider a third theme of the Proverbs of Hell: *The meaning and intrinsic value of each man's individuality.*

By expressing the desire he feels, without submitting to the worldly and collective demands of society made upon him, man is able to make manifest that which marks his being as unique. But an important precondition to the achievement of individuality, according to Blake, is that one must recognize that what is valid for his way of life is not necessarily valid for that of another. Blake does not believe in equality and has some serious doubts about fraternity although he does believe in freedom. Each life has its own intrinsic nature, to which it must conform if it is not to waste itself in endless conflict between will and desire. The choice lies between the fulfillment of man's unique potential, and something less:

> The eagle never lost so much time as when he
> submitted to learn of the crow.

> The apple tree never asks the beech how he shall
> grow; nor the lion, the horse, how he shall take
> his prey.
> If the lion was advised by the fox, he would be
> cunning.
> The best wine is the oldest, the best water the
> newest.

One aspect of the process of self-realization which Blake commends to the reader is an appreciation of the natural psychological differences between the sexes. "Let man wear the fell of the lion, woman the fleece of the sheep." The lion is already familiar to us as Blake's symbol for maleness. He dominates the jungle as king, he is present at the rising and the setting of the sun, his roar makes the floor of the forest tremble. God provides him with food. Before he can achieve full manhood the youth must, like the legendary hero Heracles, struggle with the great Nemean lion. And just as Heracles ever afterwards wore the skin of the slain lion as a cloak, the head forming a kind of hood over his own head,[20] so must man go forth as a lion whose destructive nature he has subdued and whose fearlessness and might he has assumed.

Blake characterizes the nature of woman in a way that reveals his concept of the feminine disposition; she is to wear the fleece of the sheep. He sees her as a creature who must be provided for; it is not she who goes after the hunt. Indeed, she is to be protected, for it is her art to be relatively passive and to fall into a panic in the face of danger. Softness and warmth are her covering, and she can bring man comfort and a kind of quiet peace. Unlike the lion, she does not go forth alone, but is one of the flock, giving her presence to others and receiving from them. She must be guided, for she is incapable of finding her own way. In relationship she is secure; separated from the flock she may become lost. No animal permits herself to be more easily mastered than the sheep.

One feels in Blake's advice directed toward woman the quality of his attitude toward his own wife, Catherine, who assumed the fleece of the sheep if any woman ever did, fulfilling the role which her husband had set forth. But there is another aspect of the sheep which evidently was not in the forefront of Blake's consciousness when he wrote his Proverbs —that is the mountain sheep which has never been tamed. While it is clear that the domesticated sheep has become a weak-minded vassal in the service of man, it must be remembered that the tame sheep is only a shadow of the wild one. Her free sister is lively, fast, and of the most nimble movement. Her skill at climbing is unsurpassed, her perception is keen, and she is quick and facile at avoiding danger. Faced directly with an enemy, however, she is courageous and loves the fight.[21]

Is this wild creature the feminine aspect which Blake has repressed in his own nature? We recall his love for a callous beauty who did not respond to him. Was she internalized as the free-spirited partner of his maleness? Or was that frivolous maid only an image of the untamed feminine aspect within the man, the anima who inspires him to participate in that mysterious inner union which makes possible the conception of art?

There is another Proverb, in which Blake says in six words what he feels to be the essential creative relationship between the masculine and the feminine:

"The cistern contains: the fountain overflows."

The male is the fountain, in eternal movement; the female is the vessel "to give form and rest to what is formless and flowing . . . to mark off a configured unity from the flowing energy of life, to give form to life." [22] The stream that fills the urn "is male-generative, like the archetypally fecundating power of innumerable river gods all over the world. In relation to the feminine psyche it is the overwhelming male-numinous power of that which penetrates to fructify, that is, of the paternal uroboros." [23] How like the fountain that Blake calls up for an image, the fountain that rises and falls, always the same water, over and over, into and out of the cistern that contains it! The cistern represents woman, the eternal mother; and the fountain is son, lover and father, all in one. Where once a man has become differentiated to the point where he sees himself as an individual unlike any other, he then can, if he is so psychically structured, adopt the subjective view toward his own environment. This suggests a fourth theme which emerges from a study of the Proverbs:

The essential subjectivity of perception through the five senses plus the non-sensory dimension of perception, which is imagination.

This view is identifiable in Blake's belief that "All things exist as they are percieved." Or, "A fool sees not the same tree that a wise man sees." Blake's is an earlier and cruder formulation of an attitude which Jung was later to designate as introverted (in contrast to the extraverted attitude), and which he described for the first time in *Psychological Types*. Jung's concept of introversion so applies to the nature of Blake as it appears in his writings, that it will be helpful to examine it. Jung writes:

Introverted consciousness doubtless views the external conditions, but it selects the subjective determinants as the decisive ones. . . . Two persons . . . see the same object, but they never see it in such a way as to receive two identically similar images of it. Quite apart from the differences in the personal equation and more organic acuteness, there often exists a radical difference, both in kind and degree, in the psychic assimilation of the perceived image. Whereas the extraverted type refers pre-eminently to that which reaches him from the object, the introvert principally relies upon that which the outer impression constellates in the subject.[24]

Through the subjective view which his introverted nature demands, Blake is able to disentangle himself from the trite, the commonplace, the conventional descriptions of his environment, and perceive in a way that is his and no one else's. This attitude moved him to write in a letter to Dr. Trusler on August 23, 1799:

I see Every thing I paint In This World, but Every body does not see alike. To the Eyes of a Miser a Guinea is more beautiful than the Sun, & a bag worn with the use of Money has more beautiful proportions than a Vine filled with Grapes.[25]

In *The Gates of Paradise* he had already said the same thing:

"The Sun's light when he unfolds it/Depends on the Organ that beholds it." [26]

Perhaps it is here that the difference lies between creativity and productivity. Creativity is essentially subjective: it is focused on the act itself and the important thing is the ability of the actor to express himself through the act. Productivity is essentially objective: it is concerned with the product, and with how the product will fulfill the function for which it was made. Blake's intense involvement with his vision or idea and his relative lack of concern with the mastery of the techniques of rendering indicate the introverted attitude of creativity which pervades his life and work.

This attitude brings him to assert, "Where man is not, nature is barren." For Blake, nothing exists in nature except as seen through the eye of the subject.

That this eye is directed by his basic nature, rather than by any effort of will, is expressed in the Proverb:

The rat, the mouse, the fox, the rabbet watch the roots; the lion, the tyger, the horse, the elephant watch the fruits.

The meaner animals are born to inquire into causes and sources while the nobler beasts see the ripening consequences of all that has gone before.

The final limitations on man's perception are expressed in the line:

No bird soars too high, if he soars with his own wings.

This reminds the individual that he may imagine anything he will, as long as he remains true to his own reality. This reality acquires meaning and form for the individual in the course of the process of individuation. And individuation is clearly the consciously directed journey into Self, into the gradual understanding of one's own essence to its highest level of functioning. Man's reality, seen this way, is subjective. He has become aware that whatever he experiences is affected by himself as experiencer, and that there is a subtle difference between his experience and that of anyone else.

Having withdrawn from the necessity to assign an objective valuation to what is perceived, man now can free his creative powers to experience his world in a fuller way than would be possible under the restrictions of objectivity. Perception is no longer limited to sense impressions which, theoretically at least, could be measured objectively. His perceptual capacity is widened by another aperture—it is as though a floodgate were flung open, permitting contents of the infinite to flow into the individual. The gate would be, of course, the imagination; and the individual man who can contain the flood and give form to it is the Poetic Genius. This tremendous concept, experienced by the great in every generation, must be almost too much to hold. Blake has projected it back onto the universe, fulfilling the archetypal pattern of the man who cannot hold within himself the numinosity of truth, but must find a larger vessel for it: "One thought fills immensity," he cries.

S. Foster Damon recognized an archetypal pattern inherent in that brief line, but not the projective aspect of it, when he commented as follows:

A single thought is infinite, unbound by the laws of Time and Space, therefore it can be said to "fill immensity." Traherne had written the same thing earlier: "One soul in the immensity of its intelligence is greater and more excellent than the whole world. The Ocean is but a drop of a bucket to it, the Heavens but a center, the Sun obscurity, and all Ages but as one day." (Centuries, II.70;); and Coventry Patmore repeated it later: "A moment's fruition of a true felicity is enough, and eternity not too much!" (Aurea Dicta, 55); but neither of these quotations equals Blake's either in depth or in brevity. It should be remarked that of these three it is very unlikely that any of them had ever read the works of any other. This is merely an excellent example of mystics talking the same language and uncovering the same truths.[27]

Blake's view of the interdependent relationship between imagination and truth is expressed in three Proverbs which should be read together:

What is now proved was once only imagin'd.
Every thing possible to be believ'd is an image of truth.
Truth can never be told so as to be understood, and not be believ'd.

This is a daring declaration of the supremacy of the imagination and the subjectivity of truth. It is certainly not to be universally adopted, but is it not a path that must be explored by the person who would utilize whatever creative potential he may possess? Unchecked, it leads inevitably to a dangerous doctrine; the elevation of excess. Let us see how the consequences of this doctrine manifested themselves in Blake's Proverbs as we consider the next of the major themes:

The necessity of knowing excess in order to achieve balance.

The sea which surrounds the continents is a symbol for the collective unconscious. These waters can overwhelm, and we may sometime find ourselves faced with the threatening maelstrom of excess. The man of imagination could be sucked up into this dangerous wash, as indeed the history of those creative geniuses whose lives ended in madness bears witness. Yet many men of great imagination have been able to maintain a balance, however uneasy, between the demands of living in the outer world which requires a degree of social adaptation, and the necessities of an inner life centering about attention to the surge of inspiration when it appears. Blake understands this pendulation between the opposites as a kind of "law of excess" in which too much energy expended in one direction must result in a reversal of energy flow into a compensating direction. Awareness of the value of excess in clarifying the relationship of one attitude to its opposite makes it possible to face the terrible tension of holding or containing the stream of energy which comes from imagination, and directing it into creative activity. He states the problem succinctly: "The road of excess leads to the palace of wisdom."

It is as though a man must experience that which is important to him in the fullest degree, learning to know every aspect and facet of it, before he is able to loose himself from its grip. Therefore, Blake says, "Dip him in the river who loves water." And the corollary precept is that "If the fool would persist in his folly he would become wise." He praises the extreme, and is relatively heedless of its danger. This is not surprising in view of his often expressed negative reaction to imposed discipline. Blake may sense that there is a self-regulating function of the psyche, but he does not concern himself with trying to control this consciously. He permits the flow, crying, "Exuberance is Beauty," and trusts that the contrary movement will take place at the proper time—when it must. Therefore he is able to move with the energy stream in his own being, confident that by being true to his nature he will be able to live in the full intensity of his experience until the course changes. Thus, with a sober awareness of the contraries inherent in all emotions, he says: "Excess of sorrow laughs. Excess of joy weeps," and "Joys laugh not! Sorrows weep not!"

This is not to say that each man is required to live out every experience in its very depths. Blake acknowledges the possibility of learning from others when he asserts: "If others had not been foolish, we should be so." Nevertheless, he continues to hold that others have not been nearly foolish enough—therefore the man of courage has usually to go through the trials of excess, before he will be satisfied. It is as Blake insists, "You never know what is enough unless you know what is more than enough." And, from the other point of view, the last of his Proverbs brings together the eternal dilemma: "Enough! or Too much." Excess and balance—one follows the other or the psyche of man is utterly torn apart.

From time to time, as we read the Proverbs, we catch a glimpse of the single theme which orders all the rest. Although it appears, flickers, and disappears, and is in no sense schematic, it suggests that all of Blake's "excesses" have a quite unsuspected underlying purpose:

The establishment in life of an orderly system alternating between purposive activity and restorative passivity, or progression and regression.

There must finally be a basic pattern of order, in which the throbbing mind and cramped hand of man can pause and be refreshed before taking up the renewed task of giving form to yet another idea. Blake acknowledges in two of his Proverbs the truism that to everything there is a season. The first of his Proverbs is: "In seed time learn, in harvest teach, in winter enjoy." And later: "Think in the morning, Act in the noon. Eat in the evening. Sleep in the night."

Clearly Blake expresses his sensitivity to the necessity of finding the proper moment for activity and the proper moment for cessation from activity. While this was frequently forgotten by him in his own eccentric way of working, he was nevertheless aware of the need in man for an inner order, limited only by his own nature.

First, man must be receptive: this is seed time. He must permit the idea to take root and slowly to develop what is within the kernel. Only with the harvest, when the idea has fulfilled itself and borne its fruit may man share it with the world. Then he may find some brief joy in it, before the cycle begins again.

So it goes with the endless repetition of days. Each day is a model of man's life, and his life, as Blake sees it, has the transitory quality of the day. Yet the life is not extinguished forever, for its essence continues, though in another form, through an eternity of days and years and lifetimes. "Eternity is in love with the productions of time."

Blake's credo may be discerned in these "Proverbs of Hell." He expands upon it and follows it through all its ramifications, in his later prophetic works. But the essential nuclei of meaning are found scattered through these pages.

PLATE 11

The ancient Poets animated all sensible objects
with Gods or Geniuses, calling them by the names
and adorning them with the properties of woods,
rivers, mountains, lakes, cities, nations, and
whatever their enlarged & numerous senses could
percieve.

And particularly they studied the genius of
each city & country, placing it under its mental
deity;

Till a system was formed, which some took
advantage of, & enslav'd the vulgar by attempting to realize or abstract the mental deities
from their objects: thus began Priesthood;

Choosing forms of worship from the poetic tales.

> And at length they pronounc'd that the Gods
> had order'd such things.
> Thus men forgot that All deities reside in the
> human breast.

With these words, Blake summarizes the history of religion
as it developed out of a view of the world which was fluid to
man's perceptions and later developed into elaborate systems
fixed by deductive reason. Thus religion came to support rigid
habits of thought.[1]

Man as poet in ancient and, indeed, prehistoric times lived
in close communion with natural objects. His own consciousness, not so well developed that he was able to separate entirely his concept of himself from that of his environment,
endowed woods and rivers, mountains and lakes with properties of his own essence. That is to say that the spirit which man
could not perceive directly, but nevertheless felt as a motivating
force in his activities, he tended to identify with objective
nature. When man declared that each object had an indwelling
spirit, he was projecting his own animating principle into
what he seemed to find outside of himself. Jung comments on
this phenomenon in *Psychology and Religion: West and East,*
stating:

> First in remote times (which can still be observed among primi-
> tives living today), the main body of psychic life was apparently in
> human and in nonhuman objects: it was projected as we should say
> now. This fact accounts for the theory of animism.[2]

Blake had written that the ancients called these animating
principles "gods" or "geniuses" and adorned them with properties of woods, river, cities or nations. Particularly important to
them were the geniuses of each city and country, for these were
not only identified with individuals but were also the collective
forces to which the group owed its protection and its survival.
Blake's explanation of how the priesthood began discloses
his objection to the forces of enslavement which he ascribed
to organized religion. Here he seems to agree with Paul Radin
who states that the first religious formulators were primarily

concerned with the development of deities from spirits, the elaboration of evidence for the existence of the supernatural, and the construction of definitions of the nature of the supernatural.[3] Radin goes on to say that medicine men organized and developed the theory that they alone were in communication with the supernatural, and, moreover, that they exploited the concept of the supreme deity to further the attempts of an intellectual aristocracy to buttress its own position and give its activity a semi-sanctity. The medicine man, and later the priest, undertook the function of mediation between the individual and the supernatural.[4]

Blake makes a similar remark concerning the office of the priesthood, objecting on the basis that when man as poet permits someone to mediate the relationship between himself and the divine, he loses touch with the source of his inspiration. The vital flow of energy is diverted, then, from its natural channel into an elaborate superstructure of worship. Blake's use of the word "choosing" suggests that he conceives of the development of cults and rituals out of the mythology of a city or a nation as a more or less arbitrary construct "chosen" by some members of the priesthood in an effort to enslave the vulgar.

Here Blake betrays the limitations of his classical background in his failure to recognize the deep emotional involvement of the "vulgar" in the mythology of his time. Far from being a "poetic tale" manipulated by religious leaders, the myth was the expression of the deep unconscious yearnings of the collective for those aspects of life which its members were unable to experience consciously, that is, to "live out" in their personal and collective environment.

Let us take for an example the universal incest taboo.[5] Incest was from earliest times set about with prohibitions which are interpreted by modern anthropologists and psychologists as expressing the exogamous drive of man to protect the tribe against the enemy by taking the enemy's daughter or sister to wife, and at the same time enriching his own tribe with new and variegated genetic strains. This exogamous drive was in accordance with man's nature as a social being—but set against this and buried deep in his unconscious was the infantile desire to unite with his first and most cherished love objects, his own mother and his sister. But incest has a wider meaning: man's involvement with his anima.* That this great passion in the depths of man welled up in a mighty sense of awe when he permitted himself to project his own unacceptable feeling upon gods and goddesses who did cohabit with those closest in blood relationships to themselves, representing the urge to inner incest—should have been no surprise to Blake. Perhaps it appears so obvious only when viewed from the vantage point of modern depth psychology.

Blake seemed to be unaware of the tremendous impact upon every people of its mythology—and this was probably because he had never immersed himself in the lore of pagan and primitive man. He did recognize the symbolic attraction of the myth, but was suspicious of those who seemed to profit by its dissemination. He attributed the hold of myth upon its followers to the skill with which the priesthood was able to convince the masses that the gods had ordered them to worship in the prescribed manner. W. P. Witcutt offers an explanation for this in his psychological study of Blake: "He [Blake] was essentially an uneducated man; his mind had never been nourished on a perennial philosophy; he constructed an entire philosophy of life almost without reference to any other mind; which is why his doctrines often seem strange to us as if they had been the thoughts of a man of another civilization. . . . Insofar as he knew of any other philosophy, he revolted against it." [6] Another authority, Margaret Rudd, quotes an exchange between T. S. Eliot and Rex Warner, in which Eliot says of Blake:

"What his genius required, and what it sadly lacked, was a framework of accepted and traditional ideas which would have prevented him from indulging in a philosophy of his own, and concentrated his attention upon the problems of the poet." Warner takes issue: "To me it seems that, while nearly everybody does 'need' this 'framework of accepted and traditional ideas,' Blake is one of the great exceptions to the rule. He was a self-educated mystic, and had this not been so, his peculiar and powerful vision would certainly have

---

* Cf. Jung's essay "The Sacrifice" in *Symbols of Transformation.*

been different. One must be bold indeed to suggest that it would have been in any way 'better.' " Remembering that it was Eliot who, in the same essay from which Mr. Warner quotes, puts his finger on the phrase "a peculiar honesty" to describe Blake, and who also commented that Blake "was naked and saw men naked" and that his "poetry has the unpleasantness of great poetry," we cannot altogether discard Eliot's judgment on the prophetic books, for it is sure to be considered a sensitive one. But I join Mr. Warner in decrying Eliot's too facile dismissal of Blake's "ideas," and his insistence that Blake would have been better off writing from within a tradition. Mr. Eliot of all people with his critical acumen should have taken into consideration that more than anything else Blake's vision is a severe criticism of most frameworks "of accepted and traditional ideas." Such traditions, to Blake's mind, were simply veils that must be torn away to reveal true art and true Christianity. We can hardly blame him, then, for not using one of these traditions as a vehicle as Mr. Eliot finds himself able to do. And, going a little deeper, we find that after all, Blake did belong to a tradition, albeit an untidy one, and this is the tradition of the prophets.[7]

The ancient myth as a projection of the human psyche was a concept Blake did not seem to appreciate in his evaluation of the contemporary religious scene. And, because he was not aware, he was able, later in his own life, to make the unconscious projections that were to evolve in the creation of a new system of mythology. Jung explained the nature of the process in an essay on archetypes and the collective unconscious:

Primitive man impresses us so strongly with his subjectivity that we should really have guessed long ago that myths refer to something psychic. His knowledge of nature is essentially the language and outer dress of an unconscious psychic process. But the very fact that this process is unconscious gives us the reason why man has thought of everything except the psyche in his attempt to explain myths. He simply didn't know that the psyche contains all the images that have ever given rise to myths, and that our unconscious is an acting and suffering subject with an inner drama which primitive man rediscovers, by means of analogy, in the processes of nature both great and small.[8]

Because Blake could not accept the pagan myth as an expression of the unconscious thrust in the collective psyche of a people, he was forced to find some other outlet in which his own relationship to the collective aspect of the unconscious could be enunciated. In his later years, after he had completed *The Marriage of Heaven and Hell,* Blake began to develop a mythology of his own, as complex and replete with projections onto the symbols of his own personal and collective fantasies as any body of legend that flourished in the ancient world. He had already made some tentative efforts in this direction before writing *The Marriage of Heaven and Hell. Tiriel* and the *Book of Thel* were preforms of what was to follow. His three monumental books, *Vala or the Four Zoas* (1795-1804), *Milton* (1804-1808), and *Jerusalem* (1804-1820), testify to the need of man for his myth—a principle which Blake was not yet prepared to acknowledge in 1790-1793 when, on the brink of his great creative period, he was struggling with the problems of the stormy marriage of heaven and hell.

Although the conception of the dynamism in the myth was still unrealized, the germ was already alive in the statement with which Blake ended this pronouncement against formalized religion: "Thus men forgot that All deities reside in the human breast." This was the essential recognition: that the divine is *in man*—Blake knows this instinctively but not intellectually. He is deeply involved emotionally with the world of myth whose language is the symbol. He has yet to realize that the divine in man incarnates in the god-forms which man creates. It becomes Blake's agonizing labor during the next thirty years, to live out this problem through his creative genius, by objectifying the figures of his fantasy; the myth of his own soul is projected by him into that of the collective psyche. He does not take the step of differentiation by seeing the relationship of his own soul to the collective unconscious from which his soul emerges.

We cannot conclude our discussion of Plate 11 without a word concerning the pictures which illustrate it. They may be a coda to the illustration to Plate 4, where it will be remembered we saw the feminine figure representing Energy snatching the Divine Child of Imagination away from the image of Reason enchained. She walked on the water—she was of the unconscious——but the golden sun orb of consciousness glowed behind her. Now it is as though the reader (or perhaps the artist) were enclosed in a dark cave, looking out into daylight beyond its mouth. And there in the light of morning, he sees the same lovely woman with her child. Here she is clothed in flowing robes. She seems to embody tenderest feeling and sensitivity to emotion—not passion——for that would be the color of flame, but rather love as a delicate and cherishing warmth. She could be the anima of whom Blake is enamored, the Mother of "Infant Joy." Behind this pair roars and tumbles the endless sea, but she plays with her child unmindful of the waves for she is a sea woman, an expression of the unconscious. The strange-appearing figure who may be seen emerging from the depths is colored of pure gold and from his head shine forth golden strands. This sea sprite belongs to the mother-world, and protects the frolicking pair. They are a unit unto themselves, completely alienated from the forbidding image in the section below the text.

At the bottom of the page, almost completely shrouded in murky clouds, appear the head and shoulders of a mighty and fearful god, hoary-headed and white-bearded (as Blake represented Yahweh in many drawings and especially in his *Illustrations of the Book of Job*), with arms outstretched in all-encompassing gesture of power. He is bathed in light and he stands at the right side of the page. This would lead some interpreters to suggest that he is an embodiment of the collective consciousness, since light is a precondition for consciousness and the right, symbolically speaking, is the direction associated with the environment or the collective, while the left represents the inward thrust. He brings to mind the partriarchal deity which has been imposed upon man by the priesthood. A macabre touch, just to the left, almost lost in the darkness is a slight human form. It is isolated and helpless before the might of authority. It expresses the forlorn nature of those men about whom Blake writes as having forgotten that all dieties reside in the human breast.

PLATES 12-13

A Memorable Fancy

The Prophets Isaiah and Ezekiel dined with me, and I asked them how they dared so roundly to assert that God spoke to them; and

whether they did not think at the time that they would be mis-
understood, & so be the cause of imposition.

Isaiah answer'd: "I saw no God, nor heard any, in a finite organical perception; but my senses discover'd the infinite in everything,
and as I was then perswaded, & remain confirm'd, that the voice of
honest indignation is the voice of God, I cared not for consequences
but wrote."

Then I asked: "does a firm perswasion that a thing is so, make
it so?"

He replied: "All poets believe that it does, & in ages of imagination this firm perswasion removed mountains; but many are not
capable of a firm perswasion of any thing."

Then Ezekiel said: "The philosophy of the east taught the first
principles of human perception: some nations held one principle
for the origin and some another: we of Israel taught that the Poetic
Genius (as you now call it) was the first principle and all the others
merely derivative, which was the cause of our despising the Priests &
Philosophers of other countries, and prophecying that all Gods
would at last be proved to originate in ours & to be the tributaries
of the Poetic Genius; it was this that our great poet, King David,
desired so fervently & invokes so pathetic'ly, saying by this he conquers enemies & governs kingdoms; and we so loved our God, that
we cursed in his name all the deities of surrounding nations, and
asserted that they had rebelled: from these opinions the vulgar
came to think that all nations would at last be subject to the jews."

"This," said he, "like all firm perswasions, is come to pass; for
all nations believe the jews' code and worship the jews' god, and
what greater subjection can be?"

I heard this with some wonder, & must confess my own conviction.
After dinner I ask'd Isaiah to favour the world with his lost works;
he said none of equal value was lost. Ezekiel said the same of his.

I also asked Isaiah what made him go naked and barefoot three
years? he answer'd: "the same that made our friend Diogenes, the
Grecian."

I then asked Ezekiel why he eat dung, & lay so long on his
right & left side? he answer'd, "the desire of raising other men into
a perception of the infinite: this the North American tribes practise,
& is he honest who resists his genius or conscience only for the sake
of present ease or gratification?"

The Memorable Fancy in which Blake entertains Isaiah
and Ezekiel at dinner reads like a strange and confused dream
in which time is twisted into relativity and rationalism becomes
enmeshed in the web of fantasy. The passage may be considered
as a dream related by the dreamer—as contents of the dark,

mysterious part of life which sometimes slip across the threshold of consciousness. The dream comes to man when his relationship to his environment is at its lowest level: the shades of his windows are drawn, his eyelids are closed. So, too, in fantasy, Blake was able to pull the cord which dropped the curtain between himself and the outer world.

At such times Blake experienced visions in which figures appeared and spoke with him. Their connection with outer reality may have been tenuous, but it existed. The books of Isaiah and Ezekiel were well known to Blake, who was versed in the Bible and especially in the prophetic sections. It is impossible to ascertain objectively whether his reading of the prophets had a great effect upon Blake's writing, or whether his own conviction that he was himself a prophet in intimate personal contact with God led him to meditate upon those Old Testament bearers of the divine message. This is a matter of viewpoint. Irene Langridge, who studied Blake primarily in relation to his graphic art, expressed this belief:

The sense of his great, though somewhat indefinite mission, came upon Blake gradually. Much of his time, even when engaged in designing, engraving and painting, was spent in thinking immense and original thoughts. They tyrannized over him, these thoughts, and instead of his guiding their sunward and most daring flight, they drew him along on their reckless course, sometimes bringing him to complete overthrow.[1]

The works of the Biblical prophets provided a garment in which Blake was able to clothe his ideas. He found many such garments, as often in creatures of pure imagination as in characters of legend or history. But the matrix was within Blake himself where, fertilized by the creative spirit, they might originate, take form, and develop. In this sense the writings, and especially the Memorable Fancies, are like dreams: they are out of Blake's very depths, and the outside world has barely touched them. Thus Isaiah and Ezekiel here *are* Blake. They are the carriers of his prophetic aspect, through which he may commune with God and learn what God wishes him to say.

"The prophets Isaiah and Ezekiel dined with me." Dining symbolizes a relationship in which something is taken into the individual—to dine with someone is to participate of the same

substance. It is a ceremonial union: the ancients believed that
when one has dined in your house he is under your protection
and you bear a responsibility toward him, and this tradition is
held by some peoples to this day. To sit together at the table
implies that there is a harmony between men, and to sit with the
figure of a dream suggests that there is an active and nourishing
relationship between the dreamer and that inner aspect of his
nature which is symbolically portrayed.

Blake questioned his own prophetic nature with the question
that every introspective person must inevitably ask himself:
"How do I know that the impulse I feel from within myself
is truly from the divine source within me? For God does not
appear to me palpably as in the luminous windows of a Gothic
cathedral. Can I be sure, and will men understand, if I should
express what seems to me to be of essence?"

Blake used the term "Prophet" not as a forteller of future
facts, but as a revealer of eternal truths. As Paine and others
had pointed out, the Biblical prophets were poets, corresponding to the Latin *vates*. Blake read and annotated Bacon, who
had sneered at heathen religion because "the chief doctors and
fathers of their church were the poets." Blake underlined the
last word and added "prophets." [2] He also wrote: "Prophets, in
the modern sense of the word, have never existed. Jonah was
no prophet, for his prophecy of Nineveh failed. Every honest
man is a Prophet; he utters his opinion of both private & public
matters. Thus: If you go on So, the result is So. He never says,
such a thing shall happen let you do what you will. A Prophet
is a Seer, not an Arbitrary Dictator." [3] And he underlined
Lavater's words, "every genius, every hero, is a prophet." [4]

Isaiah, upon whom Blake projects the prophetic aspect of
his nature, replies with a denial that he has seen any visual
image, while asserting that it was through the senses that a
conviction of an infinite principle in all things came to him.
At first this statement seems paradoxical, but the point seems to
be that in the very limitations of the senses man is able to perceive that there is much that lies beyond those limitations. It
is with this "beyond," whether projected into the most distant
stars or inward into the dark cavern of the unconscious, that
the poet as prophet is communicating. That "beyond" is heard

as the sound of many voices—here it speaks as honest indignation. As to the question of whether the reader of poetry will
understand it, the Isaiah aspect within Blake replies unequivocally, "I cared not for consequences, but wrote." This attitude of Blake was essential to his creative process, and it is
essential to the creative process in any man.

Blake asks whether the firm persuasion that a thing is so
makes it so. The reply is not a simple affirmative, but the remark that *all poets believe* that it does. This appears to be an
expression arising from the unconscious, compensating the
conscious attitude toward reality with the assertion that in ages
of imagination a firm persuasion was able to remove mountains.
Hamblen comments on this, saying, "The eye altering altereth
all." [5]

When Ezekiel enters the colloquy to name the creative principle, he states the first principle from which, he says, all others
are derivative. He equates the "Poetic Genius" with God, and
it is clear that this is Blake speaking, for the equation remains
throughout his work. Blake had already written, in *All Religions are One,* that the Jewish and Christian testaments are
an original derivation from the Poetic Genius. Thus he acknowledges, with the voice of Ezekiel, the truth of Isaiah's
proposition that the firm persuasion of the thing makes it so—
for just as the poets' persuasion was able to remove mountains,
so the persuasion of the vulgar that all nations would be subject
to the Jews came to pass in the sense that the God of the Bible,
as well as the moral code proclaimed in the Bible, have come
to be accepted by the nations in the western world.

If we would consider Blake's concept of the function of the
poet in relation to that of the prophet we would be able to
make a subtle but important differentiation. Blake's Poetic
Genius, as equated with God, carries with it a sense of identification with the unconscious or some aspect of it. He does not
admit the possibility of confrontation by the conscious, thinking side of man. The poet's symbolic language is largely the
language of projection upon an object. It appears as uncriti-
cized datum of subjective experience. Only later is it recognized
for what it is by the prophet, who is able to apply the insight
to a living situation. The task of the prophet, then, is to with-

draw the projections of the poet, and to see beyond the poet's symbol into its intrinsic meaning.

Jung comments on the psychological implications of this process, from his own point of view. He says that projections can be withdrawn only when they come within the scope of consciousness. That is, first they have to be objectified—the poet must compose his poem. Without that, nothing can be corrected. In parallel terms, the limitation of the poet was also that of the alchemist. Jung tells us that the adept, Gerhard Dorn, was unable to recognize what for us is clearly a projection of psychic contents into chemical substances. Evidently his understanding in this respect still moved within the confines of the contemporary consciousness, even though in other respects it plumbed greater depths than did the collective consciousness of that age. Thus it is that the psychic sphere representing the body appeared to the alchemist to be identical with the chemical preparation in the retort.[6] And correspondingly, the "firm perswasion of the poet" appears to Blake to be identical with the "truth." For both poet and alchemist there is not a dualism, but an identity. But for Jung, who stands on the side of the man who is once removed from the projection as a result of his insight—there is an apparent dualism. Truth and the chemical process, or truth and the "firm perswasion," are incommensurables that cannot be reconciled. Today, owing to our increasing knowledge of physiology we are able to differentiate neurological processes from psychological processes, though both are factors in behavior. And likewise, owing to our knowledge of the creative process, we are able to distinguish imagination from scientific objectivity. When an increase in consciousness enables us to withdraw our projections,[7] we may be said to take the prophetic (or insightful), rather than the poetic (or imaginative) view of reality.

Blake next considers his own psychological nakedness and barefootedness. This is the lot of the individual who expresses himself fully and openly, without restraint, according to the inner demand that he feels. There is no subterfuge for him who cries out that "honest indignation is the voice of God, I cared not for consequences, but wrote." Blake knew the text of the Isaianic verses:

. . . spake the Lord by Isaiah the son of Amoz, saying, Go and loose
the sackcloth from off thy loins, and put off thy shoe from thy foot.
And he did so, walking naked and barefoot.

And the Lord said, Like as my servant Isaiah hath walked naked
and barefoot for three years for a sign and wonder upon Egypt and
upon Ethiopia;

So shall the king of Assyria lead away the Egyptians prisoners . . .
naked and barefoot . . .[8]

Isaiah and Diogenes, two whose belief, or faith, or inner
necessity, was stronger than any demand of the outer world,
walk with Blake in his inner experience and personify that
aspect in him which is able to disregard convention.

The figure of Ezekiel gives form to a further ramification of
Blake's need to justify his abandonment of the environment as
he turned inward, devoting himself to his work and appearing
as an eccentric to his friends and associates on those rare occasions when he was in contact with them. Not only was it
necessary that he bare himself through expressions of his most
secret emotions, but it was also required that he subjugate the
needs and tastes of his body to the higher desire, the perception
of something of the infinite. The idea that through asceticism
and deep suffering not only his own connection with the infinite might be obtained, but also a measure of insight for
other men, corresponds to the belief in vicarious atonement.
God commanded Ezekiel:

Lie thou also upon thy left side, and lay the iniquity of the house
of Israel upon it: according to the number of the days that thou
shalt lie upon it thou shalt bear their iniquity. . . . And when thou
hast accomplished them, lie thou again on thy right side, and thou
shalt bear the iniquity of the house of Judah.[9]

As Blake experienced Ezekiel in his own vision, and shared
a meal with Ezekiel and Isaiah, he began to be a "prophet in
his own right." He had approached these two figures of the
Bible who represented the prophetic spirit, which is clarity of
insight and vigor of expression. He faced them as poet, as
visionary, as one who perceived, and dared to ask questions.
It is the dialogue with first one and then the other which performs the function of transforming Blake from pure poet to the
Poetic Genius who is allowed the grace of prophetic discrimination.

Psychologically the encounter of Blake with the prophets Ezekiel and Isaiah corresponds to the method which is used spontaneously in nature or can be taught to the patient by the Jungian analyst who utilizes that technique of "active imagination." As a rule, such an encounter occurs when the analysis or the life situation has constellated the opposites so powerfully that a union or synthesis of the personality becomes an imperative necessity. In analysis this condition tends to arise when reflection upon the patient's attitudes, and particularly upon his dreams, has brought compensatory or complementary images from the unconscious so insistently before his mind that the conflict between the conscious and the unconscious personalities becomes open and critical.[10] Blake found himself in this situation when he contemplated the apparent dichotomies between his beliefs and the views of the *consensus gentium*. This applied especially to questions of morality bared in religion.

Jung describes the outcome of such a conflict in his last book, *Mysterium Coniunctionis*. When the confrontation is confined to partial aspects of the unconscious, the conflict is limited and the solution is simple. The patient with insight and some resignation or a feeling of resentment, places himself on the side of reason and convention. Though the unconscious motifs are repressed again, as before, the unconscious is satisfied to a certain extent, because the patient must now make a certain effort to live according to its principles. In addition, he is constantly being reminded of the existence of the repressed material by annoying resentments. Eventually, however, conflict and disorientation ensue, for there comes to be an equally strong *Yes* and *No* which can no longer be kept apart by rational decision. The patient finds that he cannot transform his clinical neurosis into the less conspicuous neurosis of cynicism; in other words, he can no longer hide the conflict behind a mask. It requires a real solution and necessitates a third thing in which the opposites can unite. Here the logic of the intellect usually fails for in a logical thesis and antithesis there is no third. The "solvent" can only be of an irrational nature. In nature the resolution of the opposites is always an energic process: "(Nature) acts *symbolically*," says Jung, "in the truest sense of the word, doing something that expresses both sides, just as a waterfall visibly mediates between above and below." [11]

The process as Jung describes it has already been carried out by Blake in his dealing with this Memorable Fancy. He took the fantasy image of the two prophets who came to dine with him, and concentrated upon it simply by catching hold of it and looking at it. The image was fixed in his mind as he concentrated his attention entirely. Then the image began to alter as the figures were animated by the very fact of contemplation. This contemplation expanded into the form of a question regarding how these men looked upon themselves. As the images shifted and changed, Blake carefully noted down all that transpired.

We can see that his writing reflects the psychic processes in material relating to conscious conflicts. In this way conscious and unconscious are united just as the waterfall connects above with below.[12]

We are able to observe how Blake develops a chain of fantasy ideas which gradually take on a dramatic character. The passive process becomes an action, an interior entertainment. At first the images are observed like scenes in a theatre. This would bring about no real progress, but only an endless variation on the same theme, which is not the point of the exercise at all. The piece that is being played does not want merely to be watched impartially; it compels the participation of the poet. As observer, Blake seems gradually to become aware that this is his own drama that is being performed on the inner stage. He suddenly cannot remain indifferent to the plot and its dénouement: "I heard this with some wonder & must confess my own conviction." He is compelled to take part in the play and, instead of just sitting in the theatre, to have it out with his alter egos, the prophetic figures.

It becomes apparent that nothing in the dynamic processes of creative thinking ever remains uncontradicted. Consciousness can take no positon which will not call up a negation or a compensatory effect. The one draws forth the other, and this in turn forces a response. The creative process is now functioning dynamically. Coming to terms with the other, a dialectic which can be followed through Blake's handling of this and all his "Memorable Fancies," exposes aspects of a man's inner nature. They are often aspects which he would have allowed no one else to show him, and which he would never have admitted to himself. Yet by accepting them into consciousness and integrating them, he is able to add new and deeper dimensions to his functioning personality. It is in this way, through a rudimentary preform of the process of active imagination, that Blake was able to add prophetic wisdom to poetic genius. The union of these qualities, through the working of the "transcendent function" was eventually to make possible Blake's conception of that body of original mythology which has stunned the literary world with its depth of prophetic vision and imaginative beauty.

PLATES 14-15

Comparison of the illustrations to Plates 14 and 15 suggests that they may be considered together. Blake's occupation with the relationship of the contraries, or the tension between the opposites, is the theme of the illustrations to Plates 14 and 15. Plate 14 depicts two aspects of man's nature. The naked corpse of man lies stretched out cold and grey across the top of the page. From his left side (the side turned toward the unconscious) rises a wall of flames out of which a female figure emerges. She is the anima whom we have seen before (Plate 3), enveloped in flames, but not consumed. In the previous picture she was separated from the man: he could only contemplate her. Here she seems to be breathing life into him so that united with her he may awaken to a spiritual resurrection. Damon says of her: "She is the Emanation (the Imaginative portion of man) trying to rouse the material portion." [1] Thus she represents the feminine principle in his unconscious, the inspiring one who shows him the possibilities that lie dormant within him until he is able, with her help, to rediscover them. For what, indeed, is inspiration, but literally a "breathing into?"

On the following page, which recounts the third Memorable Fancy, what seems to be another duality in man is illustrated. But we may question whether it is really so different from the body and soul pair which Blake has termed "material man" and his "emanation." At the bottom of Plate 15 we see a golden eagle with huge wings out-stretched, flying upward as he makes his escape from the dark and threatening rocks which form the highest peaks of earth. He rises into the pale sky, grasping in his beak the lowest of all the earth's creatures, the serpent. We know from previous reading in this and other works of Blake, that the eagle carries for Blake the connotation of genius, *i.e.*, the individual who experiences a meaningful and productive relationship with the divine. This is not only Blake's concept of the eagle, for in mythology the eagle is often sacred to the king of the gods. Furthermore, the eagle's place on the coins of many lands, as well as on heraldic crests and national escutcheons, reinforces the connection of the supreme deity with his elect on earth, who hold their positions or receive their gifts by reason of his higher authority or special grace.

Of all animals, the serpent presents the most striking contrast to the eagle. The "sneaking serpent" is a favorite theme of Blake. If the eagle symbolizes the highest potential in man, that of creative activity, the serpent also symbolizes a potential, but this lies in his chthonic, instinctive nature. Bound to earth and the dark passages hollowed out of the earth, he is the creature of his impulses, by which he is enslaved. Traditionally, by his cunning he is able to manipulate man through his instincts. As the eagle represents to Blake the spiritual strivings of man, so the snake is seen by him as the bondage of his material nature.

The serpent has been a symbol of evil ever since he seduced Eve into eating of the fruit of the Tree of Knowledge. Blake gives the serpent a number of overlapping meanings, all related. One is Hypocrisy. The young Tiriel was "compell'd to pray repugnant & to humble the immortal spirit, till (he was) subtil as a serpent in a paradise, consuming all, both flowers and fruit, insects and warbling birds." [2] Hypocrisy is the result of external pressure and ruins the subject. Also the Priest is "serpentine." The Archbishop of Paris arises "in the rushing of scales and hissing of flames and rolling of sulphurious smoke . . . his voice issued harsh grating; instead of words, harsh hissings." [3] Now the sneaking serpent walks in mild humility, and the just man rages in the wilds. [4] Finally, the serpent is Nature, herself. The coils represent her dull rounds and repetitions. The serpent is often associated with material wealth, as we shall read below: "a viper folding round and round the rock and the cave, and others adorning it with gold and silver and precious stones." (Plate 15.)

The sharp talon of the eagle wrenches free the serpent from his surroundings and holds him coiling about in the air.

Is this not somehow analagous to the flame-woman's breathing into the nostrils of the man the breath of life that will enable him to rise from his inert state and to walk about upon the earth as part of it, and yet as something more than earth? This is one image of the union of the opposites. The anima has carried out her function of leading man into a relationship with the unconscious while, paradoxically enough, she gives him breath which is consciousness. Only by being awake and alive through her is he able to contemplate upon that part of life which lies beyond knowledge.

The other image of the union is implicit in the plate which shows the eagle and the serpent. Do we not see symbolized also the union of the spiritual nature of man with his primitive instinctual and sexual side? The very image of the eagle lifting the serpent off the earth shows that it is mandatory that he maintain his connection with his lower brother.

PLATE 14

How man may be liberated from the limitations of his ordinary sensory capacities is described through the metaphor of the printing process. Plate 14 contains a treatment of Blake's symbolic approach to printing, while Plate 15 elaborates through imagery this method in which knowledge is transmitted from one generation to another.

The ancient tradition that the world will be consumed in fire at the end of six thousand years is true, as I have heard from Hell.

For the cherub with his flaming sword is hereby commanded to leave his guard at tree of life; and when he does, the whole creation will be consumed and appear infinite and holy, whereas it now appears finite & corrupt.

This will come to pass by an improvement of sensual enjoyment.

But first the notion that man has a body distinct from his soul is to be expunged; that I shall do by printing in the infernal method, by corrosives, which in Hell are salutary and medicinal, melting apparent surfaces away, and displaying the infinite which was hid.

If the doors of perception were cleansed every thing would appear to man as it is, infinite.

For man has closed himself up, till he sees all things thro' narrow chinks of his cavern.

The question arises: what does Blake mean by the statement that the world will be consumed in fire at the end of six thousand years? That time has a relative, rather than an absolute, significance was expressed in "Proverbs of Hell": "The hours of folly are measured by the clock; but of wisdom no clock can measure."

Blake refers to the ancient tradition that the world will be consumed in fire at the end of six thousand years. It was said that as the Lord had created the universe in six days and rested on the seventh, so the universe in turn would labor for six ages, which would be followed by a seventh age, the Messianic Sabbath, or millennium, after which the Last Judgment would take place. According to Damon [5] all this was derived from the juxtaposition of the following Biblical texts:

In six days the Lord made heaven and earth.[6]
And on the seventh day God ended his work which he had made. And. God blessed the seventh day and sanctified it: because that in it he had rested from all his work which God created and made.[7]
One day is with the Lord as a thousand years.[8]

Is this an equation of the creative process in the work of the poet with the creative process in the macrocosm of God's creation of the world? Does Blake mean to say that the God in man carries on the creative process begun by the God who created man? And that thus six days merge into six thousand years and more? To attempt to come to Blake's intent we should read a passage in his *Milton*. Here we will not find specific answers to our questions, but a feeling about them which penetrates our minds with the dizzying effect of strong wine so that we are able, if we abandon ourselves to the lyric, to lose our sense of time in a sense of the infinite. In doing so we may experience, rather than understand, what Blake is trying to express. "Los" is a central character in Blake's mythology. He functions in the world as the creative spirit as it manifests itself in the poet and prophet.[9]

> But others of the Sons of Los build Moments &
> Minutes & Hours
> And Days & Months & Years & Ages & Periods, wondrous
>   buildings;
> And every Moment has a Couch of gold for soft repose,
> (A Moment equals a pulsation of the artery),
> And between every two Moments stands a Daughter
>   of Beulah
> To feed the Sleepers on their Couches with maternal
>   care.
> And every Minute has an azure Tent with silken Veils:
> And every Hour has a bright golden Gate carved with
>   skill:
> And every Day and Night has Walls of brass & Gates
>   of adamant,
> Shining like precious Stones & ornamented with
>   appropriate signs:
> And every Month a silver paved Terrace builded high:
> And every Year invulnerable Barriers with high Towers:
> And every Age is Moated deep with Bridges of silver
>   & gold:
> And every Seven Ages is Incircled with a Flaming Fire.
> Now Seven Ages is amounting to Two Hundred Years.
> Each has its Guard, Each Moment, Minute, Hour, Day,
> Month & Year.
> All are the work of Fairy hands of the Four Elements:
> The Guard are Angels of Providence on duty evermore.
> Every time less than the pulsation of the artery
> Is equal in its period and value to Six Thousand Years,
>
> For in this Period the Poet's Work is Done, and all the
>   Great
> Events of time start forth & are conciev'd in such
>   a Period,
> Within a Moment, a Pulsation of the Artery.[10]

Time, then, has a meaning relevant only to the process which it encompasses, and when six thousand years—or the pulsation of the artery—is at an end, then the creative process is at an end and the world may be consumed. But at the same time that the corporeal creation is consumed, it takes on the appearance of the infinite. We refer again to the picture on this page and note that at the same time the soul maiden breathes life into the corpse of man, the flames which envelop her must inevitably consume his flesh.

The cherub, whose symbol is the eye, is the spirit of knowledge in Blake's writings. In Christian tradition cherubim are of the second order surrounding God, inferior only to seraphim, the spirit of love, whose symbol is the wing. This cherub is the agent of Reason. With the flaming sword of Prohibition he drove man from Eden.[11]

And the Lord God said, Behold, the man is become as one of us, to know good and evil: and now, lest he put forth his hand, and take also of the tree of life, and eat, and live forever:/Therefore the Lord God sent him forth from the garden of Eden, to till the ground from whence he was taken./So he drove out the man; and he placed at the east of the garden of Eden Cherubims and a flaming sword which turned every way, to keep the way of the tree of life.[12]

Blake never uses the word "cherub" in a good sense. He implies here that when Reason ceases imposing its prohibitions upon man, man will be free to approach the tree of life. It is from that time forward that man will be able to distinguish what is finite and corrupt, from what is infinite. Out of this an improvement in sensual enjoyment will come to pass, for with man's greater knowledge derived from the tree of life he will be able to enjoy the experiences of the senses on an entirely different level. That release from limitations of the body, man's material aspect, elevates the whole of mankind, is Blake's hypothesis. He found this corroborated by Isaiah and Ezekiel when he held his "conversations" with them.

Here, then, is the task of the prophet or poet—to "melt apparent surfaces away" and to cleanse the "doors of perception." It is his task to use the word—concretized into the printing process which is literally the work of Blake's hands—to liberate man who has closed himself up in the cavern [13] of his own body and who sees only through the aperture of the five senses.

In commenting on this section, Northrop Frye observes that "All philosophies founded on sense experience are founded on a timid fear of expanding the powers of the mind, which uses the senses. All life lived on such principles takes caution and fear to be cardinal virtues. That is why 'reason' in the bad sense is the same thing as morality." [14]

PLATE 15

A Memorable Fancy

I was in a Printing house in Hell, & saw the method in which knowledge is transmitted from generation to generation.

In the first chamber was a Dragon-Man, clearing away the rubbish from a cave's mouth; within, a number of Dragons were hollowing the cave.

In the second chamber was a Viper folding round the rock & the cave, and others adorning it with gold, silver and precious stones.

In the third chamber was an Eagle with wings and feathers of air: he caused the inside of the cave to be infinite; around were numbers of Eagle-like men who built palaces in the immense cliffs.

In the fourth chamber were Lions of flaming fire, raging around & melting the metals into living fluids.

In the fifth chamber were Unnam'd forms, which cast the metals into the expanse.

There they were reciev'd by Men who occupied the sixth chamber, and took the forms of books & were arranged in libraries.

This could be the kind of dream one might expect an inspired printer to have. The inert surroundings of his trade take on in sleep a fantastic surcharge of energy which is expressed as incessant devilish activity. One can conjecture that the Printing house in Hell is the infernal version of 28 Poland Street, from which the plates for this book actually proceeded. Gilchrist has placed us in a frame of mind in which it is not difficult to imagine Blake in his printshop, hunched over his worktable, oblivious that midnight has long since chimed its welcome to the spirits of the night. He is weary, his hand no longer steady, so he pauses for a few moments to rest from the precise labor of engraving the copper plate. Darkness presses forward from the corners of the room, and the oil lamp on the table before him seems burning-bright to his smarting eyes. He bends to it, turns down the wick and blows out the small flame. The dark envelops him for only an instant, then the flickering glow of distant fires casts tongue-like shadows upon the wall. He is in a Printing house in Hell. The flames are the corrosives by which "apparent surfaces" have been melted away—and the "infinite which was hid" now emerges before his eyes.

The Printing house vision, if we believe Gilchrist, is taken seriously enough by William Blake. But, as with all his visions, he is more than a passive observer. We saw this in the interchange that took place in the Memorable Fancy in which he entered into lively argument with Isaiah and Ezekiel very much as a participant. Northrop Frye suggests that Blake is able to experience the vision on yet another level. He is able to abstract it, to objectify it. The result of this is that vision goes full circle. Arising from the collective unconscious, it comes to Blake in the form of an archetypal dream. He then experiences it through the medium of his own personality—he participates, observes, converses, and is completely at home in the action that takes place. He sees the vision as having implications which again involve the external world. Supported by his visionary experience he is able to comment upon that world, which he can do from a detached and often sardonic position. This leads Frye to make the declaration that *The Marriage of Heaven and Hell* belongs in the tradition of great satire. Satire, of course, has always been one of the most effective weapons of the poet and the prophet. It is an acid that corrodes everything it touches. Blake saw the acid bath which he gave his engravings as a symbol of his approach. He had first to expunge the idea that man has a body distinct from his soul, and he proposed to do this by printing in the infernal method, by corrosives which melt the apparent surface away and disclose the infinite, or truth, which is hidden behind it.

This implies that condemnation is only part of the satirist's work: his attack on the evil and foolish merely allows what he reveals to stand out in clearer relief. As Frye says, the satirist who does nothing but watch people make fools of themselves is simply pouring acid all over the plate, and achieves only a featureless disintegration. But the great satirist is an apocalyptic visionary like every other great artist, if only by implication, for his caricature leads us irresistibly away from the passive assumption that the unorganized data of sense experience are reliable and consistent, and afford the only contact with reality.[15]

We must then look at the other kind of data, the symbols that come into consciousness in the course of the visionary experience. These lead us to another contact with reality, with the non-rational side of reality. For if we accept, as we must, that man is not only a rational being, but that he is also affected by such non-rational factors as emotions and instinctual drives, then the rational approach will not provide the only contact to the whole of reality. We must look at the various elements that appear in Blake's visions and turn them this way and that, according to the method of amplification. This is, of course, the method by which Jung approaches the dream symbol. He tries to illuminate the symbol by examining the projections that have been made on this symbol in literature and mythology and history. This enables him to place it in a wider context, so that he can then select from this wider context the most meaningful application as it may apply to the dreamer. So too, we utilize the method of amplification to elaborate upon what Blake is "seeing," in order that we may discover what his images have to impart about reality itself.

Readers and critics of Blake have offered many widely differing interpretations of his symbols. This is an intrinsic problem when people try to understand a symbol, inasmuch as the symbol is a bridge between consciousness and something which is unknown. The ambiguity of the symbol must be accepted as the essence of its nature. For a symbol to retain its strange and compelling attraction, one part of it may be visible but the other must remain forever obscure. Thus, with the Printing house vision of the six cave-chambers and their occupants.

The number six, in itself, has a striking affinity for the motif of his study. Jung states that according to old tradition six means creation and evolution, since it is a product of two and three (even and odd = female and male). He quotes Philo

Judaeus, who calls the *senarius* (six) the "number most suited to generation." [16]

The use of the word "generation" here may be considered in more than one sense, and Blake's intent is not altogether clear. As used by Philo Judaeus, it suggests "the act of producing off-spring." But, in a less concrete sense it could also mean the "process of coming into being" or "origination." A "generation" as a period in the history of mankind is perhaps Blake's intended implication in the use of the word—but the question may be asked whether, on quite another level, Blake is really speaking of how apparently spontaneously an idea bursts into form, *i.e.*, how an idea is "generated."

The six-pointed star, as an ancient mystic symbol referring to the sexual union of the male and female, is represented by the masculine triangle $\triangle$ being superimposed upon the feminine triangle ∇ , thus $\hexagram$. All that is necessary for generation, for the creation of something new and living, is implicit in the *coniunctio* which is symbolized by the number six.

The six chambers, except for the last one, are really caves—dark womb-like openings in the earth where the inhabitants are isolated from the world of outer events and where their activities are directed inward. This is the area into which Blake can enter at will for, in his vision, he is now the devil's printer who has with corrosives cleansed his doors of perception. He is no longer required to peer through the narrow chinks of his cavern which are the five senses.

In the first chamber he sees a Dragon-man. We do not know if Blake had ever heard of a dragon-man although surely he was familiar with stories of dragons in the legendary history of England as well as many other lands. But of a monster half man and half dragon, we cannot determine whether Blake had any prior knowledge. We can only draw inferences from the fact that his works show some evidence of familiarity with the mythological patterns of ancient Greece, where a parallel does exist.

The first king of Attica, as Ovid recounts the tale,[17] was called Cecrops. He had no human ancestor and was himself only half human, that half being the head, arms and upper part of the torso.

> Cecrops, lord and hero,
> Born of a dragon,
> Dragon-shaped below.

He was the creature usually held to be responsible for
Athena's becoming the protector of Athens. Poseidon was in
contention with her for the city. To show what a great benefac-
tor he could be, he struck open with his trident the great rock
of the Acropolis so that salt water leapt forth from the cleft
and subsided into a deep well. But Athena achieved even more.
She caused an olive tree to grow there, the most prized of all
the trees of Greece.

> The gray-gleaming olive
> Athena showed to men,
> The glory of shining Athens
> Her crown from on high.

In return for this good gift, Cecrops, who had been made
arbiter, decided that Athens was hers. But Poseidon, who was
greatly angered, punished the people by sending a disastrous
flood. In one version of the story of the contest between Athena
and Poseidon, woman's suffrage plays a part. In those days
women voted as well as men. All the women voted for the
goddess in the contest, and all the men for the god. There was
one more woman than there were men, so Athena won. But
the men, along with Poseidon, were greatly chagrined at the
triumph of the feminine; and while Poseidon proceeded to
flood the land the men decided to take the vote away from the
women. Nevertheless, Athena kept Athens.

This tale is related to indicate the importance of attempting
to appreciate the deeper symbolism of the use of the Dragon-
man figure. The Dragon-man is the arbiter between the feminine and the masculine principles. The feminine is embodied
by Athena in the myth and in Blake's writings by that fiery
maiden who brings inspiration. The masculine principle is seen
as Poseidon in the myth and in Blake as the capacity for clarifying the abstract idea. It is this figure of the Dragon-man, then,
who serves the transcendent function of mediating between the

two and making a new development possible. He is able to clear away the rubbish that is the debris of materialism, which prevents entrance into the first chamber. He is aided by "a number of Dragons" who are creatures of fancy widening the area which can be perceived. The beginning of knowledge, as we have seen, is perception.

Now comes the second chamber, and in it a viper folding round the rock and the cave. The lower wisdom of mankind lurks in the chthonic depths, bound to earth and unable to free itself. The snake is in continuous intercourse with the earth-mother, ever penetrating her and ever emerging from her caverns—thus symbolizing the primal instincts of man. The snake is dynamic and procreative; he is essential to the nature of mankind and because of his presence the blood and flesh of life is able to come forth. He is Satan in disguise, the therio-morphic Dionysus, and the dark and active side of a hundred other gods who, in their lighter and more acceptable forms are publicly worshipped by the human race.

The viper, and the others with him, are seen adorning the cave with gold and silver and precious stones. He spreads about all kinds of material treasures prized by man. Like the serpent in Eden, he holds before man's eyes that for which he yearns. It is the fruit of the tree of knowledge, and it tempts man to procure for himself all the advantages of power and wealth. This is what Blake believes makes the attainment of knowledge desirable to so many people, and this is what he fears and dis-trusts as he would the venom of the viper. This is why he de-tests the tools and machines of the Industrial Revolution; he sees them as becoming the masters of men as they grope blindly after the treasures of the earth. Blake regards them as the blandishments of the serpent, and he believes that rather than freeing mankind, the use of knowledge for material production enslaves him. This idea was later crystallized in *Jerusalem,* where he wrote of the tyranny of the material aspect of man over his spirit:

I turn my eyes to the Schools & Universities of Europe
And there behold the Loom of Locke, whose Woof rages dire,
Wash'd by the Water-wheels of Newton: black the cloth

In heavy wreathes folds over every Nation: cruel Works
Of many Wheels I view, wheel without wheel, with cogs tyrannic
Moving by compulsion each other, not as those in Eden, which.
Wheel within Wheel, in freedom revolve in harmony & peace.[18]

As the viper symbolizes all that is material and sensual in man, the eagle represents the polar opposite to Blake. The third chamber, then, releases corporeal man from the coils of the serpent. No longer need he be bound to earth, for this eagle's feathers and wings are of air—the whole bird is wind or spirit. What under the viper's domination was a rocky cave now dissolves its walls and becomes infinity. This is Blake's feeling about the power of imagination as embodied in the great bird: it surpasses time and space and reveals that which is beyond the limit of man's experience. We note that in the first chamber the activity of the dragons was the clearing away of rubbish, in the second chamber the vipers are busily engaged in placing valuable baubles about; and it is only in the third chamber that something new actually comes into being. It is with the emergence of the eagle-men—Blake's conceptualization of the poetic genius—that creativity begins to take place.

If one can feel into this dream of Blake, he may be able to fathom how the unconscious represents itself as a cave without walls. This seeming paradox (and in dreams paradoxes abound) takes form as the night sky, walled in by darkness, the extensity of which is limited only by man's ability to penetrate it with a ray of consciousness. It is this infinite cave of which Blake speaks, and within it, if they can be said to be contained, are constructed palaces in the immense cliffs. It appears that Blake is projecting his own strivings after the holy into the dwelling places of these superior beings, in much the same way as did the ancient Greeks project their own aspirations onto the Olympian heights.

Blake describes perception in the first cave, acceptance of sensual desire in the second, development of the creative spirit in the third, and now his dream brings him into the fourth chamber: a fiery furnace in which flaming lions are the agents of a process of transformation. Their rage as they stalk about is the reaction to the ceaseless conflict between the viper aspect and the eagle aspect in man, as Blake experiences it in his own being. In the interaction which takes place in this fourth chamber the metals, or elements, combine and "living fluids" are the result. The fluid state is that condition which can take the form of any vessel into which it is poured—it might be said to resemble free energy which has the capacity of being directed into a limitless number of channels. Blake feels this energy burning within him, it is too intense for him to endure, and he must swiftly advance into the next chamber.

What are the "Unnam'd forms" of the fifth chamber? Hamblen suggests that they are

. . . those ideal structural principles within the growing object which determine its final appearance and function. *La forme* the French call it, and some of our artists can find no English equivalent which so well expresses the inner constructive principle of a living and developing thing.[19]

At the very time that Miss Hamblen was writing her book, *On the Minor Prophecies of William Blake* (first published in 1930) in solitude on her lonely New Jersey farm, C. G. Jung had been laboring for some years in Zurich to illuminate the concept she was attempting to describe but for which she could find no adequate word.

Jung discusses the problem of how new ideas arise out of the treasure-house of primordial images, using for his example the idea of conservation of energy as it was conceived of by Robert Mayer in 1844.[20] Since the whole problem of energy and its implications for the creative process was of such basic concern to Blake, and specifically in the work under consideration, we are interested in Jung's scientific formulation of the process which was to Blake a vague yet essential awareness, expressible only in the language of the poet. Jung asks, "Whence this new idea that thrusts itself upon consciousness with such elemental force?" He suggests that the idea of the conservation of energy must be an archetype of the collective unconscious, and further goes on to say that such a conclusion obliges us to prove that a primordial image of this kind really did exist in the mental history of mankind and was operative through the ages. He then proceeds to demonstrate that in the so-called "dynamistic religions" there exists this universal magical power about which everything revolves, termed "primitive energetics" by Arthur O. Lovejoy, and that this power concept is also the earliest form of a concept of God among primitives, and is an image which has undergone countless variations in the course of history. He shows that in the Old Testament the magic power glows in the burning bush and in the countenance of Moses; in the Gospels it descends with the Holy Ghost in the form of fiery tongues from heaven. In Heraclitus it appears as world energy, as "ever-living fire"; among the Stoics it is the original heat, the power of fate. He continues to trace this energy motif through history and legend up to the modern example of Mayer's "discovery," and he concludes: "So this idea has been stamped on the human brain for aeons." [21] From this position Jung develops his theory of the archetypes, in which he asserts that the greatest and best thoughts of man shape themselves upon these primordial images as a blueprint. It should be added that the archetype encompasses the sinister and infernal thoughts as well. The archetype is a kind of readiness to produce over and over again the same or similar mythical ideas. Archetypes, according to this explanation, are not only impressions of ever-repeated typical experiences, but at the same time they behave empirically like agents that tend toward the repetition of these same experiences.

This very brief summary of Jung's theory of the archetypes will perhaps suffice to indicate the resemblance of the concept of the archetype to Blake's "Unnam'd forms," which give shape and expression to energy, represented as flaming fire. Blake says that these "Unnam'd forms . . . cast the metals into the expanse," that is, from these inner constructive principles ensues the dynamic action which results in the transmission of knowledge from generation to generation. And Jung says: ". . . when an archetype appears in a dream, in a fantasy, or in life, it always brings with it a certain influence or power by virtue of which it either exercises a numinous or a fascinating effect, or impels to action." [22] It is hardly deniable that Jung has at last elucidated the concept which Blake also perceived, and that Jung has given a name to that which Blake could only speak of as "Unnam'd forms."

The sixth chamber is the end of the historical process, when a man is finally able to understand something of which he was not aware before. What he has done is to accept certain contents which come up from the unconscious and to make those contents conscious. Blake recognizes intuitively that this is the way man learns. And man as printer commits this learning to books which are placed in libraries.

We can interpret the whole passage as Blake's projection of the mystery of his personal creative activity, beginning with a vision and being brought into reality through a magical and devilish printing process. Or, we can take the passage in a broader aspect, as the paradigm in one man, possessed of an unparalleled ability to express his experience, of the manner in which unknown mysteries become psychological facts.

PLATES 16-17

The Giants who formed this world into its sensual existence, and now seem to live in it in chains, are in truth the causes of its life & the sources of all activity; but the chains are the cunning of weak and tame minds which have power to resist energy; according to the proverb, the weak in courage is strong in cunning.

Thus one portion of being is the Prolific, the other the Devouring: to the Devourer it seems as if the producer was in his chains; but it is not so, he only takes portions of existence and fancies that the whole.

But the Prolific would cease to be Prolific unless the Devourer, as a sea, recieved the excess of his delights.

Some will say: "Is not God alone the Prolific?" I answer: "God only Acts & Is, in existing beings or Men."

These two classes of men are always upon earth, & they should be enemies: whoever tries to reconcile them seeks to destroy existence.

Religion is an endeavour to reconcile the two.

Note: Jesus Christ did not wish to unite, but to separate them, as in the Parable of sheep and goats! & says: "I came not to send Peace, but a Sword."

Messiah or Satan or Tempter was formerly thought to be one of the Antediluvians who are our Energies.

Giants symbolize the great primeval powers within us, which are mostly hidden within our fleshy bodies; also they symbolize the great thinkers, those individuals who transcended their ap-

parent earthly limitations and realized their powers. When
separated from humanity, giants become its fiercest enemies.

The illustration heading this passage of text shows a narrow
cell in which crouch a group of five giants, huddled together
upon the floor, their wrists and ankles fastened together by
chains. The walls are dark and shadowy, and a feeling of
despair is pervasive. We are reminded of the cosmogonal legends in which giants roamed the earth before mankind had
come into being, giants who had to be engaged in battle by the
gods, and who finally were assigned to exile or imprisonment
in faraway places. In the mythology of ancient Greece, the race
of Titans, who were the sons and daughters of Mother Earth
(Gaea) and Father Sky (Ouranos) and who preceded the Olympian gods, ruled the earth for untold generations. The Titan
Cronos was lord of the universe, with his sister-queen Rhea,
until one of their sons, Zeus, succeeded in dethroning him.
There followed a terrible war between Zeus with his five
brothers and Cronos helped by his brother Titans, a war which
almost wrecked the universe. At last, with the help of his
irresistible weapons, thunder, lightning and earthquake, Zeus
conquered. He punished his enemies by having them

> Bound in bitter chains beneath the wide-wayed earth,
> As far below the earth as over the earth
> Is heaven, for even so far down lies Tartarus.
> Nine days and nine nights would a bronze anvil fall
> And on the tenth reach earth from heaven.
> And then again falling nine days and nights
> Would come to Tartarus, the brazen-fenced.[1]

These words are appropriate to the mood of the picture
Blake has drawn of "The Giants who formed this world into
its sensual existence and now seem to live in it in chains . . ."
Their cave, hewn out of bedrock and barely large enough to
house the huge immortals, has about it the quality of isolation
that is expressed by the depths of Tartarus. But the giants are
more than quasi historical figures: they are a primordial image,
like that of fire-energy, which recurs over and over in the
mythological memory of mankind.

In Norse lore, also, giants preceded the gods. The *Elder Edda* of Iceland, with which Blake was familiar, recounts how at the beginning of time there was nothing but two realms, the cold realm of death in the north and the land of fire in the south. From the latter came fiery clouds that turned the ice to mist. Drops of water fell from the mist and out of them were formed the frost maidens and Ymir, the first giant. His son was Odin's father, whose mother and wife were frost maidens. The saga goes on to tell how Odin and his brothers killed Ymir. From him they made the earth and sky—the sea from his blood, the earth from his body, the heavens from his skull. A great wall defended the place where mankind was to live, and this was built out of the giant's eyebrows, and the space within was called Midgard, or the world. The race of giants continued to live, according to the Norse myth, in Jotenheim, where they vied continually, and not always successfully, with the gods for power.[2]

Genesis renders an account of giants who ruled the earth before the deluge; the offspring of the angelic Sons of Elohim and human women. The loves of their parents were described in the apocryphal book of Enoch, for which Blake began illustrations depicting the power of sex.

There were giants in the earth in those days; and also after that, when the sons of God came unto the daughters of men, and they bare children unto them, the same became mighty men which were of old, men of renown.[3]

The *Midrash* refers to a race of giants before the Fall, of which Adam was one, as was his son Seth, but not Cain. Seth had commanded his descendants to keep aloof from the daughters of Cain, and for seven generations they obeyed his injunction, but then they cohabited with the accursed breed and the results were the Anakim (or Niphilim), the giants who led a shameful life and caused God to send the Flood.[4]

Giants, as we can see from these extracts from literature of antiquity with which we know Blake was acquainted, typically emerge from a paradisiacal existence where day has barely begun to be differentiated from night, where there is neither good nor bad, and where consciousness has not yet come into being. Thus we may assume that for Blake the giant was a symbol for the primeval wholeness in which all potentialities exist, but have fallen into a confused, chaotic state. The giant image is a natural one for this concept. Fairy tales are rife with episodes concerning giants who are clumsy, sleepy, poorly-coordinated creatures. They have a certain formlessness in their nondescript appearance, being usually so huge that it is impossible for the human eye to take them in all at a glance. Their movements are slow and sluggish, and any quick young Jack can manage to outwit them. Everpresent, however, is the danger that the giant, if Jack is not quick enough, may suddenly devour him.

Prolific and Devouring: this is the concept that Blake has before him when he considers the nature of the giant. In one sense the concept is dual, for it is inconceivable that fecundity and fruitfulness could reproduce indefinitely without a countermovement of consuming and emptying out. The relationship of Prolific and Devouring in another, larger sense, however, is unitary and undifferentiated. It is a merging of the swallower with the one who is being swallowed.

The symbol of this psychic state of the beginning, of the original situation in which man's consciousness and ego were still amorphous and undeveloped, may be expressed in the uroboros, the circular snake biting his tail. "As symbol of the origin and of the opposites contained in it," writes Erich Neumann, "the uroborus is the 'Great Round,' in which positive and negative, male and female elements of consciousness, elements hostile to consciousness, and unconscious elements are intermingled. In this sense the uroboros is also a symbol of the state in which chaos, the unconscious, and the psyche as a whole were undifferentiated . . ." [5]

Psychologically, the giant who contains the aspects of the Prolific and the Devouring could be said similarly to represent the pre-conscious state of mankind, a state of primordial wholeness which has to be destroyed before a new level of consciousness can come into being. It is the condition of primitive man, who scarcely differentiates himself from his tribe, whose activities are merged with those of the group according to custom and practice, so that his awareness of himself is minimal. This state may be said to have its parallel in the condition of the newborn infant nursing at the breast who does not yet conceive of himself as an entity separate from his mother.

What Blake seems to be saying here, is that with the development of ego consciousness, a sense of identity as "I," man takes the place of the giant. Man differs from the giant in that the prolific and the devouring aspects in man are separated, whereas in the giant they were combined as two portions of one being. The two aspects are expressed, according to Blake's thinking, in two types of men, in whom either one or the other of these aspects predominates.

At this point recognition is given to the conventionally accepted idea that all creativity stems from the Creator God, and that he alone is prolific. This was the attitude of Swedenborg, with whom Blake has taken issue before. Once more Blake reiterates his theme that God is not a remote and heavenly being, but that he operates and exists only through men. He distinguishes two classes of men: the Prolific, which he may equate with the poet, the genius, the man of imagination; and the Devourer, who is the man of convention, of organized religion, of reason.

He insists upon the necessity to separate these two and to consider them as irreconcilable enemies. This he did throughout his own life, by carrying on a constant war against the forces of reason and restraint, and insisting upon his right and his need to express his ideas as they came to him, straight from the dictates of his imagination. He would brook no compromise with his prolificness, using for his model the parable of the Sheep and the Goats, in which those who in their generosity have delighted the Creator are invited to sit at the right hand of Jesus and to inherit the kingdom of God:

For I was an hungred, and ye gave me meat: I was thirsty, and ye gave me drink: I was a stranger and ye took me in.
Naked, and ye clothed me: I was in prison, and ye came unto me.[6]

while those who have failed to serve the Creator are told:

Depart from me, ye cursed, into everlasting fire, prepared for the devil and his angels . . .[7]

Blake's view of the eternal struggle between the freely flowing energies and their binding restraints characterizes his approach to the creative problem which he faced. Herein lie the
elements of his greatness and perhaps herein also the source of
his inability to achieve that universal recognition which is
accorded to men of genius who have, in addition to their enormous talents and commensurate capacities to express them, that
other quality which Blake degrades as "chains" which are "the
cunning of weak and tame minds." These chains which make
slaves of the energies, in Blake's thinking, are reason and restraint. But other artists have welcomed these limitations upon
the aimless outpourings of inspiration, and called them by the
sweeter names of "discipline" and "craftsmanship" and "order"
and "control."

It would be well to consider, then, set against Blake's de-
fiance of all attempts to reconcile these two inimical aspects of
man, the following statement attributed to Leonardo da Vinci,
an indisputable genius, yet a man of this world and a supreme
realist:

Force is a spiritual power, an invisible energy arising from motion
which by impact of violence from without causes bodies to be distorted or displaced, imparting to them a marvelous animation; it
compels all created things to assume new shapes and places. It runs
with fury to its own desired undoing, expending itself as opportunity offers. Slowness strengthens it and speed weakens it. It is born of
violence and dies through liberty.[8]

PLATES 17-20

A Memorable Fancy

An Angel came to me and said: "O pitiable foolish young man!
O horrible! O dreadful state! consider the hot burning dungeon
thou are preparing for thyself to all eternity, to which thou are
going in such career."

I said: "Perhaps you will be willing to shew me my eternal lot, &
we will contemplate together upon it, and see whether your lot or
mine is most desirable."

So he took me thro' a stable & thro' a church & down into the
church vault, at the end of which was a mill: thro' the mill we went,
and came to a cave: down the winding cavern we groped our

tedious way, till a void boundless as a nether sky appear'd beneath us, & we held by the roots of trees and hung over this immensity; but I said: "if you please, we will commit ourselves to this void, and see whether providence is here also: if you will not, I will:" but he answer'd: "do not presume, O young man, but as we here remain, behold thy lot which will soon appear when the darkness passes away."

So I remain'd with him, sitting in the twisted root of an oak; he was suspended in a fungus, which hung with the head downward into the deep.

By degrees we beheld the infinite Abyss, fiery as the smoke of a burning city; beneath us, at an immense distance, was the sun, black by shining; round it were fiery tracks on which revolv'd vast spiders, crawling after their prey, which flew, or rather swum, in the infinite deep, in the most terrific shapes of animals sprung from corruption; & the air was full of them, & seem'd composed of them: these are Devils, and are called Powers of the air. I now asked my companion which was eternal lot? he said: "between the black & white spiders."

But now, from between the black & white spiders, a cloud and fire burst and rolled thro' the deep, black'ning all beneath, so that the nether deep grew black as a sea, & rolled with a terrible noise; beneath us was nothing now to be seen but a black tempest, till looking east between the clouds & the waves, we saw a cataract of blood mixed with fire, and not many stones' throw from us appear'd and sunk again the scaly fold of a monstrous serpent; at last, to the east, distant about three degrees, appear'd a fiery crest above the waves; slowly it reared like a ridge of golden rocks, till we discover'd two globes of crimson fire, from which the sea fled away in clouds of smoke; and now we saw it was the head of Leviathan; his forehead was divided into streaks of green & purple like those on a tyger's forehead: soon we saw his mouth & red gills hang just above the raging foam, tinging the black deep with beams of blood, advancing toward us with all the fury of a spiritual existence.

My friend the Angel climb'd up from his station into the mill: I remain'd alone; & then this appearance was no more, but I found myself sitting on a pleasant bank beside a river by moonlight, hearing a harper, who sung to the harp; & his theme was: "The man who never alters his opinion is like standing water, & breeds reptiles of the mind."

But I arose and sought for the mill, & there I found my Angel, who, surprised, asked me how I escaped?

I answer'd: "All that we saw was owing to your metaphysics; for when you ran away, I found myself on a bank by moonlight hearing a harper. But now we have seen my eternal lot, shall I shew you yours?" he laugh'd at my proposal; but I by force suddenly caught him in my arms, & flew westerly thro' the night, till we were elevated above the earth's shadow; then I flung myself with him directly into the body of the sun; here I clothed myself in white, & taking in my hand Swedenborg's volumes, sung from the glorious clime, and passed all the planets till we came to saturn: here I stay'd to rest, & then leap'd into the void between saturn & the fixed stars.

"Here," I said, "is your lot, in this space—if space it may be call'd." Soon we saw the stable and the Bible, and lo! it was a deep pit, into which I descended, driving the Angel before me; soon we saw seven houses of brick; one we enter'd; in it were a number of monkeys, baboons, & all of that species, chain'd by the middle, grinning and snatching at one another, but withheld by the shortness of their chains: however, I saw that they sometimes grew numerous, and then the weak were caught by the strong, and with a grinning aspect, first coupled with, & then devour'd, by plucking off first one limb and then another, till the body was left a helpless trunk; this, after grinning & kissing it with seeming fondness, they devour'd too; and here & there I saw one savourily picking the flesh off his own tail; as the stench terribly annoy'd us both, we went into the mill, & I in my hand brought the skeleton of a body, which in the mill was Aristotle's Analytics.

So the Angel said: "thy phantasy has imposed upon me, & thou oughtest to be ashamed."

I answer'd: "we impose on one another, & it is but lost time to converse with you whose works are only Analytics."

Opposition is true Friendship.

This long and complicated section follows Blake's attack upon orthodox religion which, he had suggested, seeks to transcend the strife of existential contraries by absorbing the Prolific into the Devourer. This may be paraphrased to refer to the absorbing of the energies of men into the constricting dogma of the Church. The religious believe that God alone is the Prolific; but Blake is a pragmatic humanist on this issue: "God only Acts and Is, in existing beings or Men." And Blake's Christ, ironically like "Satan or Tempter" is identified in the last plate as another of the Antediluvians who are our Energies, the Titans repressed by the Sky-gods of reductive reason.[1] Blake's demonic impiety in making this identification provokes an Angel into commencing the longest of the Memorable Fancies, which we have just read, a fantasy which has been called a "Swiftian exercise in direct satire." [2]

The Angel has undergone several successive metamorphoses since we read of Blake's first recorded vision. We recall his wandering through the fields near his home at the age of eight or nine and coming upon a tree whose boughs were bespangled with dancing angels. In *Songs of Innocence* we read in "Night" and "Cradle Song" that angels guard children and give them sleep. Angels also mercifully bring death. In the same work, the lion of "Little Girl Lost" and "The Little Girl Found" is a golden-haired Angel who unites the child and her parents in his realm.

Writing later, on Lavater, Blake proposes, "Every man's lead-ing propensity ought to be called his leading Virtue & his good Angel." [3] Blake had one,[4] "The Angel that presided o'er my birth." [5] Thus, in Blake's earlier writings the Angel carries the traditional meanings of "guardian" and "guide."

Now that Blake has become disenchanted with all traditions, the Angel becomes the symbol of the change. He reverses roles with the Devil and, in *The Marriage of Heaven and Hell*, Blake's Angels are the orthodox, "good" people, the contraries of the Devils, who are the unorthodox geniuses, the "evil" upsetters of established social orders.

Blake, as has been evident in earlier parts of *The Marriage of Heaven and Hell*, identifies himself with the side of hell, and much of what he says is purported to be a transcription of the words of the "mighty Devil" who writes with "corroding fires." Blake regards himself as the Devil's own interpreter, and his "Printing-house in Hell" is the dark and shadowy aspect of his own printer's workshop. In this place he dedicated himself to the task of following in the direction of his ideas. He takes them up precisely in the forms in which they appear to him. He is burning with the fire of energy that is fanned by the uncritical acceptance of inner perceptions. His labor is to trans-late the dazzling images into forms that can be looked at and read and meditated upon. It is Blake's unique way, and while he invites anyone whose nature permits to participate in it, he does not preach.

The Angel represents the antithesis of everything Blake says he stands for. Some writers have seen the Angel as a metaphor for Swedenborg, and this Memorable Fancy as a satire on the Swedenborgian· system in particular and through that upon any rationalistic scheme of values.[6] There is little doubt that this was one point Blake wanted to make when he set forth this account of his twisted Odyssey, but the Angel means far more. He is the vehicle of the personal forces that Blake felt had restricted him in his own life—from the theological teaching to which he had submitted in his childhood and youth, to political limitations on his personal freedom,[7] to the conventionally moral attitudes which inhibited his sexual liberty. The Angel concept, however, extends beyond the embodiment of limiting reason upon Blake as an individual; he is also the representation of the counter-revolutionary forces in France and America. The Angel guides the powerful hand of William Pitt who, for fear that the revolutionary fever would break out in England as well, had not only ceased from his political and social reforms, but had entered upon a policy of coercion at the time Blake was writing this work.[8] When the American Revolution did not spread to England, these "Angels" and weak men governed the strong for twelve years.[9]

In addition, the Angel is the voice of religion, as expressed either through the established church as an intermediary between God and man, or through any number of splinter movements, like Swedenborg's, which were established as were other systems claiming to be able to interpret for man the proper method to be used in approaching the holy.

To the Angel, Blake is a "pitable, foolish young man," for he has not been enlightened by any responsible authority. He goes his own way, apparently oblivious to social mores and religious proscriptions. The Angel begs him to consider the nature of the eternity for which he is unwittingly preparing himself.

Since this Angel is a figure of Blake's fantasy, as every character in every dream belongs wholly to the dreamer, it is necessary to view him not only as a symbolic representation of a situation or situations in the environment—but he must be taken, as well, as a subjective figure, that is, an aspect of the dreamer's or poet's own psychological makeup. Blake carries within himself this Angel, as well as his Devil; and the two are locked in continuous battle. It is the same situation as that in which the Prolific and the Devourer were bound together, one being unable to move without the counter-thrust of the other.

While Blake braces himself with all his strength against the Angel, at the same time the Angel is part of him, and without the combat there would have been an unproductive stasis. It is important to bear in mind that the Angel is that part of Blake which he has not recognized as belonging to him. Although at this stage of his development he cannot integrate the Angel, the Angel is nevertheless as essential to his nature as is the Devil.

Blake as he appears in this Memorable Fancy may be equated with the conscious ego; that is, he is Blake as Blake conceives of himself. The Angel is a representative of one aspect of his total nature which is not conscious in Blake, but whose effect upon him is nonetheless powerful because it is unrecognized. Blake recognizes the Angel's symbolism as being connected with the problems of society at large, but he misses completely the point that the Angel also refers to his own inner problems. Thus the inner personal situation is projected upon the collective, and Blake finds his sociological *raison d'être*. To the analytical psychologist, however, this is not very convincing as motivation for this "Fancy."

The Angel takes Blake through a stable, a church, a church vault, a mill, and then into a cave. The movement is downward, into the lower aspects of the unknown, or the unconscious. The Angel must pass first through his own territory, for he dwells far from the place where he supposes Blake is to spend his eternity. First the stable: this is a place where the animals ("the horses of instruction" representing the domesticated animal instincts in man) are neatly tended, where they are fed just the proper amount so that they will not hunger after forbidden food. What these stabled animals require to keep alive and healthy, according to human standards, they have. The one thing they do not have is their freedom. Man's animal nature is bound and controlled in this way-station of the Angel.

The stable may also be the place of Christ's birth, ironically leading into the grander structure of the church.[10] The Christian church has always served a mediating and protective function between man and God, and furthermore, it has had the responsibility of determining whether a revelation is authentic. This would, of course, agree with the Angel's concept of the church as the unchallengeable authority of established dogma. Beneath the church are the church vaults where lie the sanctified dead of the past. Blake may be referring here to the dogmas of organized religion which seem to him no longer to have validity, but which continue to be reverenced by the Angel. The vault is emblematic of Christ's burial. In the resurrection of the body Christ passes out of the vault, but the Angel aptly leads Blake to the vault's other end where there is a mill, the last stronghold of the Angel. The mill is where man's cleverness at devising machinery makes it possible for him to transform one kind of product into another. It is where, by the use of reason, man is able to provide for himself the nutriments and other goods he requires. Furthermore, the mill is the prototype of all machinery, which is originally conceived to serve man but in the end enslaves him, according to Blake's belief. Margaret Rudd, in writing about "the much discussed 'dark Satanic mills'" in Blake's works, says:

The image of the mill which Blake uses fairly frequently has always to do with the naturalistic 'laws' which seem to be imposed by reason, whether these laws occur in religion, in art, or in practical life. We remember that in *The Marriage of Heaven and Hell* the false 'Angel' had to go through a mill before he could impose his magical delusions on the honest 'Devil.' The so-called 'laws' . . . are akin to magical delusion . . . for such abstract laws pay no attention to particularity and fact, but simply put into motion all the supposedly infallible and mill-like machinery of 'Your Reason,' arriving at something that is far from the truth, but almost magically persuades us that it must be true.[11]

Having passed through the mill, the two grope their tedious way to a cave. They now enter the earth and turn their backs on the daylight, which is equated with consciousness. The cave or cavern is the Platonic symbol of the body in which man is confined. "For man has closed himself up, till he sees all things thro' the narrow chinks (the four senses) of his cavern." [12] On Plate 11 in one copy of *The Marriage*, the "chink" through which the world of nature is perceived is actually painted as the eyehole of a skull.

The Angel and Blake wind through a cavern ever deeper and deeper until they reach a void which Blake calls "as boundless

as a nether sky," thus likening it to the heavenly sky, except
that in this infernal realm everything is upsidedown and Blake
and his Angel must hang over the immensity, held only by the
roots of trees.

Blake is prepared to commit himself into the void, but the
angel cries out, "do not presume, O young man, but as we here
remain, behold thy lot . . ." Here we have evidence that the
Angel is an essential part of Blake, for it is the restraining influence of the Angel which forces Blake to maintain his hold
upon reality, however tenuous that hold becomes at times.
Without the Angel, whom he avowedly despises, one feels that
Blake would surely have flung himself into the depths of the
abyss and been completely overwhelmed by it.

Now Blake pictures himself as sitting in the root of a twisted
oak, while the Angel is suspended in a fungus. The oak is a tree
that has a long history of association with enormous strength
and with a special power derived from the supernatural. Oaks
and terebinths in the Old Testament, were oracle trees.[13]
Among the ancient Greeks the oracle of Zeus was Dodona, in
the land of the oak trees. The will of the ruler of the gods was
revealed by the rustling of oak leaves, which the priests interpreted.[14] In the legendary history of Blake's own England, the
oaks were sacred to the Druids, and in the groves the ancient
priests felt most intimately their relationship with the divine.
In the same spirit we may assume that Blake felt that his protected position within the twisted root of an oak tree kept him
in the closest contact with his divine essence. There was no
room for an intermediary there. This protection prevented him
from falling headlong into the abyss that stretched before him,
even as did the restraining words of the Angel.[15]

Blake refers to the Druids and their oaks in his long poem,
Jerusalem, as follows: "Your Ancestors derived their origin
from Abraham, Heber, Shem and Noah, who were Druids, as
the Druid Temples (which are the Patriarchal Pillars & Oak
Groves) over the whole earth witness to this day. You have a
tradition, that Man anciently contained in his mighty limbs all
things in Heaven and Earth: this you recieved from the
Druids." [16]

It is interesting to compare Blake's positioning of himself

within the root of the oak, while he shows the Angel suspended in a fungus. A fungus plant is one which contains no chlorophyll and therefore cannot make its own food. So the kind of spirituality which the Angel represents is dependent upon some kind of an external structure: it requires a parasitic construct, a superstructure upon the living source of its nourishment. Blake regards his personal faith as an intimate working relationship with God, while he regards the Angel's religion as removed and less essential in its connection with the divine.

As they remain together, the vision which the Angel has promised Blake appears out of the abyss. It is described as being fiery as a burning city. One has no doubts about the fiery aspect of Blake's unconscious: he has written enough about that, beginning with the opening lines of *The Marriage of Heaven and Hell:* "Rintrah roars and shakes his fires in the burden'd air . . ." The fire in the abyss is portrayed by the Angel as being destructive; for Blake himself, fire is quite the opposite. It is the energy source without which any kind of creative activity would be unthinkable. The abyss as shown to Blake by his Angel contains a black sun which is at an immense distance. The black sun is an idea found also in alchemical writings, where it is referred to as the *sol niger,* in other places called the "dark light." Jung quotes a saying attributed to the alchemist, Hermes Trismegistus: *Ego (lapis) gigno lumen, tenebrae autem naturae meae sunt* (I the lapis beget the light, but the darkness too is of my nature).[17] The Angel, who in his collectively acceptable and therefore conscious form lives in a world of light, now in his hidden or unconscious below-the-earth form reveals a black sun, which is the "light" of chaos. And chaos indeed it is, with vast spiders crawling after their prey which abound in the infinite deep, and so many weird and strange animal shapes springing out of corruption that the very air seems to be composed of them. The Angel tells Blake that his lot is between the black and the white spiders.

Black and white spiders are symbols of opposites, perhaps, as S. Foster Damon suggests, of Angels and Devils fighting over their prey which is the souls of men.[18] In the angelic point of view when opposites come together there is and there must be a terrible catastrophe. To avoid this, the Angels in their religious and even Swedenborgian sense forbid the recognition that there is a shadow side as well as a light side in every individual. They deny the need of men sometimes to behave in an asocial way and to do what is unacceptable to the arbiters of the collective morality. The Angel shows Blake what happens when the dark side is allowed to come into contact with the light side—from between the black and white spiders comes a cloud and a burst of fire and a tempest in the depths in which clouds and waves mingle with a cataract of blood and fire. Out of this blazing horror appears the most frightening creature that ever cursed the nightmare of a man, whom Blake describes in words of unparalleled intensity in the literature of hellish brimstone. He is pictured in Plate 20 as a huge serpent, twisting and writhing in a dark and foaming sea, with three coils visible out of the water and with head turned upward, mouth agape with menacing teeth and a forked tongue striking at the sky. This monster is none other than that awesome symbol of the might of God: he is the Leviathan. We read in the Book of Job:

Then answered the Lord unto Job out of the whirlwind, and said
Gird up thy loins now like a man: I will demand of thee, and
  declare thou unto me. (40:6-7)

Canst thou draw out leviathan with an hook? or his tongue with
  a cord which thou lettest down?
Canst thou put an hook into his nose? or bore his jaw through
  with a thorn?
Will he make many supplications unto thee? will he speak soft
  words unto thee?
Will he make a covenant with thee? wilt thou take him for a
  servant for ever?
Wilt thou play with him as with a bird? or wilt thou bind him for
  thy maidens?
Shall the companions make a banquet of him? shall they part him
  among the merchants? (41:1-6)

None is so fierce that dare stir him up: who then is able to stand
  before me?
Who hath prevented me that I should repay him? Whatsoever is
  under the whole heaven is mine. (41:10-11)

That the appearance of the monster, Leviathan, is a manifestation of a negative, power-thirsty aspect of God (Yahweh), is expressed by Jung in his commentary upon this passage in his "Answer to Job." In that essay, Jung writes:

Truly Yahweh can do all things and permits himself all things without batting an eyelid. With brazen countenance he can project his shadow side and remain unconscious at man's expense. He can boast of his superior power and enact laws which mean less than air to him. Murder and manslaughter are mere bagatelles, and if the mood takes him he can play the feudal grand seigneur and generously recompense his bondslave for the havoc wrought in his wheatfields. "So you have lost your sons and daughters? No harm done, I will give you new and better ones." [19]

Another interpretation of the meaning of the Leviathan's appearance in the dark and foaming sea is offered by S. Foster Damon, who sees the "crooked serpent" as a representation of Hobbes's Leviathan.[20] Thomas Hobbes, (1588-1679), an astute and cynical materialist, insisted that our knowledge originates in what we learn through our senses. Imagination, says Hobbes, "is nothing but *decaying sense.*" [21] He used the Leviathan to symbolize "a Commonwealth of State," [22] which he depicted as a giant composed of human bodies. The giant wears the crown of absolute authority; and the sword of secular power is in one hand while the other holds the crozier of religious power. Hobbes asserts that this social order originated not in any divine ordinance, as commonly supposed, but only in a human social contract, caused by the fearful need of men for self protection in their natural state of war. Hobbes' Leviathan, therefore, could be the logical outcome of the Angel's argument from good and evil (the black and the white spiders); he would be the wrathful and repetitious system of Natural Morality. Blake makes his point that this and essentially all else the Angel showed him was only an illusion: "All that we saw was owing to your metaphysics."

At the sight of the monster, whose presence is either the sign of the dark and terrifying aspect of God or its manifestation in the authoritarian State, the Angel flees from his fungus in panic. Blake is left alone to face his fate. The vision of the abyss which the Angel has conjured up, and especially the monster commanding its depths, has proved to be too much for him, and he returns to the mill, *i.e.,* to his former state as a functionary of the proper social order. Blake, to whom the hellish aspect of the divine is no surprise, remains behind.

As soon as the Angel is gone, a strange transformation takes place. Left alone, Blake finds that the horrible vision is no more. The storm-tossed sea of time and space, which the Angel said was Blake's eternal fate, disappears as quickly as the Angel who brought it to view. In its stead Blake finds himself seated on a pleasant bank beside a river by moonlight.

Like the sea, a river is also a body of water; but unlike the limitless sea, its boundaries are well defined and it has a definite direction. It is the stream of life as it flows through the unconscious, the night side of man which is feminine as symbolized by the moonlight. Blake suggests that when he is alone and free of the torments of the Angel, his life flow becomes ordered and pleasant, in diametric opposition to the turbulent-sea experience during his conflict with the forces of the Angel.

In the image of the harper who sings to his harp, Blake personifies a new psychological condition. We may conjecture that Blake believed he would find himself in the harmonious position of the harper vis-à-vis Nature, were he to be left by the Angel to follow his desires and his inner necessity. The selection of this symbol also suggests Blake's spiritual connection with a tradition older than recorded history. The earliest delineations of the harp in ancient Egyptian art point to its having had its origin in the taut string of the warrior's bow. From this to the grand vertical harps in the Egyptian frescoes of the time of Rameses III, themselves more than 3000 years old, numerous varieties from the simple bow form to the almost triangular harp comprise one family.[23]

The Bible says that the harp was invented by Jubal,[24] and its role as the instrument by which David accompanied his psalms of praise to God is well known.

The earliest records of the Celtic race give the harp a prominent place, and harpists a peculiar veneration. The Welsh harp, like the Irish, was often a hereditary instrument, preserved with great care. It was used by the bards of the family who were alike poets, musicians and historians. A slave was not permitted to touch a harp, and it was exempted by Welsh law from seizure for debt.[25] Thus it may be said that the harp was a sacred instrument reserved to the prophet-poet type of individual. The nation legally recognized the special nature of this instrument and set it apart from objects of everyday use. It was employed by men like a book of prayer to arouse their feelings in their contact with the divine. For music is a feeling art, and particularly the music of the harp: the senses are alive to the musical tones, testing and evaluating them in terms of the beauty of their harmony and the perfections of their clarity. There is no intellect in this process, there is no reason, only the union of the harper with his harp, bringing a feeling of the glory of God and a responding echo within man. Blake is the harper who, although feeling tormented by the "angels" in the outer world, finds joyous refreshment in the moonlight of his inner life.

The harper sings an often repeated theme of Blake, "The man who never alters his opinion is like standing water, and breeds reptiles of the mind." This is Blake's comment upon the rigid moral structure which the Angel strives to uphold.

Blake now returns to the mill and there he finds his Angel sitting smugly in the security of his machinery, startled to find that Blake has "escaped" from the jaws of the abyss whence the Angel had fled. But Blake only laughs, and asserts that the horrifying apparitions were brought onto the scene by the Angel himself, and that the moonlit river and the harper were the contribution of the poet. "Now that we have seen my eternal lot," says Blake, "shall I shew you yours?"

The Angel tries to get away, but Blake catches him up in his arms and an upward flight begins. The Angel had previously sought to show Blake his fate by taking him downward into hell, which may be regarded as the polar opposite of the Angel's conscious attitude, containing the dark contents repressed from his avowed way of life. Now Blake flies upward out of the hell with which *his* conscious attitude seems to be identified: the Printing-house where he works with corrosives trying to clean up the mess which obscures the perception of truth. Blake's is an upward flight away from consciousness. Far from being the light of clarity, this is the light directly in the "body of the sun" and such a light must be equally as blinding as total darkness. The upper sphere, far above earth, belongs to the unconscious as much as does the lower sphere.

Marie-Louise von Franz, a collaborator with C. G. Jung, points out that people generally think of consciousness as above and the unconscious below, which leads to a word which, both in German and English, distorts the concept. In German, people speak of *unterbewusst* instead of *unbewusst,* and in English, the term *subconscious* is used instead of *unconscious.* In mythology, consciousness is generally projected onto the geographical surface of the earth. The depths of the earth appear as a symbol of the unconscious, with emphasis on its instinctual aspects; and the faraway sky and what is beyond the clouds serve also as a symbol of the unconscious; with emphasis on its more orderly aspects. This coincides with Jung's definition of consciousness as a "field" of things known to our ego with the unconscious surrounding it in all directions—just as on old maps the uroboros snake surrounds the known world from the end of the world in the west to the end of the world in the east, and above and below. So if we construct a geography of consciousness derived from our own myths, it would be right to think of consciousness as about the center of where we live and the unconscious could be symbolized by all other surrounding areas. But the unconscious areas of above and below, west and east, are characterized differently in their *quality.* They illustrate different aspects of the unconscious.[26]

Blake's upward flight with the Angel in his arms exposes yet another area of the unconscious, one with which Blake has actively concerned himself. Here is the brightness of the sun which Blake has often contemplated as a source of energy. Here he dons the white clothing symbolizing the purity of desire for "the soul of sweet delight can never be defiled." [27] With a touch of wryness, he takes in hand Swedenborg's volumes and their weight makes him sink with the Angel from "the glorious clime." He brings the Angel to a heavenly abyss, and there in the void they plant themselves between Saturn and the fixed stars. Again the stable and the church appear, and this time Blake leads the way into the church. There he opens the Bible to show the Angel the true aspect of established religion. The two fall into a pit and before them they see seven houses of brick [28] which turn out to be monkey houses. They enter one of them and in it they see a number of monkeys grinning and snatching at each other, but chained by the middle so that they are somewhat restrained. The "seven houses of brick," as Swinburne surmised, are the seven churches in Asia to whom St. John the Divine addressed his revelation.[29] The gruesome lewdness of Blake's vision of a theological monkeyhouse has not lost its shock value; it still offends orthodoxy.[30]

The monkeys pictured here are filthy and repulsive. We must, however, take into consideration the reality of the monkey and note that he bears a most interesting relationship to man. If in the evolutionary process of the mammalian order, the two species developed from a common ancestral strain, the courses of their adaptation have greatly varied. Organically, the monkey is the better-developed animal in almost every sense: his feet are far more flexible and multi-purposed than man's, his hands are more powerful, his strength is greater, his musculature is more highly developed. In only two areas is the monkey organically inferior to man: his brain lacks the capacity of man's and his thumb is relatively underdeveloped and scarcely used. Thus, monkeys cannot exercise their intellectual faculties to the degree that man does, nor can they fashion complicated material objects with their hands because their thumbs do not permit the highly controlled and variegated movements which man has.

Blake shows the Angel his fate, which is the fate of man when his animal aspects are chained or restricted. Man may be in a church, he points out, but it is only a vile monkey house if the two qualities which distinguish the human from the monkey—the superior brain and the creative hand—are not permitted to exercise themselves freely.

The Angel and Blake return to the mill, where the Angel reproaches Blake for imposing his fantasy upon him. Blake replies, "we impose upon one another," which in a satiric way notes his belief that there can be no real rapprochement between the agents of heaven and those of hell.

In the end of the Memorable Fancy, Blake likens the Angel's work to Aristotle's *Analytics*, a copy of which he has found in the mill, and which he also refers to as the skeleton of a body. It is interesting that Blake, in no sense a scientist, should attack Aristotle who, at that time, was revered by many for his basic work in forming the conceptual structure of classical physics. Aristotle (384-322 BC) was the culmination of Greek speculative philosophy and the forerunner of modern science. Blake referred to him once as one of the great lights of antiquity [31] but in *The Marriage of Heaven and Hell* he disapproves of him and his *Analytics,* the great opus on logic.

It was not until the present century that some of the Aristotelian ideas were acknowledged by certain scientists to be exactly what Blake called them. For example: in their work, *The New World of Physics,* Arthur March and Ira Freeman, professors of theoretical physics at the University of Innsbruck, relegate Aristotle's "scientific method" to a kind of limbo like the mill where Blake symbolically came upon the *Analytics* around 1790.

"There is no good reason," these modern physicists write, "for natural scientists to concur in the veneration in which Aristotle is generally held. His denial of atomism, whose development could certainly have led to significant results even in ancient times, held up the progress of science by two thousand years. And, even worse, this man who originated an intellectual movement which denied every foundation of physical thinking, threw the whole weight of his tremendous authority into a blighting influence on the later development not only of physics but of all other natural sciences. . . . Mankind had blindingly trusted Aristotle through two thousand years. Now at last it was able to break the spell and witness the dawn of a new era in which truth would no longer be sought in the writings of Aristotle, but in nature itself." [32]

It is then no meaningless coincidence that Blake, with tongue in cheek, says farewell to the Angel, chiding him that his works are only *Analytics.* For indeed, March's and Freeman's view of Aristotelian physics resembles Blake's views of systematic theology: both are looked upon as the dry bones of doctrines based on questionable "axioms" as contrasted with the living flesh of concepts developing out of experiment and experience.

The alienation of Blake from his Angel at this point creates a situation which corresponds to one described by Jolande Jacobi:

The two "halves" of the marriage (of opposites) have separated in enmity and withdrawn, each into its one-sided domain. The raw material of imagery, the content of the unconscious, lacks the formative power of the conscious mind, and consciousness dries up because the nourishing source of the image no longer reaches it.[33]

The concluding line of the Memorable Fancy, "Opposition is true Friendship," has been obliterated in some copies. Blake's ambivalence in respect to this statement is not difficult to appreciate. The Angel and the Blake who associates himself with the infernal powers are both Blake. He seems vaguely to sense this—but it appears that at this moment he is not ready to accept fully the psychological implications of this essential reality.

PLATES 21-22

Above the text of this passage is the picture of an idealized form of a man, seated on a grassy hillside looking toward the sky. Behind him is a dazzling white light from which extends a yellowish glow. The brightness is contained by a wreath of clouds in deepening tones of purplish grey. And beyond this, on all sides, we see the blue of a limitless heaven. This figure appears more than once in Blake's works of art. Damon describes him as "the newly resurrected man with the skull beneath his feet." [1] This same figure is seen in Plate 8 of *America*, and an especially fine example is the illustration of "Death's Door" which Blake designed for Blair's *Grave*, published in 1808. He opposes the youthful free spirit of the picture to the hardened and dying doctrines which he criticizes in the text below.

I have always found that Angels have the vanity to speak of themselves as the only wise; this they do with a confident insolence sprouting from systematic reasoning.

Thus Swedenborg boasts that what he writes is new: tho' it is only the Contents or Index of already publish'd books.

A man carried a monkey about for a shew, & because he was a little wiser than the monkey, grew vain, and conciev'd himself as much wiser than seven men. It is so with Swedenborg: he shews the folly of churches, & exposes hypocrites, till he imagines that all are religious, & himself the single one on earth that ever broke a net.

Now hear a plain fact: Swedenborg has not written one new

truth. Now hear another: he has written all the old falsehoods.

And now hear the reason. He conversed with Angels who are all religious, & conversed not with Devils who all hate religion, for he was incapable thro' his conceited notions.

Thus Swedenborg's writings are a recapitulation of all superficial opinions, and an analysis of the more sublime—but no further.

Have now another plain fact. Any man of mechanical talents may, from the writings of Paracelsus or Jacob Behmen, produce ten thousand volumes of equal value with Swedenborg's, and from those of Dante or Shakespear an infinite number.

But when he has done this, let him not say that he knows better than his master, for he only holds a candle in sunshine.

Blake shows that Swedenborg, while setting himself above the established Church of England, is nevertheless of the Angel's party. Swedenborg's religion is only another way of applying the tyranny of the religious doctrine. The inflexible authority of Swedenborgianism holds the same place in Blake's estimation as did that of the State in Hobbes' *Leviathan*.

The Church Universal [2] was the only church that Blake recognized. Its doctrine is the Everlasting Gospel, its congregation the Brotherhood of Man, its symbol the Woman in the Wilderness, its architecture Gothic. Blake rejected all other churches with the dissenter's loathing. The Church and the State, or their representatives the priest and the king, symbolize the twin evil ruling powers of society. In his *Notebook* he writes in 1793:

"Remove away that black'ning church:" [3]

And in *Songs of Experience:*

The Chimney Sweeper

A little black thing among the snow,
Crying "weep! weep!" in notes of woe!
"Where are thy father & mother? say?"
"They are both gone up to the church to pray.

"Because I was happy upon the heath,
"And smil'd among the winter's snow,

"They clothed me in the clothes of death,
"And taught me to sing the notes of woe.

"And because I am happy & dance & sing,
"They think they have done me no injury,
"They are gone to praise God his Priest & King,
"Who make up a heaven of our misery." [4]

The discourse on Angels needs little elucidation. It is a commentary on the attitude of superiority which Blake attributes to the systematizers of reason. Swedenborg, in his assertion that his interpretation of religion is wiser than that of the monkey churches, is likened to the man who carried a monkey about and, because he was wiser than the monkey, became highly inflated with the concept of the greatness of his intellectual powers. But in comparison with Boehme and Paracelsus and Dante and Shakespeare, says Blake, the writings of Swedenborg are the commonplace recapitulations of superficial opinions. He views Swedenborg's insights against those of the truly great poetic geniuses who are his masters, as a candle against the light of the sun.

Swedenborg's exalted opinion of himself seems to Blake to be a result of the theologian's limiting himself to consideration of the Angel's demands upon man, and to his denial of the Devil's. Swedenborg would have his followers meditate upon his religious views and emulate the examples of upright and moral behavior which he sets forth. As a consequence of disregarding those devilish instincts and urges with which Blake has occupied himself, Swedenborg turns aside the creative energy that Blake sees as flowing from unrestrained elemental forces within man.

One wonders if there is not a deep problem of Blake's own behind his remarks on Swedenborg. This problem he sees not as a part of himself but rather experiences in its projected form as vituperative utterances against Swedenborg. Why has Blake such an uncommon amount of vehemence when he speaks of his former idol? It is suggested that the figure of Swedenborg and the Angel with whom he is identified, symbolize that aspect of Blake which, though unconscious, holds a fascinating attraction for him. Blake protests that he will have no part of Swedenborg and his Angel. He refuses to have dealings with them; yet throughout his works he is engaged in pursuing, entreating or persuading the Angel, which is one aspect of himself, to accept the Devil, which is another.

Clearly we see here the play of attraction and counter-attraction which creates the tremendous tension between the opposites of Blake's nature. Were Blake's ego, as central conscious personality, either to give way to the Devil altogether and refuse further intercourse with the Angel, or were he to be seduced by the Angel to give up his frequent meanderings through his private hell, one feels that he would lose that throbbing tension which makes him what he is, and that he would suddenly become as useless as a bow whose cord has snapped. Blake's ego, if we think of it metaphorically as the one who draws the bowstring, must be exceedingly strong, for the bow is often bent to the extreme limit of its resiliency. It is just for this reason, however, that the arrow—the idea Blake is aiming to express—is able to go very far, and often very straight.

PLATES 22-24

A Memorable Fancy

Once I saw a Devil in a flame of fire, who arose before an Angel that sat on a cloud, and the Devil utter'd these words:

"The worship of God is: Honouring his gifts in other men, each according to his genius, and loving the greatest men best: those who envy or calumniate great men hate God; for there is no other God."

The Angel hearing this became almost blue; but mastering himself he grew yellow, & at last white, pink, & smiling, and then replied:

"Thou Idolater! is not God One? & is not the visible in Jesus Christ? and has not Jesus Christ given his sanction to the law of ten commandments? and are not all other men fools, sinners, & nothings?"

The Devil answer'd: "bray a fool in a morter with wheat, yet shall not his folly be beaten out of him; if Jesus Christ is the greatest man, you ought to love him in the greatest degree; now hear how he has given this sanction to the law of ten commandments: did he not mock at the sabbath and so mock the sabbath's God? murder those who were murder'd because of him? turn away the law from the woman taken in adultery? steal the labor of others to support him? bear false witness when he omitted making a defence before Pilate? covet when he pray'd for his disciples, and when he bid them shake off the dust of their feet against such as refused to lodge them? I tell you, no virtue can exist without breaking these ten commandments. Jesus was all virtue, and acted from impulse, not from rules."

When he had so spoken, I beheld the Angel, who stretched out his arms, embracing the flame of fire, & he was consumed and arose as Elijah.

Note: This Angel, who is now become a Devil, is my particular friend; we often read the Bible together in its infernal or diabolical sense, which the world shall have if they behave well.

I have also The Bible of Hell, which the world shall have whether they will or no.

One Law for the Lion & Ox is Oppression.

In this last and wisest of the Memorable Fancies, Blake illustrates the Proverb that Angels generally will not learn: [5]

"Opposition is true friendship."

Yet it is in this section that Blake brings about the beginning of a rapprochement between his Devil and his Angel. To suggest that this represents the union of heaven and hell is to mistake the momentary surge of emotion that comes when the opposites feel the first strong impact of the one upon the other for a deep and enduring relationship. Yet there is something of the Angel in the Devil, if only that every swelling passion carries with it the longing that it might be sustained. The capacity to sustain it is quite another matter: it must be developed slowly and over a long period of time.

The initiative in this final dialogue comes from the Devil. He emerges from a flame of fire, summoning all his infernal energies to challenge the very foundations of the Angel's dogma. The Angel, seated passively upon a cloud, is assaulted by a statement of belief calculated to deny altogether the concept of a God whose authority is beyond and outside of man and is brought to bear upon him through a system of universal law. Far from worshipping that quality of universal wisdom beneath which men are to be judged as equals under God, the

Devil sees divinity in those qualities of greatness which set apart certain men from the so-called "common man." In a completely undemocratic concept, the first type is sacred, the second profane. He proclaims once more that the creative capacity of the poetic genius is the embodiment of the divine, and that there is no other God. Except as man experiences God in his own life, God is incomprehensible to him. In this, Blake's Devil takes the position that the magnitude of God is somehow measurable by the perceptions of man and that God's work is what he accomplishes through men.

The Angel is shocked and angered by the blasphemous words of the Devil. But in his very emotional reaction, the beginning of a transformation takes place. Blake states this in the matter-of-fact language of the physical phenomena—when one's emotions are touched one colors, and almost every part of the body responds in some way. The Angel becomes blue, and we know that he can no longer remain passive, aloof and superior. It is this total involvement, not alone on an abstract plane, that makes it possible for the conversion to take place. As heat applied to the alchemical vessel causes the contents to undergo a series of changes characterized by specific colors, so the pressure which the Angel must undergo effects a transformation. Whether he will or no, the Angel takes into himself some of that fierce energetic force which must affect the status of his conventional belief. The Angel becomes "volatile," active and participating, and when he speaks out for the traditional morality supposedly sanctioned by Jesus, it is the last proud rallying cry in defense of a citadel which he knows is already falling.

The Angel calls upon God in his capacity as the absolute ruler of men, who makes himself visible in the symbol of Jesus Christ, the sanctifier of the Law. With his concept of the divine as the supreme authority over men, he reinforces the belief that all good, all wisdom, all justice and all power reside in a God whose abode is heaven, and that these qualities are not within the reach of men, whom he describes as "fools, sinners, & nothings." He takes the extreme position, and by doing so he exposes his vulnerability to the Devil who gives him no quarter.

The Devil counters with the statement that a fool remains

a fool even as the Angel has said, but he does not deny that the man of genius possesses wisdom. He accepts fully the greatness of Jesus, and does not take issue with the statement that God is visible in him. Whatever he may believe concerning the divinity of Jesus, he says clearly that Jesus is the greatest *man*, thereby announcing his contention that divinity *is* visible in man, even as it is visible in Jesus.

The Devil sees the symbol of Jesus in a quite different light than does the Angel. To the Angel, whose law is reason, one who breaks the law must indeed forsake the way of goodness. But the Jesus described by the Devil has a dark side as well as a light side, he is the sanctifier of the law and the abrogator of the law. "Think not that I am come to destroy the law or the prophets: I am not come to destroy but to fulfill." [6] Blake's Devil points out that Jesus supplies that element which a Christianity of strict dogma requires: the awareness of another kind of law which may at times supercede the collective compact. It is the law that recognizes the unique spark of divinity within the individual, which may present itself as impulse or as desire. Jesus' virtue, the Devil shows, was that he acted from impulse and not from rules. Virtue, as Blake used the word, was the individual natural aspect of man, expressing itself freely, and thus uniquely.

In Jesus Christ as fulfiller of the law and Jesus Christ as lawbreaker, a bridge is formed upon which two contraries represented by Angel and Devil can approach one another. Out of their intimate confrontation arise the imagination and the vision which make it possible to relate reason and restraint to energy and desire.

The Angel accepts the fire and embraces it, and the vision tells us that he is consumed and arises as Elijah. The inclusion here of this prophet is significant in letting us know what sort of a transformation is taking place in the Angel. Elijah was witness to the dramatic reality of a God who does not simply create and leave his creation to operate on its own, as the Deists had announced, but rather as a God who is deeply involved in the ongoing life of man. God speaks from time to time through Elijah, and the words are prophecy—in the same sense that the inspired words of the Blakean prophetic figures are words dictated by the "Eternals," the divine aspect of man's nature. The Lord makes himself known to Elijah in this way:

And behold, the Lord passed by, and a great and strong wind rent the mountains, and brake in pieces the rocks before the Lord, but the Lord was not in the wind; and after the wind an earthquake: And after the earthquake a fire; but the Lord was not in the fire: and after the fire a still small voice.[7]

And Elijah, hearing, says the words and performs the acts that the voice within him assigns. In doing so, time and again he is associating with the cleansing and transforming agent of fire. He asks for a manifestation of God, so that the people will know who is God and who is Baal. The sacrificial bull of Elijah is placed on the altar and four jars of water are poured over it and over the wood beneath it and into the trench surrounding the altar. No man puts a fire to it but

. . . the fire of the Lord fell, and consumed the burnt offering, and the wood, and the stones, and the dust, and licked up the water that was in the trench.[8]

And when the messengers of the sick king, Ahaziah, encounter Elijah on their way to inquire of the god Baalzebub if their king shall live or die, Elijah again shows that he is a man of the true God. Fire as the symbol of divine potency comes down from heaven and consumes the captain and his fifty messengers.

When it is time for Elijah to die, Elisha stands with him and Elijah asks what he shall do for him before he is taken from him. Elisha replies, "I pray you, let me inherit a double share of your spirit." And Elijah charges him: "You have asked me a hard thing; yet if you see me as I am being taken from you, it shall be so for you; but if you see me not, it shall not be so."

And, as they still went on and talked, behold, there appeared a chariot of fire and horses of fire, and parted them both asunder; and Elijah went up by a whirlwind into heaven.
And Elisha saw it . . .[9]

Now Blake's meaning is clear when he proclaims: "I beheld

the Angel who stretched out his arms, embracing the flame of fire, & he was consumed and arose as Elijah." Blake identifies himself with the cosmic drama and insists that the importance of the entire act is the *seeing* of it. This refers to the perception beyond that of the five senses, the capacity to observe the mysterious process as an inner process, as well as a vision which appears to be taking place in the outer world. Blake's ability to pass through the "doors of perception" secures for him the special grace with which the Lord had endowed Elisha. For, as Elijah went up into heaven and disappeared, his mantle fell from him, and Elisha took it up, and with it the mana of the prophet. Afterwards, never doubting his capacity for a moment to do so, he smote the waters with the mantle exactly as Elijah had done. And the waters separated as they had done for Elijah, and Elisha was able to cross back to dry ground. Elijah is reborn in the fire through Elisha, and the prophetic work continues. And Blake's observation of the identical process taking place with his Angel being risen, indicates his own acceptance of the prophetic commitment, the mantle of Elijah.

Blake's particular prophetic charge is to mediate the transformation of the Angelic principle. The Angel is a dynamic symbol as we have seen, and its various metamorphoses indicate the manner in which a symbol may actively lead a man through his own development in the individuation process. Recalling the first Angels which appeared to Blake as a child, and reviewing how their original ephemeral loveliness became solidified through association with the collective morality, we have watched the symbol in flux. When the Angel becomes identified with the Swedenborgian doctrine, it becomes identified also with the side of Reason and is split off from the more energetic side, which is then identified with the Devil. The Angel "loses its fire," as Blake so dramatically shows us at the beginning of this Fancy by seating him upon a cloud. Only when the opposites are set against each other can the real confrontation take place. It did here, in the argument over the Virtue, that is, the calling of Jesus Christ. In the heat generated by the conflict, the fire produced the change.

We know that the phoenix motif of destruction by fire precedes the phenomenon of rebirth in a new and purified

form. The new being, or idea, is tempered and therefore stronger than it was before its exposure to the flame. It is also more
flexible. Thus it is that after his conversion, the Angel is able
to accept the principle that discipline need not be a negative
force from outside the individual, imposing stultifying and inhibiting rules. He can recognize that the moment we cease to
conform to external discipline, in that moment life imposes
upon us the necessity of conforming to a far more rigorous
discipline—the self discipline upon which individuation depends.

The discipline which has its origin in the individual nature
of man is more representative of the workings of the divine
than are the laws imposed by the collective in which man lives.
The inherent question here is whether man can lay aside the
authority of the "ten commandments" which he believes to
have been inspired in the hearts of certain men and through
their hands revealed to all mankind. Blake suggests that the
creative man must, like Jesus, reinterpret the law in his individual way, and that the age of revelation did not end with
the teachings of Jesus any more than it began with them.

Blake proposes that the two aspects of man, Devil and Angel,
be joined together and that they participate in coming to new
and revolutionary understandings. The Bible, formerly the
Angel's book, is not discarded; rather it is read in the diabolical
—that is, in its originally poetic—sense. It is read by Blake in
friendly companionship with the Angel "who is now become a
Devil." In his ironic Note to the Fancy, Blake blandly in-
sinuates that if the world behaves well, it shall have this
reading. It will be read as an expression of the lower as well
as the higher aspects of man and as a document subject to
penetration by imaginative contemplation.

In any case "The Bible of Hell' is to be written to com-
pensate The Holy Bible, and the world shall have it "whether
they will or no." This means that the dark side is present in
man whether or not he chooses to acknowledge it. Blake, however, will not rest until he brings this side of man, and of
nature, and of the cosmos, to the attention of his readers. He
finds himself embarked upon a task of huge proportions, a
task which will occupy him for the remainder of his life.

The appearance of this name of Jesus Christ precedes the momentary union of the two opposites and the climax of *The Marriage of Heaven and Hell*. It precipitates the *coniunctio* out of which the new creative energy was to be born. The contact, catalytic as it is, does not represent a completed process. It is more in the nature of a first glimpse into the possibility of union, a glimpse that makes one a candidate for the long process of striving through alternating experiences of differentiation and synthesis, toward wholeness. Jesus is symbolic of the whole man, who was all goodness and yet could bear all guilt upon his shoulders. His name provides the kind of symbolic expression that Jung must have had in mind when he wrote:

A symbol really lives only when it is the best and highest possible expression of something divined but not yet known even to the observer. For under these circumstances it provokes participation. It advances and creates life.[10]

That the particular symbol of Christ is placed here is neither an accident nor an act of will. For symbols are never consciously devised, according to Jung, but rather result from "a psychological process of development which expresses itself in symbols." [11] The appearance of the Saviour signifies a reconciliation of the opposites as predicted in Isaiah 11:6:

The wolf also shall dwell with the lamb, and the leopard shall lie down with the kid; and the calf and the young lion and the fatling together; and a little child shall lead them.

The appearance of the Christ-symbol as a unifying force, and its healing effect on the split in the psyche of William Blake represented by Angel and Devil, is explained as an individual application of a collective phenomenon:

. . . experience shows that religions are in no sense conscious constructions but that they arise from the natural life of the unconscious psyche and somehow give adequate expression to it. This explains their universal distribution and their enormous influence on humanity throughout history, which would be incomprehensible if religious symbols were not at the very least truths of man's psychological nature.[12]

The coming together of the opposites, as expressed in this final chapter is, however, anything but a stable relationship, as is evidenced by the continuing struggle related in succeeding books. Out of *The Marriage of Heaven and Hell* emerges Blake's realization that contrary forces exist in man and produce a dynamic which is necessary in order to activate his creative potential. Almost unbearable tension may be produced in this relationship. There are times when the tension cannot be borne. The opposites break apart and the split cannot be healed without the symbol which reestablishes the relationship between consciousness and the unconscious. In its absence one of two possibilities may occur. The individual may so identify with the side of consciousness that he lives on a completely superficial level, unaware of the mysterious and powerful forces which direct his thoughts and his behavior. He is a shallow, unthinking, "mass man," and his "ideas" are dull repetitions of what he reads in the daily press, sees on television, or hears across the dinner table. Or, if he identifies with the side of the unconscious, he may lose his grasp upon the problems and issues of the objective world, and become lost in the psychotic limbo of his fantasy.

Most of us, whether consciously or not, utilize symbols to deal with these psychic splits or potential splits. We find them in the principles by which we live, in religious ideas, or in the images of people whom we feel impelled to imitate. Every politician and every salesman knows how to present the attractive symbol which will help to unify a conflict between belief and resistance, and win a convert to his cause or to his product.

For the person who feels the need of resolving or expressing a deep-seated conflict, either of a personal of collective nature, a ready-packaged symbol will not serve. Recognition of the conflict, of its issues, is of the first order. It is often a very painful state to be in because the wound is bared and there is nothing that can be done about it through an act of will alone. At the crucial moments when this occurs, the symbols arise, which when translated into art brings into being all truly original work. In this way also the symbol forms the core of Blake's poetry and visionary prose and much of his painting, making it possible for Blake to discharge in some measure the tension of the opposites—at least for the time being.

The Marriage of Heaven and Hell is concluded with a Proverb which sums up Blake's leitmotif: that the intrinsic individuality of man takes precedence over any authority imposed from the outside.

"One Law for the Lion & Ox is Oppression."

For amplification of this theme we can do no better than to turn to its first appearance in *Tiriel*, a narrative poem of Blake's which preceded the work under consideration by about a year. In it he tells of an old man and his wife who exchange love and liberty, *i.e.*, imagination, for logic—and of the dessication of their lives which is the result. In the course of their wanderings, all relationships with human beings and with art and poetry end in debasement and emptiness, until at the time of his death Tiriel cries out:

Why is one law given to the lion & the patient Ox?
Dost thou not see that men cannot be formed all alike,
Some nostril'd wide, breathing out blood. Some close shut up
In silent deceit, poisons inhaling from the morning rose,
With daggers hid beneath their lips & poison in their tongue;
Or eyed with little sparks of Hell, or with infernal brands
Flinging flames of discontent & plagues of dark despair;
Or those whose mouths are graves, whose teeth the gates of eternal
   death.
Can wisdom be put in a silver rod, or love in a golden bowl? [13]

As he proceeded with his writing and engraving of *The Marriage*, Blake evidently arrived at the central organizing principle of his life work. The experiments in the pastoral of *Poetical Sketches* and *Songs of Innocence* suggest to critic Harold Bloom [14] an emulation of the classical kind of canonical principle, as Blake follows Virgil, Spencer and Milton in preparing for epic by exploring man's golden age. But now, in *The Marriage*, says Bloom, Blake declares himself a Biblical poet, in the tradition of Milton who repudiated the classicism of Greece and sought the Hebrew sources instead. The English Bible, as Blake read it, began with a Creation that was also a

Fall, and then proceeded to a history with cyclical movements of vision alternating with collapse, and reached successive climaxes with the idyllic art of the Song of Solomon, the tragedy of Job, and the triumphant prophecy of men like Isaiah and Ezekiel. The entrance of these works into history in the Gospels culminating in the Apocalypse sets a model for the Christian epic, a pattern that Milton, in Blake's view, had almost succeeded in emulating. [15]

In order for Blake to put this pattern to poetic use it was necessary for him to achieve complete freedom from the interpretative tradition of Rome. The Protestant passion for the Bible as a possession of the individual, to be read finally by the inner light of each believer's spirit, is Blake's most direct heritage from the radical elements in English religious tradition. Blake's "Bible of Hell," the sequence of his engraved poems, is the first of the great Romantic displacements of the Biblical revelation into the poetic world of the individual creator. Bloom speaks of this work as the "first of the heterocosms." [16]

The text of *The Marriage of Heaven and Hell* is underlined with a final illustration. It is the compelling picture of a man of huge and powerful body stripped naked and crawling upon all fours, a look of unbelieving terror in his eyes. The figure is the prototype of one which Blake painted a few years later and called "Nebuchadnezzar." It depicts the dream of the mighty ruler of Church and State whose dominion had grown so great that it reached "to the end of the earth." Daniel interpreted the dream:

. . . this is the decree of the most High, which is come upon my lord the king:
That they shall drive thee from men, and thy dwelling place shall be with the beasts of the field, and they shall make thee to eat grass as oxen, and they shall wet thee with the dew of heaven, and seven times shall pass over thee, till thou know that the most High ruleth in the kingdom of men, and giveth it to whomsoever he will.[17]

It is as though Blake wanted to say through this illustration that it is neither by law nor by the power of authority that greatness is achieved, but that the kingdom of God—that is, Imagination—is a gift of grace to be found in those men who have been chosen to receive it.

PLATES 25-27

A Song of Liberty

1. The Eternal Female groan'd! it was heard over all the Earth.

2. Albion's coast is sick, silent; the American meadows faint!

3. Shadows of Prophecy shiver along by the lakes and the rivers, and mutter across the ocean: France, rend down thy dungeon!

4. Golden Spain, burst the barriers of old Rome!

5. Cast thy keys, O Rome, into the deep down falling, even to eternity down falling,

6. And weep and bow thy reverend locks.

7. In her trembling hand she took the new born terror, howling.

8. On those infinite mountains of light, now barr'd out by the atlantic sea, the new born fire stood before the starry king!

9. Flag'd with grey brow'd snows and thunderous visages, the jealous wings wav'd over the deep.

10. The speary hand burned aloft, unbuckled was the shield; forth went the hand of jealousy among the flaming hair, and hurl'd the new born wonder thro' the starry night.

11. The fire, the fire is falling!

12. Look up! look up! O citizen of London, enlarge thy countenance! O Jew, leave counting gold! return to thy oil and wine. O African! black African! (go, winged thought, widen his forehead.)

13. The fiery limbs, the flaming hair, shot like the sinking sun into the western sea.

14. Wak'd from his eternal sleep, the hoary element roaring fled away.

15. Down rush'd, beating his wings in vain, the jealous king; his grey brow'd councellors, thunderous warriors, curl'd vet-

erans, among helms, and shields, and chariots, horses, elephants, banners, castles, slings, and rocks.

16. Falling, rushing, ruining! buried in the ruins, on Urthona's dens;

17. All night beneath the ruins; then, their sullen flames faded, emerge round the gloomy king.

18. With thunder and fire, leading his starry hosts thro' the waste wilderness, he promulgates his ten commands, glancing his beamy eyelids over the deep in dark dismay,

19. Where the son of fire in his eastern cloud, while the morning plumes her golden breast,

20. Spurning the clouds written with curses, stamps the stony law to dust, loosing the eternal horses from the dens of night, crying:

Empire is no more! And now the lion & wolf shall cease.

Chorus

Let the Priests of the Raven of Dawn no longer, in deadly black, with hoarse note curse the sons of joy. Nor his accepted brethren—whom, tyrant, he calls free—lay the bound or build the roof. Nor pale religious letchery call that virginity that wishes but acts not!

For every thing that lives is Holy.

A Song of Liberty is clearly a separate poem, yet it is always found included with *The Marriage of Heaven and Hell*, at the end of that work. Max Plowman is of the opinion that *The Marriage of Heaven and Hell* deals with Blake's personal spiritual liberation, and that *A Song of Liberty* tells the same story from the standpoint of eternity.[1] Hamblen takes the more subjective view that the meaning of his own life and place in history at times held Blake tightly in its grip, and at times released him to the sway of certain contemporary influences. She feels that Blake's mind at this time was filled with the conception of a new age and a new prophecy with which he could not but closely associate himself and his work.[2] What both of these writers seem to be saying is that *A Song of Liberty* is written in another mood, from another viewpoint, and that in it Blake is no longer speaking out of his own personal experience. He has now become involved in the *mysterium tremendum* in which time and space melt away as do the characteristics of the individual, and the eye is left to wander over distant skies, and here and there to focus on a brilliant pinpoint of light in a dark encompassing firmament.

As we read *A Song of Liberty*, we are struck by its difference in style from *The Marriage of Heaven and Hell*. *The Marriage* was composed of a number of short passages, each one propounding a particular facet of Blake's major theme: his personal struggle for liberation from a paralyzing tension of opposites. In *A Song of Liberty*, there is no dialogue, there are no opposing forces as such and, most remarkably, no single voice speaks out. There is an impersonal quality which contrasts sharply with the pages we have read which began: "I saw a Devil" . . . "I have always found" . . . "An Angel came to me and said" . . . "As I was walking among the fires . . ." It is as though all through *The Marriage of Heaven and Hell* Blake's aim has been to open up the caverns of perception to a wider image of himself and his own soul, and that now having completed this opus as far as he could, he steps outside to view the world in its vast impersonal aspect. His insistence upon individual liberty suddenly gives way to concern with the *idea* of liberty, which overrides any personal consideration. Blake is now possessed of an idea, and since the idea is collective and archetypal, he tends to lose his former standpoint to a sense of overwhelming awe. The fantasies which he was able to express formerly in images which, despite their wildness, could nevertheless be visualized by the reader and responded to because of their intimate connection with the writer—these fantasies have now become so extensive and embracing that the eye can no longer hold them nor the mind measure them.

A Song of Liberty is about the birth of the Deliverer of man —the archetypal image of the Saviour. The Eternal Female (Blake's image for what others have called the primordial Great Mother) is about to bear a child, and those who wait for freedom—Albion (England), America, France and Spain—remain in the anteroom. The power and tyranny which enslave man's spirit is called by Blake "Rome," and Rome is falling.

The infant is described as a "terror, howling." How apt a

phrase for a newborn child whose cry, outrageously loud for the tiny body which emits it, holds the promise of life and every possibility of how a man may live it! Then comes a section exhorting the citizens of the world, symbolized by the Londoner, the Jew and the African, to change their attitudes in a new era proclaimed by the birth of the Divine Child. Lastly, the death of the old king, "the hoary element," and all his minions, is recounted. His fiery limbs fall into the western sea, his sun sets into night, he falls into the underworld, and all through the long night-sea journey his sullen flames fade. He wanders through the wilderness and the deeps, through the realm of darkness which is the forerunner of salvation and rebirth.

Then rises "the son of fire in his eastern cloud, while the morning plumes her golden breast." It is he who stamps the stony law—immovable tradition—to dust, as Jesus did the ten commandments.[3] "Empire is no more"—no collectively imposed supernatural God or political despot or theological doctrine shall be imposed forcibly upon humanity. "The lion & wolf shall cease" foresees the time at the birth of the Redeemer when Isaiah proclaimed: "The wolf shall dwell with the lamb [4] . . . and the lion shall eat straw like the ox." [5]

The Black Priests are no longer to curse the sons of joy, the tyrant shall no longer make his subservient worshippers "lay the bound" (fix boundaries upon the vision of the imagination) or "build the roof" (shelter man from nature and his own natural aspects by cutting him off from the open sky). Nor shall hypocrisy be mistaken for virtue. "For every thing that lives is Holy"—each man in his essentiality and individuality partakes of and participates in the Godhead.

The source of the mighty impact of *A Song of Liberty* upon the reader is the tremendous numinosity which is associated with the concept of the birth of the Saviour. The meaning of this great archetypal theme was treated by Jung, and his words cast light upon the deeper significance of this impressive *Song:*

The birth of the deliverer is equivalent to a great catastrophe, since a new and powerful life issues forth just where no life force or new development was anticipated. It streams forth out of the unconscious, *i.e.*, from that part of the psyche which, whether we desire it or not, is unknown and therefore treated as nothing at all by the rationalists. From this discredited and rejected region comes the new tributary of energy, the revivification of life. But what is this discredited and despised region? It is the sum of all those psychic contents which are repressed on account of their incompatibility with conscious values, hence the ugly, immoral, wrong, irrelevant, useless, etc.; which means everything that at one time appeared so to the individual in question. Now herein lies the danger that the very force with which these things reappear as well as their new and wonderful brilliance, may so intrigue the individual that he either forgets or repudiates all former values. What he formerly despised now becomes a supreme principle, and what was formerly truth now becomes error. This reversal of values is tantamount to a destruction of previously accepted values; hence it resembles the devastation of a country by floods.[6]

A Song of Liberty, which follows *The Marriage of Heaven and Hell* and yet is not a part of it, foreshadows what is to come in Blake's writing during the remainder of his life. Ambiguous and cumbersome as this poem is, one cannot help but feel the gripping power behind it. It is this dynamism which is to characterize the later, so-called "prophetic works." It is as though the act of confronting the personified demons of heaven and hell prepared Blake for a larger work of a totally different kind, in which he was to explore the reaches far beyond the personal unconscious. *A Song of Liberty* is a beginning step in another direction, and therefore is to be considered as a first chapter of the later writings rather than as the concluding chapter of *The Marriage of Heaven and Hell*.

4
The Bible of Hell

THE SONG OF THE LIBERATION OF MAN FROM THE INHIBIT-
ing factors that limit his enjoyment of delight now beats an
incessant theme in Blake's ear. He must follow the strains with
their endless variations, and give them voice. Restless, he leaves
Poland Street and the familiar Printshop, and moves across
Westmister Bridge to Lambeth, to a rowhouse at number 13
Hercules Buildings. Here within a couple of years or more, he
writes a series of short works in the prophetic style: *Visions of
the Daughters of Albion, The Book of Urizen, The Book of
Ahania, The Book of Los, The Song of Los, Europe* and
America. The prophetic style is the taking up of the grand
motifs of human passions and treating them as though they
were the moving forces in single individuals. Implicit in the
power of the phraseology is the sense that the individuals are
symbols of all of the various aspects of the human personality,
and that their drama is microcosmic and macrocosmic at the
same time.

> To see a World in a Grain of Sand
> And a Heaven in a Wild Flower,
> Hold Infinity in the palm of your hand
> And Eternity in an hour.[1]

177

The prophetic writing speaks at once of the struggle of the many instinctive and intellectual components of the individual, and of the moods and philosophical orientations of the masses. These writings do not really concern themselves with persons, but rather with supra-personal ideas which are anthropo-morphically expressed. Each of these fairly short poetic works contains narratives of the beginnings of the human race, and yet we will recognize later that they were all fragments of a grand legend which had not yet begun to be cohesive.

Were these works the "Bible of Hell" that Blake had promised the readers of *The Marriage*, "which the world shall have whether they will or no"? S. Foster Damon [2] seems to think that some of them were. *The Book of Urizen* deals with the origins of life on earth, but it has no real parallel with Genesis. *The Book of Los* retells the story of *The Book of Urizen*, but with strong parallels from Genesis. *The Book of Ahania* seems to be a sequel to *The Book of Urizen*, and con-tains certain parallels to Exodus. Therefore we may suppose that these works, at least, were already in Blake's mind when he was working on *The Marriage*, and that possibly he had already written down parts of them and expanded in them some of the ideas that had been germinating while he was in the process of committing *The Marriage* to the copper plates and then coloring them. The long and tedious hours that fol-lowed after the swiftly moving pen which had responded to inspiration were the hours in which the mind was free to fancy while the hands were occupied with the task. We realize that Blake was reaching further and further back into the past, at-tempting to cross the threshold of his own personal memory and dig into the collective unconscious heritage common to all men.

If it is possible to recapture infantile memories in the ex-perience of psychoanalysis and to relive them with all of their affect and emotional texture, can this not be done also without the participation of an analyst, by a person who has the capacity to distance himself sufficiently from his perceptions? Cases of self analysis have been reported, most notably Freud's own. One of the goals of the analytic process is, of course, develop-ment of the ability to objectify one's own experience, to be able to apply to a new experience the psychological insight derived from the understanding of previous experiences. It is clear that Blake was one of those to whom this ability comes quite naturally, as it does to many creative people without their having to be taught through the didactic method.

The question must arise—are the "experiences" which flood consciousness in the course of this process in reality evocations of what actually occurred in the past, or are they new "Fancies" about what might have occurred in the past? For our purpose the question cannot be answered unequivocally, but the relevant point is that these experiences are *psychologically valid as recollections* because that is the way they are understood. It is *psychologically true* that man regards his apparent penetrations of the forgotten past as memories. They belong to the unconscious, more specifically to the personal unconscious insofar as they are concerned with events or supposed events in the life of the inward-looking man. But what about those fantasies, or "memories" if you will, that concern themselves with the collective experience of a people, and which extend beyond the contemporary era of the individuals who "recall" them? They appear as tales of the emergence of the human animal, of races, of civilizations. As such they are formed by man into images which take the form of myths. They are discovered by the same kind of reaching backward that takes place in analysis, only now the limits of the individual personality are shattered by the dynamic of imagination and "memory" goes beyond a man's lifetime or his personal experience. Memory is defined in *Webster's Unabridged Dictionary* as the "power or process of reproducing or recalling what has been learned or retained, especially through non-conscious associative mechanisms." Blake reached back, or tried to reach back, into the mythology of the Judeo-Christian culture. In doing this he probed his "memory." He then gave these "memories" another context, reading them as he stated in *The Marriage*, "in the infernal sense."

The "Bible of Hell" evidently was suppressed by Blake, for only a few copies of these early works exist, and *The Book of Los* and *The Book of Ahania* survive in single copies only. These tentative cosmogonies became the bases for a new poem, in which all of Blake's earlier prophetic work is recast. During the years 1795 to 1804 the longest and most comprehensive of Blake's books was written: *The Four Zoas*. This all-inclusive epic is an effort to establish the complete formula of man. Damon says, "This attempt puts Blake in the company of Homer, Dante, Spencer and Milton, whether or not we think he was a worthy companion." [3] *The Four Zoas* was written and rewritten over and over; it contains much brilliance and strength and beauty, but it often becomes entangled and confused. Damon explains this by saying that in this work Blake invented the dream technique, which was the cause of greatest confusion among his earlier critics. We have seen the beginnings of this in *The Marriage of Heaven and Hell*, where from the standpoint of analytical psychology we were able to deal with the "Memorable Fancies" much in the manner in which the dreams of an analysant might be dealt with by the analyst. But now in *The Four Zoas*, it is stated outright by the author that this is the dream of mankind, thus a revelation of the collective unconscious as Blake would understand it. The first form of his title for this work is:

VALA
OR
The Death and Judgement
of the Ancient Man
A DREAM of Nine Nights
by William Blake 1797

The second form for the title is:

The Four Zoas
The Torments of Love & Jealousy in
The Death and Judgement
of *Albion* the Ancient Man
Rest Before Labour [4]

Here we see in the last line the observation that the regression to the unconscious sources of energy in "rest" is required before the creative effort can move forward.

The Four Zoas, monumental as it was, was never completed,

and Blake moved on to another work which took up his relationship to the poet with whom he closely identified himself and of whom he wrote: "Milton lov'd me in childhood & shew'd me his face." [5] The poem was titled *Milton, A Poem to Justify the Ways of God to Man*. If *The Four Zoas* was Blake's rewriting of *Paradise Lost*, the leading purpose of *Milton* was avowedly to correct Milton's errors. Blake had told his friend Robinson Crabb that "I saw Milton in imagination, and he told me to beware of being misled by his *Paradise Lost*." [6] Milton's "coming to Blake" in order that his work might be better understood produced an opportunity for Blake to criticize Milton's ideas and to observe their effect upon him. Damon stated the problem taken on by Blake by saying that *Milton* is "the autobiography of the poem itself, a study of the psychology of creation; like Joyce's *Ulysses*, it is a book whose subject is its own composition." [7]

The last of the great prophetic works of Blake was the magnificently engraved book of one hundred plates titled *Jerusalem: The Emanation of the Giant Albion*. Begun in 1804, it was probably not completed before 1820, seven years before Blake's death. Again we have a dream plot which proceeds not so much by actions as by sequences of ideas. "Jerusalem" in all of Blake's works is the symbolic term for Liberty. She who is unnamed but envisioned in *A Song of Liberty* is, in this final epochal work, separated from man—and the world suffers the catastrophic consequences. Through the long and agonizing experience of contention between the many aspects of human nature bringing about the distintegration of the human spirit, man learns what isolation and alienation mean. Only with this knowledge is he in a position to discover the glorious possibility of relating the disparate elements of his nature in a new way, so that a new synthesis may take place, of a totally different kind from that which existed in the primordial chaos out of which the world was framed. At the end of *Jerusalem* there is a Divine Vision of Eternity which completes the cycle that began in the conceptualization of *The Marriage of Heaven and Hell*.

Was the starting point of this Divine Vision the roar of the tiger of wrath, of Rintrah, who begins "The Argument" not with a statement of the way things are but with a fiery blast which fills the "burden'd air"? Was it the intrusion of Energy, the creative force that is also the terrifying side of God in man, that gives impetus to the poetic genius? Perhaps the inspiration for these later works had its inception in the doctrine that "Without contraries there is no progression." Blake dared to identify Good, which is passive, with Reason — and Evil, which is active, with Energy. In the third plate of *The Marriage* we saw Blake's first attempts to find out the nature of the relationship between these two, and later sections gave varied forms to the dynamism that developed out of the conflict between them. The entire *Marriage* might have been seen as an effort to deal with that apparent split, in whatever way it manifested itself. This seeming paradox of inimical opposites which must somehow be reconciled represents the dilemma of every person who labors in the process of coming to consciousness. How appropriate it is that Blake, instead of resolving the problem in an inner way by self-analysis takes the poetical challenge to project the problem upon the screen of the world's face and expand it into a mythological vision of the development of human consciousness!

Perhaps the sources for these later works came out of the Devil's own proclamations, as Blake perceived and transcribed them, that "Energy is the only life, and is from the Body, and Reason is the Bound or outward Circumference of Energy." The image is of Energy, with its capacity for infinite expansion, pressing against the boundaries set for it by the various forms of discipline associated with reason. The tension exists and grows until the man-made structure of logic becomes inadequate at some point. Somewhere there is an opening, a break through which fantasy can carry a man beyond what he has ever known. He is able to escape from the fixated patterns of thinking that always become attached to any body of accepted knowledge or tradition and to find his way into the realm of the undiscovered, the unknown. If Hell were thought of as that pole of the unconscious which harbored the violent thrashing impulses, either rejected and repressed by man or else unrecognized altogether, Heaven was the opposite pole, a symbol for potential cosmic order beyond the limited order comprehensible to the limited vehicle of man's consciousness. It is through the opening, through the breach in the "outward circumference of Energy" that Blake has entered into the archetypal city, which he called "Jerusalem."

> I give you the end of a golden string
> Only wind it into a ball,
> It will lead you in at Heaven's gate
> Built in Jerusalem's wall.[8]

We take up the string and follow it through these later works, stopping here and there to find what we are looking for: evidence of the products of that consummation which occurred when the Angel embraced the flame of fire and arose as Elijah. We will not approach these prophetic works of Blake as literary critics who look for sources in earlier or contemporary works. Nor will we attempt to discover their philosophical roots, since much has already been written about Blake's later prophetic works from this point of view. We will take our cue from the title of one of Blake's own poems: "The Mental Traveller." We will journey with the writer as bard, following the trail of his thoughts through some later works, observing how the images were gradually filled out and embellished, yet how they continued to refer to their archetypal matrices which were first disclosed in *The Marriage of Heaven and Hell*. We will become aware of the basic structure of the archetype by observing its manifestations in image and symbol, in much the same way that the adolescent Blake became aware of the long lost plans of Gothic cathedrals by pondering their vaults and buttresses, sketching their clustered piers and mullioned windows. In the process we will have the possibility of experiencing the numinous quality of the archetype. In our study of Blake's development, as in personal therapeutic analysis carried on under the Jungian method, we may come to an awareness of the reality of the archetype and its effect upon the creative process. Jolande Jacobi describes what we may expect to find: ". . . the deeper the analysis penetrates, the more clearly the effects of the archetypes appear; the symbol becomes increasingly dominant, for it encloses the archetype, a nucleus of meaning that is not representable in itself but charged with energy. It is very much as when we print an engraving: the first print is extremely sharp, its slightest details are discernible and its meaning is clear; the following prints become poorer in detail and definition; and in the last perceptible image the outlines and details are quite blurred, though we can still distinguish the basic forms which leave all the possible aspects open or combine them. The first dream of a series, for example, gives a detailed image of the real mother in her limited diurnal role; but gradually the meaning becomes wider and deeper until the image is transformed into a symbol of Woman in all her variations as the contrasexual partner; then rising up from a still deeper stratum, the image discloses mythological features, becomes a fairy or a dragon; in the deepest stratum, the storehouse of collective, universally human experience, it takes the form of a dark cave, the underworld, the ocean, and finally it swells into the one-half of creation, chaos, the darkness that receives and conceives." [9]

The Marriage of Heaven and Hell provided the initial condition, comparable to the first dream or the early parts of the dream series as Jacobi has described. *A Song of Liberty* gives us a glimpse of the vision that was to be realized in *Jerusalem.* The chronological order of these shorter prophetic works is not altogether clear. It is likely that Blake was working on several at the same time, as there are overlappings and interweavings of subject matter and theme. It seems clear that the *Visions of the Daughters of Albion,* a manuscript consisting of eight illuminated plates, was already in process while Blake was completing *The Marriage of Heaven and Hell.* A symbolic narrative, cohesive in itself, it takes up the issue of the contraries and the nature of their opposition to one another. In a sense it provides a mythological counterpoint to the more allegorical and satirical *Marriage,* and illustrates another dimension of essentially the same problem.

The other works have a continuity about them; they are loose and not clearly ordered, but the "golden string" is there. Beginning with primordial chaos and ending in the revolutionary spirit of Blake's times, they may be said to represent the emergence of the archetypal images which were to take hold of Blake and possess him and express themselves through his prophetic tongue.

Visions of the Daughters of Albion

In this book we see for the first time names of the characters who will inhabit the archetypal world of Blake's mythology. Each one represents a specific quality or aspect of human nature. The antagonists in this *Vision* are called Theotormon and Bromion. They are incarnations of the opposing principles of Desire and Reason, respectively. We could interpolate their names as we read in *The Marriage:* "Those who restrain desire, do so because theirs is weak enough to be restrained; and the restrainer or reasoner usurps its place & governs the unwilling."

The Visions of the Daughters of Albion weaves this concept into a cloth of imagery. Theotormon, as Desire, is loved by Oothoon who is his feminine counterpart. She is related to him on two levels. The positive or conscious relationship is their mutual desire, the wish for the joyous union of the opposites in the sexual relationship which is possible only because of their differing natures. The negative or unconscious relationship is the unrecognized hostility brought about by the very tension between them—his desire is capable of being restrained, and hers is utterly free. The figure of the Restrainer emerges, called Bromion, a symbol of Reason. Theotormon and Bromion, as will be divulged in a later work, are brothers; in the total mythological scheme they are two of the four sons of Los, who is the personification of Imagination. These two, representing the forces of Reason and Desire, find themselves in the presence of Oothoon, who is betrothed to Theotormon. She expresses her openness to nature and to natural love in *The Argument* which opens the *Visions:*

I loved Theotormon,
And I was not ashamed

> I trembled in my virgin fears,
> And I hid in Leutha's vale!
>
> I plucked Leutha's flower,
> And I rose up from the vale! [1]

Leutha here, and in the subsequent works, refers to sex under law, and hence she may be most easily understood as the sense of sin, or guilt.[2] In later works she will appear as the feminine counterpart of Bromion, having in common with him the respect for legalism, but also bringing him the fulfillment of lust on his own terms. In the act of plucking Leutha's flower, Oothoon is responding to the energetic spirit who in the form of a golden nymph whispers seductively in her ear:

> Pluck thou my flower, Oothoon the mild!
> Another flower shall spring, because the soul
>   of sweet delight
> Can never pass away.

We recall from the "Proverbs of Hell": "The soul of sweet delight can never be defiled." [3] Then we read on in *Visions*

that Oothoon pluck'd the flower saying:

> I pluck thee from thy bed,
> Sweet flower, and put thee here to glow between my
>   breasts,
> And thus I turn my face to where my whole soul seeks.[4]

In doing so, she disregards the inhibiting conventions imposed by Reason; she has taken sexuality (the flower) from the garden of marriage, and has not considered the possible implications. In her unconsciousness—

> Over the waves she went in wing'd exulting swift delight,
> And over Theotormon's reign took her impetuous course.

But Bromion by his nature must subdue this winged creature

whose newly won independence he compares with that of America—after whom he lusts even as he rages at Oothoon for disturbing Leutha's tranquility.

> Bromion rent her with his thunders; on his stormy bed
> Lay the faint maid, and soon her woes appall'd his
>   thunders hoarse.[5]

Having raped the virgin Oothoon, Bromion speaks as Theotormon listens:

> ". . . Behold this harlot here on Bromion's bed,
> And let the jealous dolphins sport around the lovely maid!
> Thy soft American plains are mine, and mine, thy north &
>   south
> Stampt with my signet . . .
> Now thou maist marry Bromion's harlot, and protect the
>   child
> Of Bromion's rage . . ."[6]

Theotormon, as Desire which is weak enough to be restrained, now becomes possessed by Jealousy. He cannot find it within himself to take Oothoon back, but binds her back-to-back with Bromion, and he weeps impotently over the adulterous pair. So all are chained because the reconciling element is lacking, the element of love. Love, as Blake begins now to develop the concept, requires an openness and generous giving of pleasure to the other without ever making a demand or placing a restriction upon the beloved. Theotormon knows nothing of love in this sense. If Oothoon cannot experience with him the pleasure she anticipated, well then, at least she can experience its antithesis, the agony that presages redemption. She calls upon Theotormon's Eagles to prey upon her flesh.

> "I call with holy voice! Kings of the sounding air,
> Rend away this defiled bosom that I may reflect
> The image of Theotormon on my pure transparent breast."
> The Eagles at her call descend & rend their bleeding prey.[7]

Now the free open expression of Desire, as personified by Oothoon, has mingled her blood with that of the Eagles. Like Prometheus she would not be dominated by authority, even if it were that of the Almighty, and like Prometheus she must undergo the torture demanded of her by that powerful bird which symbolized the poetic spirit. Even so, she is not overwhelmed. Blake had written in his "Proverbs of Hell": "When thou seest an Eagle, thou seest a portion of Genius; lift up thy head!" [8] In the commitment of her body, her wholeness, to the Eagle, she is able to see that in her former innocence she had been enclosed completely in the cavern of the five senses:

> "They told me that the night and day were all that I
>   could see
> They told me that I had five senses to inclose me up
> And they inclos'd my infinite brain into a narrow circle,
> And sunk my heart into the Abyss, a red, round globe,
>   hot burning,
> Till from all life I was obliterated and erased." [9]

Now she is freed from those limitations. She can express herself in inspired poetry which echoes the sublime lyric of the book of Job when God out of the whirlwind reminds Job that the universe has magnitude and mystery of which he had scarcely the faintest concept. Oothoon perceives in a new way, because she now has spiritual vision which is a sense beyond the senses. She reads the world in the "infernal" way, in the passage which follows. She is carrying further what Blake began in the "Proverbs"—a new and therefore creative insight into the intuitive forces that exert their influence in every living creature including man.

> "With what sense is it that the chicken shuns the
>   ravenous hawk?
> With what sense does the tame pigeon measure out the
>   expanse?
> With what sense does the bee form cells? have not the
>   mouse & frog
> Eyes and ears and sense of touch? yet are their habitations

And their pursuits as different as their forms and their
   joys.
Ask the wild ass why he refuses burdens, and the meek
   camel
Why he loves man: is it because of eye, ear, mouth, or skin,
Or breathing nostrils? No, for these the wolf and tyger
   have.
Ask the blind worm the secrets of the grave, and why her
   spires
Love to curl round the bones of death; and ask the
   rav'nous snake
Where she gets poison, & the wing'd eagle why he loves
   the sun;
And then tell me the thoughts of man, that have been
   hid of old." [10]

But Theotormon's jealousy is as stifling as Oothoon's free
love is creative. Thus Theotormon answers her in blind and
bitter righteousness: "Tell me, what is night or day to one
o'erflowed with woe?" [11]

Bromion, as Reason, is able to recognize the infinite varieties of response to situations which grow out of the intrinsic
differences in the nature of individuals. Where Oothoon had
accepted this in a feminine way, allowing these unique qualities to come to consciousness and grow within her, Bromion cannot be so passive. He must attempt with masculine
logic to order them and to control them. Recalling the final line
from *The Marriage of Heaven and Hell:* "One Law for the
lion and the ox is Oppression," [12] we now see this concept in
the context of Bromion's lamentation:

"Thou knowest that the ancient trees seen by thine eyes
   have fruit,
But knowest thou that trees and fruit flourish upon the
   earth
To gratify senses unknown? trees, beasts, and birds
   unknown;
Unknown! not unperciev'd, spread in the infinite
   microscope,

In places yet unvisited by the voyager, and in worlds
Over another kind of seas, and in atmospheres unknown:
Ah! are there other wars beside the wars of sword and fire?
And are there other sorrows beside the sorrows of poverty?
And are there other joys beside the joys of riches and ease?
And is there not one law for both the lion and the ox?
And is there not eternal fire and eternal chains
To bind the phantoms of existence from eternal life?" [13]

Now for the first time the name of Urizen appears in the
Visions of the Daughters of Albion. He was the "Starry King"
in *A Song of Liberty,* who presided over the birth of the "newborn terror," and who in a jealous rage hurled the infant into
the night. Then the King was possessed of the attributes of the
Old Testament Jehovah: "With thunder and fire, leading his
starry hosts thro' the waste wilderness, he promulgates his ten
commands, glancing his beamy eyelids over the deep in dark
dismay . . ." [14] Urizen now appears as the formulator of the
collective mores, whom Oothoon blames for loss of the possibility of further intimate relationship with her beloved Theotormon:

"O Urizen! Creator of Men! mistaken Demon of heaven!
Thy joys are tears, thy labour vain to form men to thine
    image.
How can one joy absorb another? are not different joys
Holy, eternal, infinite? . . ." [15]

Oothoon sees Urizen's legalistic system as a means to hold
man in the social condition into which he is born. The clergy
guards that system, as Blake had already pointed out in *The
Marriage.* There he had written in his very brief synopsis of
the history of religion: ". . . a system was formed, which some
took advantage of, & enslaved the vulgar by attempting to
realize or abstract the mental deities from their objects: thus
began the Priesthood . . ." [16] In the *Visions of the Daughters
of Albion,* Oothoon, in her plaint against Urizen, questions the
function of an organized religion which demands that its dicta

be obeyed at the price of spontaneity and freedom. Theology is to her the castle of the lordly authority, in whose dungeon the natural man is enchained.

"With what sense does the parson claim the labour of the
  farmer?
What are his nets & gins & traps; & how does he surround
  him
With cold floods of abstraction, and with forests of
  solitude,
To build him castles and high spires, where kings and
  priests may dwell;
Till she who burns with youth, and knows no fixed lot,
  is bound
In spells of law to one she loathes? and must she drag
  the chain
Of life in weary lust? must chilling, murderous thoughts
  obscure
The clear heaven of her eternal spring; to bear the
  wintry rage
Of a harsh terror, driv'n to madness, bound to hold a rod
Over her shrinking shoulders all the day, & all the
  night . . ." [17]

"Father of Jealousy, be thou accursed from the earth!
Why has thou taught my Theotormon this accursed
  thing?" [18]

Now Oothoon expresses the ideal of human relationship which Blake seeks in his doctrine of openness to experience. Putting aside the dogma of every organized system—designed to protect the weak and fearful—she makes herself utterly vulnerable to the play of life, to the drama of human relationships. She becomes Blake's anima in the noblest sense, for she can take lightly the rhythms of passions, and enjoy them whether they involve her alone or whether only the beloved, or the two of them together. For it is the harmonious interrelationships in life which are important, rather than the ego which is invested in them. She denies that possessiveness can ever be a part of love, and insists that there is no joy greater than the pure delight which one can offer to another. She addresses herself to Urizen:

> "I cry: Love! Love! Love! happy happy Love! free as the
> mountain wind!
> Can that be Love which drinks another as a sponge
> drinks water,
> That clouds with jealousy his nights, with weepings all
> the day,
> To spin a web of age around him, grey and hoary, dark,
> Till his eyes sicken at the fruit that hangs before his
> sight?
> Such is self-love that envies all, a creeping skeleton
> With lamplike eyes watching all around the marriage
> bed.
>
> But silken nets and traps will Oothoon spread,
> And catch for thee girls of mild silver, or of furious gold.
> I'll lie beside thee on a bank & view their wanton play
> In lovely copulation, bliss on bliss, with Theotormon:
> Red as the rosy morning, lustful as the first born beam,
> Oothoon shall view his dear delight, nor e'er with
> jealous cloud
> Come in the heavens of generous love, nor selfish
> blightings bring." [19]

It must be clear that Oothoon, as feminine ideal for Blake, compensates his consciously masculine viewpoint as expressed in his way of life. She does what he does not do and thus completes him. She in turn requires Leutha's flower in order to be complete. Leutha, who represents Blake's marital tie under law with Catherine, exists in an eternal tension with Oothoon as Impulse. The two are not distinct personalities, but states of the human soul. So also are Theotormon and Bromion: as Desire which can be frustrated, and as Law which can be tyrannical. These latter two are the opposites implicit within the masculine creator-god, Urizen, whose instrument of creation is Logos, the word. Blake presents them all: these four—Oothoon, Leutha, Theotormon and Bromion, giving names for the first time to the personifications of the warring opposites. They are to gather a mighty company unto themselves as Blake pursues the theme of co-existent states fighting the battles of Eternity. The archetypal image of opposition was present in *The Marriage* as the Prolific and the Devourer who "are always upon earth, & they should be enemies . . ." yet Blake recognizes and proclaims ". . . the Prolific would cease to be Prolific unless the Devourer, as a sea, received the excess of his delights." [20] Thus opposition is essential to the dynamism of life. It should not be mitigated or minimized, but kept full in the light of the day [21] which is consciousness.

The Minor Prophecies

Five books foreshadowed the major prophetic works like grey clay mock-ups for a monumental piece of sculpture. Blake sweated and strained over them during the years of 1794 and 1795. They were roughly and wildly written for the most part, as though to capture and hold a full clear view into eternity that would otherwise surely vanish. They were fiercely claimed as the dictation of the Eternals who, through the mythology of mankind, reveal timeless secrets to the human mind. Later on they were to be shaped and reshaped into *The Four Zoas*, the first of the major prophetic works. In that book we shall begin to see the fulfillment of the promise in *The Marriage of Heaven and Hell*, perhaps a new cosmology to replace the beginnings of Genesis, or perhaps another projection of the long and arduous story of individual man's development from the primordial chaos of his material conception, through ego consciousness and beyond, to his spiritual emancipation from the mundane world. What *The Four Zoas* is we shall determine as we read it in the light of our understanding of the creative process in Blake; but first a brief review of the shorter works will allow us to see the nature of the thoughts that were preparing the way for the major opus.

The Book of Urizen

The Book of Urizen is the first of Blake's creation stories. Urizen is pictured as the dark demon that "hath form'd the abominable void, the soul-shudd'ring vacuum." [1] He is unproductive, always

> Dark, revolving in silent activity:
> Unseen in tormenting passions:
> An activity unknown and horrible,
> A self-contemplating shadow,
> In enormous labours occupied. [2]

In those days

> Earth was not: nor globes of attraction
> The will of the Immortal expanded
> Or contracted all his flexible senses:
> Death was not, but eternal life sprung. [3]

Urizen's first abortive efforts at creation are efforts to find the absolutes which his authoritarian nature requires:

> "Hidden, set apart, in my stern counsels . . .
> I have sought for a joy without pain,
> For a solid without fluctuation." [4]

He binds the merciless winds and, after the manner of the God in Genesis who made the firmament and divided the waters, Urizen

> . . . repell'd
> The vast waves, & arose on the waters
> A wide world of solid obstruction. [5]

Before man is made, or even a god in the image of man, Urizen appears with his books. These recall to us the Printing house in Hell where molten metals were cast into the expanse and ultimately took the forms of books as they were received by man. Urizen proclaims that his law will be the equivalent of knowledge for the race of Man as yet unborn:

> "Here alone I, in books form'd of metals,
> Have written the secrets of wisdom,
> The secrets of dark contemplation, . . .
> Lo! I unfold my darkness, and on
> This rock place with strong hand the Book
> Of eternal brass, written in my solitude:
> Law of peace, of love, of unity,
> Of pity, compassion, forgiveness;
> Let each chuse one habitation,
> His ancient infinite mansion,
> One command, one joy, one desire,
> One curse, one weight, one measure,
> One King, one God, one Law." [6]

These laws, these patterns of ideal attitudes, are from the beginning stereotyped in Urizen, and they must therefore imply the existence of their opposites, the seven deadly sins of the soul. Urizen is caught in a conflict, which is described in terms of fierce anguish and quenchless flames, in whirlwinds and cataracts of blood, and, at last, in wrenching away from another form, which has until now been a part of Urizen himself. Los, who will hereafter stand for the Creative Imagination, no longer must circle "round the dark globe of Urizen." He is freed by the appearance of the first dichotomy, only he is freed into suffering

>   . . . for in anguish
> Urizen was rent from his side, . .
> . . . But Urizen laid in a stony sleep,
> Unorganiz'd, rent from Eternity.
> The Eternals said: "What is this? Death.
> Urizen is a clod of clay."
> Los howled in a dismal stupor,
> Groaning, gnashing, groaning,
> Till the wrenching apart was healed.

But the wrenching of Urizen heal'd not . . .
Till Los rouz'd his fires, affrighted
At the formless, unmeasurable death.[7]

Now, in words of fantastic imagery, the symbolic representation of Creative Imagination fashions a bodily form for Urizen, which is to be the prototype of the body of Man. Over a period of seven ages, Los shapes the various parts, from the head, "a roof, shaggy, wild, inclos'd in an orb the fountain of his thought," to the skeleton, heart and circulatory system, the eyes, ears, nostrils, and other sensory apparatus, the stomach and digestive system and at last the arms and legs:

He threw his right Arm to the north,
His left Arm to the south,
Shooting out in anguish deep,
And his feet stamp'd the nether Abyss
In trembling and howling and dismay.
And a seventh Age passed over.[8]

Urizen continues to sleep and Los, his bellows and hammers silent, his fires cooled, looks upon Urizen whose eternal life is now obliterated, and he weeps, "obscur'd with mourning." [9] Then Pity begins:

In anguish dividing & dividing,
For pity divides the soul
In pangs, eternity on eternity,
Life in cataracts pour'd down his cliffs.
The void shrunk the lymph into Nerves
Wandering wide on the bosom of night
And left a round globe of blood
Trembling upon the Void.[10]

It is clear that Blake begins to tell his version of the separation of the female out of the male, corresponding to Genesis 2:23: "This is now bone of my bone and flesh of my flesh and she shall be called Woman, because she was taken out of Man." She who is about to come into being will be the archetypal or Eternal Female and the spouse of Los, the Eternal Prophet. We know her already, from her appearance in *A Song of Liberty*, but *The Book of Urizen* takes us back to her creation:

> The globe of life blood trembled
> Branching out into roots
> Fibrous, writing upon the winds,
> Fibres of blood, milk and tears,
> In pangs, eternity on eternity.
> At length in tears & cries imbodied,
> A female form, trembling and pale,
> Waves before his deathy face.
>
> All Eternity shudder'd at sight
> Of the first female now separate,
> Pale as a cloud of snow . . . [11]

Now Los sees her, and she him:

> He embrac'd her; she wept, she refus'd;
> In perverse and cruel delight
> She fled from his arms, yet he follow'd.
>
> Eternity shudder'd when they saw
> Man begetting his likeness
> On his own divided image.[12]

The Eternals now begin to weave a tent which will shut the two out of Eternity, even as the first male and the first female were cast out of Paradise in Genesis 3:23-24. The pregnancy of the female, who is named Enitharmon, is described from the moment when she, "sick, felt a Worm within her Womb . . ." and all the while the Eternals are weaving, until the moment comes which was proclaimed in *A Song of Liberty* when "The Eternal Female Groaned! It was heard all over the earth." Now we see who is this first child to issue from the loins of woman, and what his meaning may be:

> The Eternals their tent finished
> Alarm'd with these gloomy visions,
> When Enitharmon groaning
> Produc'd a man Child to the light.
> A shriek ran thro' Eternity,
> And a paralytic stroke,
> At the birth of the Human shadow.
>
> Delving earth in his resistless way,
> Howling, the Child with fierce flames
> Issu'd from Enitharmon.
>
> The Eternals closed the tent;
> They beat down the stakes, the cords
> Stretch'd for a work of eternity.
> No more Los beheld Eternity . . .
>
> They named the child Orc; he grew
> Fed with the milk of Enitharmon.[13]

That Orc is Revolution is clear from the moment he is wrapped in swaddling clothes. For with his sobbings he burst the girdle in two, and over and over again as he is wrapped, he bursts it: Again:

> The girdle was form'd by day,
> By night was burst in twain.[14]

His cries rouse the passive from their lethargy:

> The dead heard the voice of the child
> And began to awake from sleep;
> All things heard the voice of the child
> And began to awake to life.[15]

Even Urizen awakens, from his deathlike trance, and now the jealousy he feels for the infant who will grow in strength begins to be his motivating impulse. He begins to organize the earth according to his plans and rules:

> He form'd a line & a plummet
> To divide the Abyss beneath;
> He form'd a dividing rule;
> He formed scales to weigh,
> He formed a brazen quadrant;
> He formed golden compasses,
> And began to explore the Abyss;
> And he planted a garden of fruits.[16]

John Middleton Murry observes that "the point of Blake's new myth is that Urizen creates nothing. Los has created him, not he Los and Enitharmon. Urizen's creation is a mere measuring, dividing, exploring of that which exists: the imposition of the Ratio upon the Infinite. All the real creation has been from Los and Enitharmon." [17]

Urizen goes on to propagate the earth with his sons and daughters, for whom he has shaped and ordered it . . . Blake pens with bitter irony:

> And his soul sicken'd! he curs'd
> Both sons & daughters; for he saw
> That no flesh nor spirit could keep
> His iron laws one moment.[18]

And so it is necessary for Urizen to work a net that will accomplish his aim of controlling his progeny. It must be delicate and appealing, yet it must provide a way of keeping man bound within a system so that he will not fall victim to the uncontrollable impulses that arise out of the revolutionary spirit of Orc. Blake explains the advent of the adversary of Liberty in this way:

> [Urizen] wander'd on high, over their cities
> . . . And where ever he wander'd, in sorrows . . .
> A cold shadow follow'd behind him
> Like a spider's web, moist, cold & dim,
> Drawing out from his sorrowing soul . . .
> Till a Web, dark & cold, throughout all
> The tormented element stretch'd

From the sorrows of Urizen's soul. . . .
None could break the Web, no wings of fire,

So twisted the cords, & so knotted
The meshes, twisted like to the human brain.

And all call'd it The Net of Religion.[19]

The Book of Ahania

This work was suppressed by Blake, who kept only one copy for himself. He introduces a character, Fuzon, who is not carried forward into his major works. Urizen in all of the other works of Blake, has the quality of being sterile, by his very nature of withholding and restraining the vital forces. In this book, the fiery figure of Fuzon is pictured as Urizen's son— and this image must be erased, lest some potency of Urizen be established. Ahania also appears for the first time in this book, but her individual meaning is not made clear. That she is the feminine aspect of Urizen and that she becomes separated from him is told, but she does not develop a significant role in the myth until she reappears later in *The Four Zoas*.

The Song of Los and The Book of Los

The Song of Los is the third of the short books leading toward *The Four Zoas*. It completes the cycle of the four continents; these are the four harps to which Los sang his song at the tables of Eternity. *The Book of Los* may be read as a prelude to *The Song of Los*. *The Book of Los* covers much the same ground as *The Book of Urizen*, that is, the Genesis creation story, but from the point of view of Los. That it is clearly a part of "The Bible of Hell" comes through also in the emotional quality of the writing. Los finds himself already separated from Urizen, and the flames of desire are running loose through heaven and hell. Now trapped in the disorganized universe,

Los, as Creative Imagination, expends his furious efforts to give it form. With violent exertion paralleling the work of the six days of Genesis, Los brings into being the creation itself as the result of his desperate wrath.

The Song of Los tells the story of mankind, from Adam in Eden through the Hebrew tradition, until Moses beholds on Mount Sinai the "forms of dark delusion." [1] Rintrah gives "Abstract Philosophy to Brama in the East" [2] and to Mohamet a "loose Bible" is given, and in the north Odin receives a "Code of War." Oothoon hovers over Judah and Jerusalem "And Jesus heard her voice (a man of sorrows) he reciev'd / A Gospel from wretched Theotormon." [3]

Los sings of the tragedy of man, how out of fear and obedience to the *logos* of authority he has lost his freedom. He weeps for him who can no longer move beyond the limitations of his sensory being:

> Thus the terrible race of Los & Enitharmon gave
> Laws and Religions to the sons of Har, binding them more
> And more to Earth, closing and restraining,
> Till a Philosophy of Five Senses was complete. [4]

It was this situation, in Blake's eyes, that obtained at the beginning of the Christian era. The nature of this era he describes in the book which seems logically to follow *The Song of Los*.

Europe, A Prophecy

Enitharmon is the central figure of *Europe*. As Great Mother, she held the dominant position in the Western world during the eighteen centuries of the Christian era by virtue of what Blake sees as two errors of official Christianity. The prophecy begins with the birth of Jesus, the Christian image of the archetypal birth of Orc.

> The deep of winter came,
> What time the secret child

Descended thro' the orient gates of the eternal day:
War ceas'd & all the troops like shadows fled to their
abodes.[1]

Now Blake, proceeding with his polemic against the doctrine
in orthodox Christianity that sex is sin, lets Enitharmon stand
here for the matriarchal role of the Church. Through her the
male is dominated by the female will, and the false doctrine
becomes the rule. She calls upon two of her sons, subdued by
their devotion to her, to proclaim her will. Rintrah, who in
The Marriage was wrath, free and wild at the gates of Paradise,
serves now as the expression of the Mother's anger against the
sons of man. She addresses him "Arise! O Rintrah, eldest born,
second to none but Orc! O lion Rintrah, raise thy fury from
thy forests black! Bring Palambron, horned priest, skipping
upon the mountains." [2] Palambron, here mentioned for the
first time, is usually paired with Rintrah, for his mild sympathy
overcomes where Rintrah is ineffective. Together, they attend
Enitharmon as she calls:

"Now comes the night of Enitharmon's joy!
Who shall I call? Who shall I send,
That Woman, lovely Woman, may have dominion?
Arise O Rintrah, thee I call! & Palambron, thee!
Go! Tell the Human race that Woman's love is Sin;" [3]

She then assigns them the task of enmeshing man in the doctrine of salvation in an allegorical—that is, false—heaven, which
exists for those who are able to avoid the temptations of joyous
and free sexuality: She has her sons declare to man:

"That an Eternal life awaits the worms of sixty winters
In an allegorical abode where existence hath never come.
Forbid all Joy, & from her childhood shall the little female
Spread nets in every secret path." [4]

Enitharmon falls asleep as the Christian tradition spreads
over Europe. England, Albion's Angel, is encompassed in a
grey mist involving Churches, Palaces and Towers; that is,

Christian materialism, the second error of doctrine in Blake's view:

> Albion's Angel rose upon the Stone of Night.
> He saw Urizen on the Atlantic;
> And his brazen Book
> That Kings & Priests had copied on Earth,
> Expanded from North to South.[5]

Blake is particularly sensitive to this restrictive development of the feminine who now is in the position of power, even as in his own personal life he feels the inhibition of the tradition into which he is born. Enitharmon, Eternal Female, is also Catherine Blake. One senses Blake's inner sense of frustration in his own marriage and his growing urge to revolt. His way of expressing it is to objectify the feeling through the word, with a sardonic twist:

> Enitharmon laugh'd in her sleep to see (O woman's
> triumph!)
> Every house a den, every man bound . . .
> Over the doors "Thou shalt not," & over the chimneys
> "Fear" is written.[6]

In this work, then, the concept of sin is shown to be the cord and sinew that keeps man enslaved. Encompass his emotions and limit their expression, and he is bound not only sexually, but politically and spiritually as well. The pre-revolutionary condition portrayed in *Europe* is the natural result of man's immature dependence upon the mother image as the major source of his nourishment. He lies long with his head against her soft seductive breast.

At the end of this dark regressive sleep, Orc rises, and beholds the morning in the east. It is the day in which the sons know that they are grown enough, and gird themselves to battle the mothers:

> The sun glow'd fiery red!
> The furious terror flew around

> On golden chariots raging with red wheels dropping
>   with blood!
> The Lions lash their wrathful tails!
> The Tigers crouch upon the prey & suck the ruddy tide,
> And Enitharmon groans & cries in anguish and dismay.[7]

The spirit of Revolution has come of age, and there will be a frightful struggle. Blake had written *The French Revolution* some years earlier (ca. 1791), and his poem was, as we saw, a horrified observation of the results of man's brutal oppression of his fellow man. Now, in *America,* Revolution is again the theme, but the scale is grander, and at the same time it penetrates deeper into the corresponding internal struggle in a man's own depths. In between, there was *The Marriage of Heaven and Hell,* and the poet who experienced that first consummation is no longer merely an observer of the ways of the human spirit.

America—A Prophecy

Here, again, Blake literally designates one of his books as "prophecy." He was not attempting to dramatize history as he had done in *The French Revolution,* but instead was revealing the formula of all revolution, utilizing the material of the American Revolution as a prototype. Orc is the name Blake gives to the personification of Revolution in the material world. We have heard of him before in *Europe,* as Jesus, and in *A Song of Liberty,* where as the unnamed "new-born terror" he threatened the status quo—embodied in the figure of the starry King. Now he appears as antagonist to the Guardian Prince of Albion. Calling upon Albion (the ancient name of England) Blake uses the name in the archetypal sense to mean the regal domain where men are ruled by law and are punished for their transgressions by loss of freedom or, rather, loss of the illusion of a freedom that they never possessed. "The King of England looking westward trembles at the vision" suggests that the archetypal figure of authority comes face to face with the vision of his own fate at the hands of Orc, or Revolution. The time of momentous change exists again, recalling that condition in which Blake found himself when he wrote in *The Marriage:* "A new heaven is begun, and it is now thirty-three years since its advent . . . Swedenborg is the Angel sitting at the tomb; his writings are the linen clothes folded up." [1] Now, in another age the Crucified is America, and she can no longer be held in the "grave" of domination.

> "The morning comes, the night decays, the watchmen
>   leave their stations
> The grave is burst, the spices shed, the linen wrapped up;
> The bones of death, the cov'ring clay, the sinews shrunk
>   & dry'd
> Reviving shake, inspiring move, breathing, awakening,
> Spring like redeemed captives when their bonds and bars
>   are burst." [2]

The Revolutionary Spirit of Orc, in rising up against the King who has flung him into the night, offers a typically Blakean declaration of independence:

> "Let the slave, grinding at the mill run out into the field
> Let him look up into the heavens & laugh in the bright
>   air;
> Let the inchained soul, shut up in darkness and in
>   sighing,
> Whose face has never seen a smile in thirty weary years,
> Rise and look out; his chains are loose, his dungeon
>   doors are open." [3]

Now the wife and children of the slave believe Orc's song is a dream, yet they raise their voices in jubilation:

> "The Sun has left his blackness and has found a fresher
>   morning,
> And the fair Moon rejoices in the clear & cloudless night;
> For Empire is no more, and now the Lion & Wolf shall
>   cease." [4]

The last line is a repetition of the close of *A Song of Liberty*.
We read on and realize with Blake that the dream *is* a dream
which may not be fulfilled because, upon hearing Orc's song,
the King feels that his authority is being threatened. Albion's
Angel, agent of the Starry King, curses Orc for being the
transgressor of God's commandments. The King, regarding
himself as the Prolific, wrapped in a sacrosanct cloak of his
office, now accuses Orc of being the Devourer:

> ". . . Art thou not Orc, who serpent-form'd
> Stands at the gate of Enitharmon to devour her children?
> Blasphemous Demon, AntiChrist, hater of Dignities,
> Lover of wild rebellion, and transgressor of God's
>   Law . . ." [5]

The "terror" of whom we read in *A Song of Liberty* now
openly declares who he is and what his purpose:

> ". . . I am Orc, wreath'd round the accursed tree:
> The times are ended, shadows pass, the morning 'gins to
>   break;
> The fiery joy, that Urizen perverted to ten commands,
> What night he led the starry hosts thro' the wide
>   wilderness,
> That stony law I stamp to dust; and scatter religion abroad
> To the four winds as a torn book, & none shall gather
>   the leaves . . ." [6]

The Revolutionary doctrine makes raw words as the new
king strives with ancient tradition and finally with all the im-
petuousness of youth casts it aside. His words spring from the
same inspiration as Hell's Proverb: "The soul of sweet delight
can never be defiled." [7] He spoke with the same conviction of
Oothoon, who had wept at the feet of Theotormon in *Visions
of the Daughters of Albion:* "How can I be defiled when I
reflect thy image pure?" [8] It is his way to enter into experience
fully and without reserve, expecting only that it will refine and
purify the spirit. By following natural impulse and shaking

free of the bonds imposed by an old order whose rules are no longer applicable, Revolutionary man can find renewed meaning and revived emotion in his life, as Orc cries out:

"For everything that lives is holy, life delights in life;
Because the soul of sweet delight can never be defil'd.
Fires inwarp the earthly globe, yet man is not consum'd;
Amidst the lustful fires he walks; his feet become like brass,
His knees and thighs like silver, & his breast and head
    like gold." [9]

In these words, with their changing contexts, the development of Blake's idea unfolds. First in "Proverbs" the lines were a provocative jab at the Genesis concept of "purity"; next in *Vision of the Daughters of Albion* it was the lamentation of the individual soul against the prevailing law, and here in *America* the same words, "the soul of sweet delight can never be defil'd," become the battle-cry which must awaken an impassive civilization.

The Four Zoas

Blake first gave evidence of his perception of the archetype of quaternity in "Proverbs of Hell." "The head sublime" with its contrary "the heart Pathos" were in tension with that other pair "the genitals Beauty, the hands & feet Proportion." [1] This germ of an idea that has been growing and developing through the minor works comes into maturity in *The Four Zoas*. In *The Marriage of Heaven and Hell,* references to the quaternity appeared as statements about the nature of man, but how the fourfold structure came into being was never questioned. Essentially, in *The Marriage,* Blake was still considering the problem of man's dualism, that is, how the opposites were related to one another. Thus we had the positing of the contraries which were expressed as soul and body, and took form as man and woman, and functioned as Reason and Energy. In "The Argument" of *The Marriage,* the just man was opposed by the villain, who was also seen as sneaking serpent. And, when the new heaven was begun, a necessary condition for its being was the existence of the Contraries. Out of them sprang Good and Evil, Good being the passive that obeys Reason and Evil the active springing from Energy. Blake insisted that dualism was an error advanced by "all Bibles or sacred codes" and that the truth was seen only when we read the Bible in its infernal sense. This was that the contraries are only artificial divisions of an indivisible unity in which Reason was the boundary or outward circumference of Energy.

How then does Blake advance from the concept of dualism within an intrinsic unity to the monistic concept of man's wholeness which has a basically fourfold structure? It may be that we can find a clue in the personal life of Blake. We were aware of Blake's mood of divisiveness during his writing of *The Marriage*. What bitterness was he projecting when he spoke, for example, of the Prolific and the Devourer? Was it not his inner struggle for survival in the face of the failure of the sexual side of his marriage—his determination to express himself with the full energy of his potency whether or not Catherine would accept him physically. He knew that "the Prolific would cease to be Prolific unless the Devourer as a sea, recieved the excess of his delights." Therefore his energy had to flow into his work and his mistress was Imagination.

In the minor prophetic works he played with the growing realization that his problems were not primarily with the opposites existing in the nature of a man and the forces in the world which seemed to be ranged against him. He came to see that he himself was of a contrary nature and the opposing forces were antagonists in an inner struggle. It is not until he wrote *The Four Zoas* that he really came face to face with the problem which most prophets have avoided, the problem of life between man and woman. He had asked in *The Marriage of Heaven and Hell*, was marriage to be just a barren and bitter struggle, a torment of love and jealousy? Or was a true union possible?

Substantially, in *The Four Zoas*, his answer is this: A creative union between a man and woman is possible only when the man has achieved creative unity in himself.[2] In *The Book of Urizen* we have already seen how Los was wrenched from the side of Urizen. In *The Four Zoas* there will have to be a reunion of the dual aspects of the man before he can come into relationship with his feminine counterpart. The whole process can be seen subjectively as an internal process, with the masculine and feminine aspects of a single individual seeking union. Artistic creativity then becomes an attempt to fulfill in an inner way what the outer world and its relationships fail to provide in the service of wholeness. At the opposite pole, neurosis is another attempt to accomplish the same thing.

The fourfold vision of Blake was beautifully conceptualized in a letter to Thomas Butts:

> Now I a fourfold vision see,
> And a fourfold vision is given to me;
> 'Tis fourfold in my supreme delight
> And threefold in soft Beulah's night
> And twofold Always. May God us keep
> From Single vision & Newton's sleep! [3]

Single vision as conceived by Blake is the vision of the Ratio only. Newton's sleep is the symbol for that unconsciousness which is aware only of that which is demonstrable and measurable. Twofold vision is the vision of *The Marriage of Heaven and Hell,* the vision of "the immense world of delight," the Infinite beyond the Ratio.[4] Threefold vision is the soft night of Beulah, where the "Contrarieties" are equally true.[5] Beulah was the name given to Palestine when it was restored to God's favor, according to Isaiah: "thy land shall be called Beulah: for the Lord delighteth in thee, and thy land shall be married." [6] In that place is the peaceful escape from the living stress of the opposition between the contraries, whether in serene imaginative contemplation, or in sexual union wherein the fact that the "Contrarieties" are equally true is bodily expressed and bodily experienced. The fourfold vision is at once to experience the conflict of the contraries, and in that same moment to transcend that conflict. It is the Eternal Moment itself, the moment in which "the Poet's Work is Done." [7]

The word "Zoa," which Blake used as an English singular, is a Greek plural. It is awkwardly translated as "beasts" in Revelations.[8] St. John the Divine on Patmos saw the four beasts standing about the throne of the Lamb. They worship him and cry out, "Come and see," revealing in turn the four disastrous riders of the Apocalypse. These beasts are the same four "living creatures" which Ezekiel beheld by the river of Chebar.[9] In conventional iconography they have the faces of a man, a lion, an ox and an eagle. Even before the time of Ezekiel, the huge statues before the gates of the Assyrian palace were sculptured with the face of a man, the head of a lion, the wings of an eagle, and the body of an ox.

Blake identified the Zoas with the four fundamental aspects of Man: his body (Tharmas): his reason (Urizen) ; his emotions (Luvah); and his Imagination (Urthona). These correspond to Jung's fourfold analysis of man in his book *Psychological Types*. Here Jung described four functions which exist within every man, and which determine the manner in which he approaches every life situation. The *sensation function* would be related to Tharmas, for it is of the body, and refers to man's response to stimuli through the five senses. Jung's *thinking function* would serve Urizen, for thinking is searching out the significance of things through the process of reason. His *feeling function* is that which Blake personifies as Luvah, the Zoa of the emotions, and his *intuitive function*, like Urthona, refers to perception of that which is not accessible through the senses, that is, Imagination.

Near the beginning of *The Four Zoas*, Blake states his proposition:

Four Mighty Ones are in every Man; a Perfect Unity
Cannot Exist but from the Universal Brotherhood of Eden,
The Universal Man, to Whom be Glory
     Evermore. Amen.[10]

We have already met with two of the four in *The Marriage of Heaven and Hell*, though they were not called by name. They were Urizen and Luvah, respectively the head and the heart or reason and emotion (in terms of Jung's functions: thinking and feeling). In *The Book of Urizen* and others of the minor prophecies we saw that Urizen was the projection of Los, who is the earthly form of Urthona, and vice versa. This means that while each is the repressed side of the other, they do not recognize this, but perceive the other as an adversary on the outside. In *The Four Zoas,* the other two "Mighty Ones" are added. They are Urthona (Los) who is Spirit and functions through Imagination, and Tharmas who is Body (more specifically the genitals) and functions through sensation. The Spirit (Urthona) beholds the conflicts of the contraries. As Intuition he is able to perceive his opposite and to recognize that in union with it there may be fulfillment. Here is the spark, the electronuminosity of love. Tharmas is the body which contains it, that is, Tharmas contains the conflict of the contraries. These four, in their mysterious and simple harmony of conflict, are the Eternal Man, of whom the individual man, typified in Los, is but a member.[11]

This prophetic work is the narration of the Eternal Man—

> His fall into Division & his Resurrection to Unity:
> His fall into the Generation of Decay & death, & his
> Regeneration by the Resurrection from the dead.[12]

The agony of the separation of the male from the female of Man may parallel the individual sense of alienation from his wife that Blake was experiencing during this writing. Blake wished to give free expression to his love, to be open and uninhibited in his passion. Catherine was fearful and restrained. The power in these lines attest to the archetypal nature of such a relationship. In the poem, the female (Enion) says:

> "All Love is lost: Terror succeeds, & Hatred instead of
>   Love,
> And stern demands of Right and Duty instead of Liberty.
> Once thou wast to Me the loveliest son of heaven—But now
> Why art thou Terrible? and yet I love thee in thy terror
>   till
> I am almost extinct & soon shall be a shadow in Oblivion,
> Unless some way can be found that I may look upon thee &
>   live . . .
> I have look'd into the secret soul of him I lov'd,
> And in the Dark recesses found Sin & cannot return." [13]

What has separated Enion from her beloved Tharmas is her growing consciousness, her looking to his "secret soul." Here

is told the pain that is attendant upon the withdrawing of projections and the individual's facing up to the reality of another
person. Reality testing is also part of any process of self examination, and it is one of the factors that makes psychological
analysis so difficult. If Tharmas looks at Enion as his separated
mate, then his cry against her is of utter despair. How much
more so is it the cry of lonely discovery in a man such as Blake,
whose examination is performed not by another person, but in
connection with that reproachful feminine aspect of himself
which Jung named "anima!" Tharmas' lament as he sits "weeping in his clouds" expresses vividly the painful horror of self-
discovery:

> "Why wilt thou Examine every little fibre of my soul,
> Spreading them out before the sun like stalks of flax to dry?
> The infant joy is beautiful, but its anatomy
> Horrible, Ghast & Deadly; nought shall thóu find in it
> But Death, Despair & Everlasting brooding Melancholy.
> Thou wilt go mad with horror if thou dost Examine thus
> Every moment of my secret hours. . . .
> O Enion, thou art thyself a root growing in hell,
> Tho' thus heavenly beautiful to draw me to destruction.
> *Sometimes I think thou art a flower expanding,*
> *Sometimes I think thou art fruit, breaking from its bud*
> *In dreadful dolor & pain; & I am like an atom,*
> *A Nothing, left in darkness; yet I am an identity:*
> *I wish & feel & weep & groan. Ah, terrible! terrible!"* [14]

The long poem, *The Four Zoas*, describes the many aspects
of man as they are differentiated from one another. The symbolism amazingly parallels the analytic process of differentiating the many unconscious contents one from the other, and
then gradually reintegrating them into a new and productive
unity. The parallel is even more impressive when we consider
that Blake uses the schema of the nine nights of dreams, since
dreams in analytical psychology provide the key to understanding the unconscious processes. It is with this key that Blake has
unlocked "the doors of perception" as he promised he would in
The Marriage of Heaven and Hell. At the end of the ninth
night man beholds the infinite vision, and he sings his Ode to

Joy (we recall the first two lines, first uttered by the enslaved wives and children of *America*):

> The Sun has left his blackness & has found a fresher
>   morning,
> And the mild moon rejoices in the clear & cloudness night,
> And Man walks forth from the midst of fires: the evil is
>   all consum'd.
> His eyes behold the Angelic spheres arising night & day;
> The stars consum'd like a lamp blown out, & in their
>   stead, behold
> The Expanding Eyes of Man behold the depths of
>   wondrous worlds!
> One Earth, one sea beneath; nor Erring Globes wander,
>   but Stars
> Of fire rise up nightly from the Ocean; & one Sun
> Each morning, like a New born Man, issues with songs &
>   joy
> Calling the Plowman to his Labour & the Shepherd to his
>   rest.
> He walks upon the Eternal Mountains, raising his heavenly
>   voice,
> Conversing with the Animal forms of wisdom night & day,
> That, risen from the Sea of fire, renew'd walk o'er the
>   Earth;
> For Tharmas brought his flocks upon the hills, & in the
>   Vales
> Around the Eternal Man's bright tent, the little Children
>   play
> Among the wooly flocks. The hammer of Urthona sounds
> In the deep caves beneath; his limbs renew'd, his Lions
>   roar
> Around the Furnace & in Evening sport upon the plains.
> They raise their faces from the Earth, conversing with
>   the Man:
>
> "How is it we have walk'd thro' fires & yet are not
>   consum'd?
> How is it that all things are chang'd, even as in ancient
>   times?" [15]

The Four Zoas does not belong to the sequence of Blake's writings published during his lifetime. It exists only in the form of a manuscript, decorated by a few beautiful and frankly sexual drawings. It was composed between 1795 and 1804, a period in which no engraved prophetic works appeared. *The Song of Los,* in 1795, had been the last one, and *Milton* and *Jerusalem* were yet to be started when Blake stopped working on *The Four Zoas.* Strangely enough, in Alexander Gilchrist's *Life of Blake* where Blake's activities and writings are described often in minutest detail, there is no mention at all of *The Four Zoas.* Blake's commercial writing and engraving productions are reviewed, as well as his relationship with friends and some political activities, but of this major work, nothing. It is as though the writing of this book were a very private experience, like a dream, that belonged to Blake alone. It was the working through of the difficult union foretold in *The Marriage of Heaven and Hell.* An inner marriage was taking place in his psyche which to him was more real than his conventional marriage with Catherine. As masculine creative force, his energy spurted forth abundantly. As feminine receptive vessel, his anima aspect functioned in his work to contain and shape that stream.

"The cistern contains: the fountain overflows." [16] It was a secret happening, a pregnancy, which could not be shown prematurely to the public. This is why, I believe, Blake never engraved this book. Murry states it well when he says, "It is the book of the travail of Blake's final rebirth." [17]

Milton

After seven productive years in Lambeth, Blake exchanged his modest house in Hercules Buildings for a cottage by the sea at Felpham. There he lived for three or four years, the only period of his life spent in the country. He was forty-three when he and Catherine were invited by William Hayley, a poet of sorts and a country gentleman, to live on his inherited estate rent free. It was understood that Blake was to illustrate certain of Hayley's poems; and he was to be free to execute independent commissions, some of which Hayley helped him to secure. It was during this period, evidently, though Gilchrist in his *Life of Blake* made no mention of it, that Blake composed *The Four Zoas,* and began working on *Milton* and *Jerusalem.* Gilchrist describes Blake's life at Felpham as "a happy one," but later writers, in scrutinizing his productions during that period which were not available to Gilchrist, thought otherwise. In any case, Blake terminated the relationship in 1804, and returned to London and poverty. He later referred to life at Hayley's as "my three years slumber on the banks of the Ocean." Not long after his return to London, the poem *Milton* was written and etched (1804-1808).

The poet Milton had been Blake's idol from earliest youth. In his opinion, Milton was England's greatest poet, taking precedence over Chaucer and Shakespeare. His influence began early in Blake's life, and was as much a foundation of Blake's poetry as was the art of Michelangelo of his painting. The lives of Blake and Milton were strangely parallel in many ways. Damon points out some of the correspondences in the biographies of the two:

Milton's father was disinherited for turning Protestant; Blake's father was a Dissenter. Milton's first poetic period was a great one, so was Blake's. Milton considered himself divorced from his first wife, who abandoned him, but he did not take a second wife when the first returned; Blake, unhappy with Catherine, considered taking a second woman into his home, but was dissuaded by Catherine's tears. When Milton abandoned poetry for politics, Blake condemned him as an atheist, "till in his old age he returned back to God whom he had in childhood" (letter to Crabb Robinson). But in his dishonored retirement, Milton wrote his three greatest poems; and Blake, after returning from Felpham into obscurity, wrote [or completed] his three greatest poems.[1]

Blake, with his independent approach to life and literature, did not read Milton's *Paradise Lost* as a versified account of past history or of the Christian epic. He was inspired by the charge that was implicit there: to understand that Milton was trying to say "things unattempted yet in Prose or Rhime." [2] Milton's work inspired Blake over and over with the challenge of his ideas.

One example of this is in the paired poems of Milton, "L'Al-legro" and "Il Pensoroso." Here the poet uses extensively "the contraries" to bind the two poems together, as day and night, the lark and the nightingale. Blake gave expression to the extremes of ecstasy and despair in the human soul in his collections *Songs of Innocence* and *Songs of Experience,* and within each volume lyrics paralleled those of the other in theme and mood. Milton's *Comus* describes a young girl on the edge of experience who avoids the snares of evil, and in Blake's early *Thel,* the virgin who fears that she shall fade away without a use is promised that "Every thing that lives/Lives not alone nor for itself." *Visions of the Daughters of Albion* corresponds to Milton's attack on unhappy marriage through his divorce pamphlets. But where Milton was content to speak out for divorce on grounds of incompatibility, Blake demanded complete freedom for love, regardless of legal sanction.

It was in *The Marriage of Heaven and Hell* that Blake for the first time disagreed openly with his idol. This book has been compared by Damon [3] to *The Christian Doctrine,* where Milton consolidated the old system, with important alterations. Blake, on the contrary, demolished it entirely, and proclaimed a totally new view of the universe, suggesting that Milton's Messiah was really Satan, and hinting that the real Messiah, the tempter, was what Milton considered the Devil. Blake had written that Milton "was a true Poet and of the Devil's party without knowing it." [4] He wrote that in elevating Reason, Milton had mistaken the figure Blake was to re-name "Urizen" for God.[5] Also, Blake saw Milton's "Son" as a "Ratio of the five senses." [6] By "Ratio," a word which often occurs in Blake's work, he means a *limited* system founded upon what facts are available and organized by Reason. In the later work, *Milton,* Blake was to say that "The Vegetable Ratio is all that the fallen senses can percieve" [7] and also that "the Reason is a State Created to be Annihilated & a new Ratio Created," [8] and he was to indicate the circumstance under which the creation of art could take place as a time when "Mathematic Proportion was subdued by Living Proportion." [9] Also:

. . . every Natural Effect has a Spiritual Cause, and Not

A Natural; for a Natural cause only seems: it is a Delusion
Of Ulro & a ratio of the perishing Vegetable Memory.[10]

As so often now, Blake begins his work with an invocation to
the creative spirit. He knows that he does not write out of
himself, but out of the inspiration, the divine breath within
him, that same *pneuma* which God breathed into clay when
he named it Adam:

Daughters of Beulah! Muses who inspire the Poet's Song,
Record the journey of immortal Milton thro' your Realms
Of terror & mild moony lustre in soft lustre in soft
    sexual delusions
Of varied beauty, to delight the wanderer and repose
His burning thirst & freezing hunger! Come into my hand,
By your mild powers descending down the Nerves of my
    right arm
From out the Portals of my brain, where by your ministry
The Eternal Great Humanity Divine planted his Paradise,
And in it caus'd Spectres of the Dead to take sweet forms
In likeness of himself.[11]

Blake then asks what moved Milton, after he had walked
about in Eternity for a hundred years "pond'ring the intricate
mazes of Providence," to descend again to earth? Milton had
been separated from his Emanation, that sixfold feminine spirit
which had embodied his three wives and three daughters while
he lived and with whom he was not truly united either in life
or in death. Therefore, his Emanation, "scattered thro' the
deep," kept him in torment, and caused him to descend again
to redeem her, even though he knew that he might himself
perish in the act of so doing.

Then follows "The Bard's Song," in which is described to
Milton the nature of the finite world which he is to enter. This
is the world which was cut off from infinity by the tent the
Eternals erected while the revolutionary Orc was yet taking
form in the womb of Enitharmon. Enitharmon, too, is a weaver.
She at her looms and Los with his hammer have created the
three classes of mortal men whom Milton had recognized: the

Elect, the Redeemed and the Reprobate. The Bard goes on to describe the Elect as those who cannot be redeemed but must be created continually, by offering and atonement in the Moral Law. The Redeemed are the Repentant Sinners saved by Christ, and the Reprobate or Transgressors are those who go their own way to damnation. Milton's Jesus and Samson were examples of the Elect, his Adam and Eve of the Redeemed, and his Satan and Dalilah of the Reprobate. Blake, reading Milton in the infernal light, inverted the classification and saw the Reprobate, like the Devil in *The Marriage of Heaven and Hell,* as the original geniuses—the poet and the prophet.

The Bard sings how Satan, "with incomparable mildness," prevails upon Los to let him take the Harrow of the Almighty, which belongs to Palambron. That tender brother of Rintrah often represents the aspect in Blake which is moved to Pity, the weakness which allows disintegration of the personality. Palambron calls Satan to account before Los, and a terrible struggle ensues with Rintrah crying out in "indignation for Satan's soft dissimulation of friendship" and with those other sons of Los, Theotormon and Bromion arraying themselves on the side of Satan. Palambron declares the truth that Blake has learned through his own experience: "That he who will not defend Truth, may be compelled to / Defend a Lie, that he may be snared & caught & taken." [12] In the vast confusion, indentities are mingled and Satan assumes Rintrah's wrath "in a feminine delusion of false pride self-deciev'd." For, in the using of female wiles, Satan has fallen from his Manhood, and he receives the condemnation of a Great Solemn Assembly. Leutha, a Daughter of Beulah, whom we have come to know as the image for legalized sexuality, offers herself as a ransom for Satan, taking upon herself his sin, saying "I am the Author of this Sin! by my suggestion my Parent power Satan has committed this transgression." She describes her sinful act whereby sexuality becomes loosed in the vegetative world called "Ulro" to serve as a weapon by which woman may dare to control the impulses of man:

"I loved Palambron & I sought to approach his Tent,
But beautiful Elynittria with her silver arrows repell'd me,

For her light is terrible to me: I fade before her
  immortal beauty.
O wherefore doth a Dragon-Form forth issue from my limbs
To sieze her new born son? Ah me! the wretched Leutha!
This to prevent, entering the doors of Satan's brain night
  after night
Like sweet perfumes, I stupefied the masculine perceptions
And kept only the feminine awake: hence rose his soft
Delusory love to Palambron, admiration join'd with envy.
Cupidity unconquerable! my fault, when at noon of day
The horses of Palambron call'd for rest and pleasant death,
I sprang out of the breast of Satan, over the Harrow
  beaming
. . . that I might unloose the flaming steeds . . ." [13]

Milton, who is in a sense Blake, hears the Bard's song, then
rises up and makes his commitment to return to earth where
his own sexuality, his relationship to the feminine, was left un-
resolved, and to redeem that aspect of himself which should
have remained inseparable, his Emanation. Taking off his
heavenly robes and ungirding himself from the oath of God,
Milton proclaims:

"I go to Eternal Death! The Nations still
Follow after the detestable Gods of Priam, in pomp
Of warlike selfhood contradicting and blaspheming.
When will the Resurrection come to deliver the sleeping
  body
From corruptibility? O when, Lord Jesus, wilt thou come?
Tarry no longer for my soul lies at the gates of death.
I will arise and look forth for the morning of the grave:
I will go down to self annihilation and eternal death,
Lest the Last Judgment come & find me unannihilate
And I be siez'd & giv'n into the hands of my own
  Selfhood. . . .
What do I do here before Judgment? without my
  Emanation?" [14]

Here is the argument of the book of *Milton*: that Milton had in his lifetime been involved too much with selfhood (which we would understand as ego identification). He had become disproportionately focused upon his own ideas and had lost sight of their eternal implications. He had also lost sight of relationship, both in the outer world with his wives and daughters, and within, with his own feminine side. He fell into the Mundane Shell, Blake's appellation for earth as seen from the viewpoint of eternity. There he had, in the past, given support and comfort to many of the doctrines of the orthodox Church and, even when he had disagreed, had sought some sort of peaceful understanding with it. Unwilling or unable to fly free in his imagination as Blake feels he should have done, Milton becomes the subject for the lamentation of the Shadowy Female who is associated in Blake with all the bounds that limit man, including the Church.

Thus the Shadowy Female howls in articulate howlings:

"I will lament over Milton in the lamentations of the
     afflicted
My Garments shall be woven of sighs & heart broken
     lamentations:
The misery of unhappy families shall be drawn into its
     border,
Wrought with the needle with dire sufferings, poverty,
     pain & woe
. . . throughout the whole Earth
There shall be the sick Father & his starving Family, there
The Prisoner in the stone Dungeon and the Slave at the
     Mill.
I will have writings written over it in Human Words
That every infant that is born upon the Earth shall read
And get by rote as a hard task of life of sixty years." [15]

Blake has Milton take the path of self-annihilation and he endows him with his own understandings. Milton has to become aware of his unconscious motivation in making Satan the hero of *Paradise Lost*. He needs to realize that he is his own Satan, and not merely that, but that Satan is that egocentric aspect which must be continually annihilated. "I in my selfhood am that Satan: I am that Evil One." [16] Secondly, the personality of Satan is hermaphroditic, which means that the contra-sexual aspects are at war within him. They include the negations: Reason and Energy (as in *The Marriage*), and Milton's God the Father and Milton's Satan, also Blake's Urizen and Blake's Orc.[17] Negations differ from contraries in the manner of their relationship. Negations tend to destroy one another, while contraries may coexist in a state of complementarity. Milton is called upon to redeem first the Satan aspect of his personality. Satan is also that dark side to which Jung was later to refer as the shadow. Only when the shadow is integrated in man's personality, according to Jung, can man fully and adequately relate to his feminine side, his anima. The sacrifice is annihilation of the impulse to be concerned primarily with one's temporal needs, and the result is a defeat for the ego. Milton has this experience of self-annihilation in the Threefold Sexual World, into which he has descended. It is here that he is able to come again into contact with his Emanation, and to recognize her in all her capacities and potentialities. He is one with her in the Sexual World, which is finite. But the act of annihilating his ego before Satan is necessary as he prepares himself to conclude his journey and to return to the condition of eternity. He knows that he cannot do this through an act of will, for that again would be an example of the very selfhood he seeks to annihilate. Therefore he can only submit his ego to the higher power and plead:

"O how can I with my gross tongue that cleaveth to the dust
Tell of the Four-fold Man in starry numbers fitly order'd,
Or how can I with my cold hands of clay! But thou O Lord,
Do with me as thou wilt! for I am nothing, and vanity.
If thou chuse to elect a worm, it shall remove the
     mountains." [18]

How magnificent this tribute to the Creative spirit, how impressive in its humility! In the end the Emanation divides and the sexual portion falls away. The daughters of memory who are associated with time are changed into the daughters of inspiration, and the anima who is the breath of God accompanies

Milton as he returns to eternity in the form of the whole or Fourfold Human.

And what has happened to Blake as he has through his imagination been one with Milton in traveling through the finite world to prepare for his eternal existence as the whole or Fourfold Human? He has become united with Los, the spirit of divine inspiration. We learn from his own words whence came to Blake the tremendous energy for creative activity:

"While Los heard indistinct in fear, what time I bound my
 sandals
On to walk forward thro' Eternity, Los descended to me:
And Los behind me stood, a terrible flaming Sun, just close
Behind my back. I turned round in terror, and behold!
Los stood in that fierce glowing fire, & he also stoop'd down
And bound my sandals on . . . trembling I stood
Exceedingly with fear and terror . . .
. . . but he kissed me and wished me health,
And I became One Man with him arising in my strength.
'Twas too late now to recede. Los had enter'd into my soul:
His terrors now possess'd me whole! I arose in fury &
 strength." [19]

JERUSALEM

From *The Holy Bible:*

And I John saw the holy city, new Jerusalem, coming down from God out of heaven, prepared as a bride adorned for her husband.

And I heard a great voice out of heaven saying, Behold the tabernacle of God is with men, and he will dwell with them, and they shall be his people, and God himself shall be with them, and be their God.

And God shall wipe away all tears from their eyes; and there shall be no more death, neither tears nor crying, neither shall there be any more pain: for the former things are passed away.

And he sat upon the throne and said, Behold I make all things new. And he said unto me, Write: for these words are true and faithful. (Rev. 21:2-5)

And there came unto me one of the seven angels which had the seven vials full of the seven last plagues, and talked with me, saying, Come hither, I will shew thee the bride, the Lamb's wife.

And he carried me away in the spirit to a great and high mountain, and shewed me that great city, the holy Jerusalem, descending out of heaven from God.

Having the glory of God: and her light was like unto a stone most precious, even like a jasper stone, clear as crystal . . . (Rev. 21:9-11)

At last we come to the longest and most impressive of Blake's completed Prophecies. *Jerusalem, The Emanation of the Giant Albion* contains exactly one hundred plates. Eight completed copies are known, three of them printed posthumously. Only one complete copy was colored by Blake and that remains. In addition there are several examples of single colored plates.

Writing about *Jerusalem,* John Middleton Murry asked: "After *Milton* can Blake add anything? It is not possible. His truth is final indeed. All that he can do is to walk forward along the past of Self-annihilation, and utter the truth again and again. . . . In *Jerusalem* Blake has nothing essential to add to his message. But that very sense of finality makes him impatient to utter it anew. He must be about his Father's business." [1] Murry sees *Jerusalem* as a summary of all that has gone before, and he compares it to Wordsworth's condition of poetry— emotion recollected in tranquility. "In *Milton* we have Blake's forward leap into Eternity, in *Jerusalem* the speech is of one who dwells therein." [2] *Jerusalem* does not, in his view, have the immediacy of either *The Four Zoas,* or *Milton.* Northrop Frye, on the other hand, sees *Milton* as a mere prelude to the longer poem whose theme it announces.[3] That theme is:

Of the Sleep of Ulro! and of the passage through
Eternal Death! And of the awakening to Eternal Life.[4]

Blake goes on to reaffirm his sense of being in complete harmony with Divine Inspiration in the opening lines of *Jerusalem.*

This theme calls me in sleep night after night & ev'ry morn
Awakes me at sun-rise; then I see the Saviour over me
Spreading his beams of love & dictating the words of this
    mild song.

"Awake! awake O sleeper of the land of shadows, wake!
    expand!
I am in you and you in me, mutual in love divine." [5]

The long poem is Blake's imaginative vision of human life, seen in a drama of four acts: a *Fall,* the *Struggle* of men in a fallen world which is what we usually think of as history, the *Redemption* of the world by a divine man in which death and eternal life achieve a simultaneous triumph, and a final *Divine Revelation*.[6]

Albion is Britain, but in a deeper sense he is fallen Man, separated from his Emanation, Jerusalem. In the first part, the *Fall*, Jesus comes and calls Albion to account saying

> "Where hast thou hidden thy Emanation, lovely Jerusalem
> From the vision and fruition of the Holy-one?" [7]

In losing her who stands for freedom, Albion has lost the essential quality of humanity, and he replies in jealous fear:

> "Jerusalem is not! her daughters are indefinite:
> By demonstration man alone can live, and not by faith.
> My mountains are my own, and I will keep them to myself:
> . . . here will I build my Laws of Moral Virtue.
> Humanity shall be no more, but war & princedom &
>   victory!" [8]

By this declaration Albion forfeits his claim to eternity, and falls into a sleep that is like death. Meanwhile Los, ever the champion of Man, is affected. He divides into his various parts, as do the four sons of Los. Yet in their effort to hold on to the possibility of creativity Los and his sons busy themselves with the building of the City of Art, the fourfold city in "Jerusalem" which is called "Golgonooza." Los beholds its four compass points in eternity:

> West, the Circumference: South the Zenith: North,
> The Nadir: East, the Center, unapproachable for ever.[9]

And he says the words which elucidate the concept of fourfold man that was first expressed in *The Marriage of Heaven and Hell:*

> "These are the four Faces toward the Four Worlds of
>   Humanity

In every Man. Ezekiel saw them by Chebar's flood.
And the eyes are the South, and the Nostrils are the East,
And the Tongue is the West, and the Ear is the North." [10]

There is a beautiful section which brings to its full flower the
concept of the Contraries which germinated in *The Marriage*.
It shows how the Contraries are essential to Love for they signify mutual acceptance, its primary condition. The Contraries
are set in contrast to the Negations, which separate and divide
because of their refusal to tolerate difference. This is a part of
the doctrine of Los who utters it in secret communion with himself as he searches for the way in which true integration of the
human personality can be achieved:

"They know not why they love, nor wherefore they sicken
    & die,
Calling that Holy Love which is Envy, Revenge, & Cruelty,
Which separated the stars from the mountains, the
    mountains from Man
And left Man, a little grovelling Root outside of Himself.
Negations are not Contraries: Contraries mutually exist;
But Negations Exist Not. Exceptions & Objections &
    Unbeliefs
Exist not, Nor shall they ever be Organized for ever
    & ever." [11]

Again in *The Marriage,* we were given a most unorthodox
image of a Jesus who was "all virtue" because he "acted from
impulse, not from rules." [12] He had given his sanction to the
law of the ten commandments not by observing them, but
rather by his ability to forgive and to pray for those who had
broken them. For "The Devil answer'd: . . . I tell you, no
virtue can exist without breaking these ten commandments." [13]
Now, in *Jerusalem,* the Divine Lamb stands beside Jerusalem
who, having been cast out by Albion, has also lost her faith in
her Lord and Saviour, and cries out:

"Babel mocks, saying there is no God nor Son of God,

That thou, O Human Imagination, O Divine Body, art all
A delusion; but I know thee, O Lord, when thou arisest
  upon
My weary eyes, even in this dungeon & this iron mill.
The stars of Albion cruel rise; thou bindest to sweet
  influences,
For thou also sufferest with me, altho' I behold thee not;
And altho' I sin and blaspheme thy holy name, thou
  pitiest me
Because thou knowest I am deluded by the turning mills
And by these visions of pity and love . . ." [14]

The Lamb entreats her to return to him, and to "Give forth
thy pity & thy love; fear not, lo! I am with thee always—Only
believe in me." [15] He then allows her to see a vision in which
his own conception is discussed by Joseph and Mary. Jesus accepts his illegitimacy as Jehovah's doctrine of Forgiveness of
Sins is enunciated:

She [Jerusalem] looked & saw Joseph the Carpenter in
  Nazareth & Mary
His espoused Wife. And Mary said, "If thou put me away
  from thee
Doest thou not murder me?" Joseph spoke in anger & fury,
  "Should I
Marry a Harlot & an Adulteress?" Mary answer'd, "Art
  thou more pure
Than thy Maker who forgiveth Sins & calls again Her that
  is Lost?
Tho' She hates, he calls her again in love. I love my dear
  Joseph,
But he driveth me away from his presence; yet I hear the
  voice of God
In the voice of my Husband: tho' he is angry for a moment,
  he will not
Utterly cast me away; if I were pure, I never could taste
  the sweets
Of the Forgiveness of Sins; if I were holy, I never could
  behold the tears,

Of love, of him who loves me in the midst of his anger in
furnace of fire."

"Ah my Mary!" said Joseph, weeping & embracing her
closely in

His arms: "Doth he forgive Jerusalem, & not exact Purity
from her who is

Polluted? I heard his voice in my sleep & his Angel in
my dream,

Saying, 'Doth Jehovah Forgive a Debt only on condition
that it shall

Be Payed? Doth he Forgive Pollution only on conditions of
Purity?

That Debt is not Forgiven! That Pollution is not Forgiven!

Such is the Forgiveness of the Gods, the Moral Virtues
of the

Heathen whose tender Mercies are Cruelty. But Jehovah's
Salvation

Is without Money & without Price, in the Continual
Forgiveness of Sins,

In the Perpetual Mutual Sacrifice in Great Eternity; for
behold,

There is none that liveth & Sinneth not! And this is the
Covenant

Of Jehovah: If you Forgive one-another, so shall Jehovah
Forgive You,

That He Himself may Dwell among You. . . .' " [16]

This is the promise made to Jerusalem, which shall be the
condition of Regenerated Man when he comes into the right
relationship with the new split-off aspects of his personality.
He must, first, forgive his many selves, and then he must be
able to forgive every other man.

Still another idea that was born out of *The Marriage of
Heaven and Hell* comes into its maturity in *Jerusalem*. It was
first uttered by Blake's Devil when he arose before Blake's
Angel in a flame of fire, saying "The Worship of God is:
Honoring his gifts in other men, each according to his genius,
and loving the greatest men best: those who envy or calumniate

against great men hate God; for there is no other God." [17] In
Jerusalem the idea is elaborated and out of it grows the procla-
mation of Los, guardian of man's creative potential:

> Go, tell them that the Worship of God is honouring his
>   gifts
> In other men: & loving the greatest men best, each according
> To his Genius: which is the Holy Ghost in Man; there is
>   no other
> God than that God who is the intellectual fountain of
>   Humanity.
> He who envies or calumniates, which is murder & cruelty,
> Murders the Holy-one. Go, tell them this, & overthrow
>   their cup,
> Their bread, their altar-table, their incense & their oath,
> Their marriage and their baptism, their burial &
>   consecration." [18]

When man shall recognize God as being within him, and
being of him, then shall God be known to man. The great unity
of the cosmos shall be seen as the eternal reality of which our
temporal observations, dependent upon the agents of the
senses, have shown us only fragments. In the end the promise of
the divine in man made in *The Marriage of Heaven and Hell*
is at last fulfilled. The promise is that the "Doors of Perception"
shall be cleansed, and that everything shall appear to man as it
is, Infinite. That appearance is the vision of the quaternio of
man, which has been called "Blake's Apocalypse," [19] and which
we read in the final chapter of *Jerusalem:*

> And every Man stood Fourfold; each Four Faces had: One
>   to the West,
> One toward the East, One to the South, One to the North,
>   the Horses Fourfold.
> And the dim Chaos brighten'd beneath, above, around:
>   Eyed as the Peacock,
> According to the Human Nerves of Sensation, the Four
>   Rivers of the Water of Life.

South stood the Nerves of the Eye; East, in Rivers of
bliss, the Nerves of the
Expansive Nostrils; West flow'd the Parent Sense, the
Tongue; North stood
The labyrinthine Ear: Circumscribing & Circumcising the
excrementitious
Husk & Covering, into Vacuum evaporating, revealing the
lineaments of Man,
Driving outward the Body of Death in an Eternal Death &
Resurrection,
Awaking it to Life among the Flowers of Beulah, rejoicing
in Unity
In the Four Senses, in the Outline, the Circumference &
Form, for ever
In the Forgiveness of Sins which is Self Annihilation; it
is the Covenant of Jehovah.[20]

Blake's fourfold image of Man is a God image, or at least it
cannot be distinguished from one. It is an expression of what
Blake saw to be the divine aspect of every human being, which
carries the creative spark. That such an image is essential to the
individual whose goal it is to penetrate and elucidate the
mysteries of the unknown was also known to the early Christian
spirit. Otherwise, as Jung has pointed out, Clement of·Alex-
andria would never have said that he who knows himself knows
God.[21] The unmistakable implication for modern psychology is
that a complete concept of man cannot properly be reduced to
its physical components—but that it must be expanded to include all that is perceived or experienced from whatever source.

5
Sources of Creative Energy

MARRIAGE IS A SYMBOL OF A UNION BETWEEN TWO SEPARATE and distinct entities—a primary purpose of which is to conceive and bring into being the third, an essence individual in itself yet constituted of the characteristics of the first and the second out of which it came. The marriage between a man and a woman—and the bearing of children—is the acting out in a personal and immediate way the fundamental drama of the spheres, the first expression of which was seen in the cosmogonic myths of ancient and primitive peoples. In these myths there was invariably a great "all" or "chaos" or "nothingness" which existed in its oneness until, through some act or desire or thought, a breaking apart took place. Then there were two: sky and earth, light and darkness, male and female, active protagonist god and shadow counterpart—uncountable variations of the representations of duality.

Jolande Jacobi, a Jungian analyst, has written that mythology, as a living reflection of world creation, is the symbolic form, the "primordial guise," assumed by archetypes in the process of becoming manifest. Since the basic forms of the archetypes are common to all nations and times, it is hardly surprising to find parallels in myths that have arisen independently in many places. There is a kinship between the great traditional mythologies with their mythologems and the archetypes with their symbols.[1] Archetypal images appear in condensed forms in the dreams and fantasies of the individual, and constitute a man's personal myth.

Individual man begins his life unconscious in the intra-uterine state, a microcosm in which are present all knowledge and all possibilities in an amorphous and undifferentiated wholeness. Very early in the psychic life of the individual, discrimination begins to take place. Every psychological phenomenon is based on the existence of opposites within a single entity. This principle underlies every discrimination: ego from environment, inner reality from outer reality, and all the rest. A breaking apart precedes every conscious development—that is to say, before an unconscious content crosses the threshold of consciousness it tends to split into its two polar opposites. We see this in dream motifs with their subjective and objective significance, and in reality with its everpresent demand for judgment or evaluation.

This is the briefest possible introduction to Jung's theory of the development of consciousness. He explored the workings of the processes of growth and transformation in as many areas as his insatiably curious mind would lead him. His deepest concern was to penetrate the workings of his own personal psychology. The reason for this was his conviction that unless a psychiatrist understood the part his subjective experience played in his observations, he could not be confident of the validity of what he was seeing in his patients. So, in considering the sources of his own attitudes, he looked to his personal biographical material and beyond—into a conglomerate mass of human experiences. Those which he could call up easily into consciousness were only the smallest part, the visible tip of the iceberg. There were also those subtle impressions which had been transmitted to him first by his mother in her glance, her special way of nurturing, her training and guidance, her angers and her habits of control. Superimposed upon these were the effects of experiences with his father, in his role of rival for his mother's affection as paterfamilias, as clergyman, as educational and social arbiter and as expositor of the moral conventions of his small Swiss canton. The values of Jung's school friends, his fury against a teacher who accused him of cheating in the preparation of a paper, the hallucinations of patients with whom he worked as a young psychiatric student—all became part of his experience. These people with whom he was in contact were all, potentially at least, as complex in their psychic structure as he, inheriting their ways, their mores, their attitudes from their own ancestors. So the circle increased in everwidening progressions as he moved out from the center of his consciousness to consider the teeming mass of human experience to which each man is heir.

Jung began to understand that it was not "his" unconscious alone with which he needed to be concerned. It was, rather, "the" unconscious—an infinitely large and active collection of happenings and reactions to them which affected his life and thought. These collective happenings stretched outward into space so that not only Switzerland was involved, but also all the world. To gain a direct and personal insight into the psychological processes common to all mankind and their infinite modes of expression in the vast variety of cultures and nations and races, Jung traveled widely. Nor did the contemporary age alone account for the aggregate of collective events which interested him. Jung studied the religions of antiquity both in the Western world and in the East. He was absorbed also in research on historical patterns in early Christendom, certain of which had expressions in Gnosticism, in alchemy and in astrology. He sought out lands in which man continued to live much as he had in primitive times.

In Mombasa, an island off Kenya, Jung wrote: "When the first ray of sunlight announced the onset of day, I awoke. The train swathed in a red cloud of dust was just making a turn around a steep red cliff. On a jagged rock above us a slim, brownish-black figure stood motionless, leaning on a long spear, looking down at the train. Beside him towered a giant labrum cactus. I was enchanted by this sight—it was a picture of something utterly alien and outside my experience, but on the other hand I had a most intense *sentiment du déjà vu*. I had the feeling that I had already experienced this moment and had always known this world which was separated from me only by a distance in time. It was as if I were this moment returning to the land of my youth, and as if I knew that dark-skinned man who had been waiting for me for five thousand years." [2]

On a trip to America he visited the Pueblo Indians and listened to a chief of the Taos Pueblos complaining about how the Americans want to stamp out his people's religion. "Why can they not let us alone?" he said. "What we do we do not only for ourselves, but for the Americans also. Yes, we do it for the whole world. Everyone benefits by it." Jung observed from the chief's excitement that he was alluding to some extremely important element of his religion. He therefore asked him: "You think, then, that what you do in your religion benefits the whole world?" The chief replied with great animation, "Of course. If we did not do it, what would become of the world?" And then, with a significant gesture, he pointed to the sun, awakening in Jung the feeling that they were approaching extremely delicate ground verging on the tribal mysteries. "After all," said the chief, "we are a people who live on the roof of the world; we are the sons of Father Sun, and with our religion we daily help our father to go across the sky. We do this not only for ourselves, but for the whole world. If we were to cease practicing our religion, the sun would no longer rise. Then it would be night forever." Jung then realized on what the dignity, the composure of the individual Indian was founded. It sprang from his being a son of the sun; his life cosmologically meaningful. And he reflected that out of sheer envy we are obliged to smile at the Indian's naiveté and to plume ourselves on our cleverness; for otherwise we should discover how down at the heels we are. "Knowledge," says Jung, "does not enrich us; it removes us more and more from the mythic world in which we were once at home by right of birth." He suggests that we should, for a moment, put away all modern rationalism and transport ourselves into the clear mountain air of that solitary plateau; and we should also set aside our intimate knowledge of the world and exchange it for a horizon that seems immeasurable, and an ignorance of what lies beyond it, and then we will begin to achieve an inner comprehension of the Pueblo Indian's point of view. "All life comes from the mountain" is immediately convincing to him, and he is equally certain that he lives upon the roof of an immeasurable world, closest to God. He above all others has the Divinity's ear, and his ritual act will reach the distant sun soonest of all. The holiness of mountains, the revelation of Yahweh on Sinai, the inspiration that Nietzsche was granted in the Engadine—all speak the same language. The idea, absurd to us, that a ritual act can magically affect the sun is, upon closer examination, no less irrational but far more familiar to us than might be at first assumed. The Judeo-Christian religion, like every other, is permeated by the idea that special acts can influence God, for example through certain rites or by prayer, or by a morality pleasing to the Divinity.[3]

The essential unity of mankind through the common participation in a collective unconscious is perceived not only by the depth psychologist. Biologist, paleontologist and philosopher Pierre Teilhard de Chardin found it of utmost importance in his scientific studies:

I repeat this same thing like a refrain on every rung of the ladder that leads to man; for, if this thing is forgotten, nothing can be understood. To see life properly we must never lose sight of the unity of the biosphere that lies beyond the plurality and essential rivalry of individual beings. This unity was still diffuse in the early stages—a unity in origin, framework and dispersed impetus rather than in ordered groupings; yet a unity which, together with life's ascent, was to grow ever sharper in outline, to fold in upon itself, and, finally, to center itself under our eyes.[4]

Jung and Teilhard, trained in objective observation and meticulous analysis and recording, are able to note and communicate the basic patterns of human experience. They make the necessary connections between what appears to be the inner adventure of a single man and the history of mankind. They do it in a conscious way, seeking insight into the nature of man and his capacity to grow, to develop and to transform himself over and over again. Both men are aware of the limitations of the conscious mind when it is closed and both perceived that what lies beyond is limitless. How then can man reach into that other realm, where all the secrets lie waiting to be discovered? The myths are all there, explaining the same mysteries, but in many tongues to suit the mystic and the scientist, the historian and the artist. We can read about them in the works of the commentators of our day and of their predecessors. But reading about them is resurrecting the past and participating in it vicariously; it is a long way from *immediate experience*.

Blake's *Marriage of Heaven and Hell* is *immediate experience*. He engraved with his own hand the words we read and the pictures and embellishments. Is he speaking metaphorically when he begins a Memorable Fancy with such words as these: "Once I saw a Devil in a flame of fire, who arose before an Angel that sat on a cloud, and the Devil uttered these words:"? Is this a literary device? Or is his writing really something that came to consciousness through his inner ear from that inner world of the unconscious? The words were not there in consciousness before Blake "heard" them. Out of nothing, nothing comes. If they were not there, then where were they? Where every idea, every potential, every innate but unrealized capacity is, before it is present and functioning—beyond the threshold of consciousness. This is the meaning of the vast underground storehouse filled with more riches than could ever be sold or spent in the story of Alladin and a thousand like it.

Metaphors, stories, myths, and pictures are all ways of expressing the inexpressible reality of the unconscious. Communication requires a device. To Blake the device was a copper plate. It was the symbol of the threshold between his consciousness and the mystery. He held it in his hand and wrote upon it, "If the doors of perception were cleansed every thing would appear to man as it is, infinite." His etching complete, he placed the plate in the acid, and the message was transferred to paper. In time it is read, and the reader may also look through the doors of perception.

He may react with his own kind of emotion; he may shudder in fear or laugh in mockery, or he may try to imagine what Blake's emotion was as he hung over the immensity of the "void boundless as a nether sky," held only by the roots of trees. Here Blake is not reliving any early traumatic experience. There is nothing exclusively personal about this, or any others of his visions in *The Marriage*. It is not only his own doors of perception that he is cleansing, but also ours, if we will let him. As

Blake was able to look straight into the face of darkness and see its shapes emerge, so is the source of creative activity accessible to any person who will accept equally the beauty and terror and the ugliness of the collective unconscious.

From time to time the question has been raised, "Was Blake mad?" Is it madness to be involved with the collective unconscious to the degree that there appears to be little if any differentiation between subjective reality and the kind of reality with which we expect to meet and deal in our everyday waking lives? For, if Blake's output seems the work of a madman then we have to ask whether a certain amount of madness may not be necessary to support a heroic creative effort. The common opinion held by many writers and artists that it would be destructive to their talent were they to receive analytic treatment for their "neurotic problems" seems to substantiate this view. Most agree that tension is necessary and that it must build up nearly to the breaking point. "Psychic energizers" are used. Long late hours are spent completing a project. Pressures, self-inflicted often, help by lowering the resistance to the barrier between consciousness and unconscious. This may make it possible to probe beneath the surface of the unconscious to bring back useful material that was once known and now must be recalled and synthesized for the purpose at hand. This may seem neurotic, perhaps, but madness is something different.

In neurosis, according to Jung, a loss of psychological equilibrium may be brought about by a conflict between some attitudes acceptable to conscious thinking and some others which are not acceptable and so are repressed into the unconscious. There, the issue acts as a magnet, drawing toward itself a complex of feelings and emotions which consume energy simply through the task of remaining hidden from view. The barrier is dropped down between consciousness and the unconscious, and the victim may be to a greater or lesser degree immobilized, like the Dutch boy who held his finger in the hole in the dike, or the bored office worker who finds it nearly impossible to drag herself out of bed in the morning even after a sufficient amount of sleep. Both the Dutch boy and the office worker somehow manage. They are not at peace and they do not accomplish as much as they might, but neither are they overwhelmed by psychoneurotic symptoms such as obsessions, hysterical paralysis or phobic reactions. Others put to work the tensions generated by the neurotic conflict, and of this we shall have more to say presently.

The madman or psychotic tends also to become caught in conflicts, but he is unable to deal with them in conscious, rational ways—for whatever reason. The cause may be psychologically, physiologically or sociologically determined—this is not the issue here. We are concerned only with the "psychological effect." He does not have a problem, a problem has him. He has been overwhelmed by the immensity of the unconscious objection to his conscious way of living, the way he "wills" to live. His ego seems like a helmsman who has lost the wheel of the ship in a storm at sea. The waves wash over the deck and he is pitched first to the port side and then to the starboard. He feels, he senses, his perception is keen, but he does not see the pattern of the moving force, he cannot relate constructively to it. Reality is no longer tested; it is avoided. A more tenable "reality" is constructed, with systems of thought that may be based upon the raw effluences from the unconscious.

When Gilchrist wrote his biography of Blake, he was faced with finding some explanation for the non-conforming behavior described by Blake's associates as typical of the man. One source of the estimate of Blake as less than sane is traceable to the "wild and hurling words" [5] he would utter in conversation, especially when provoked. In society people would make clear their disbelief of him, and this would exasperate him. They would stir him up into being extravagant, and out of a mere spirit of opposition, he would say things on purpose to startle, to make people stare. In the excitement of conversation, Gilchrist goes on to relate, Blake would exaggerate his peculiarities of opinion and doctrine, or he would express a floating fantasy in the most matter-of-fact way without the qualification he knew full well it needed, taking a secret pleasure in the surprise and opposition his views would arouse.

The visions were so familiar to Blake that he talked about them as though they were corporeal facts, as we have seen in the Memorable Fancies. "Milton the other day was saying to me . . . I tried to convince him that he was wrong, but could not." Gilchrist relates that at one party Blake was talking to a little group gathered around him, within hearing of a lady whose children has just come home from boarding school for the holidays. "The other evening," said Blake in his usual quiet way, "taking a walk, I came to a meadow, and at the farther corner of it I saw a fold of lambs. Coming nearer, the ground blushed with flowers, the wattled cote and its woolly tenants were of an exquisite pastoral beauty. But I looked again and it proved to be no living flock, but beautiful sculpture." The lady thinking this to be a good bit of entertainment for her children, interjected, "I beg pardon, Mr. Blake but *may* I ask *where* you saw this?" "Here, Madam," answered Blake, touching his forehead.[6]

Gilchrist asserts that the reply indicates the point of view from which Blake regarded his own visions. He says it was by no means the mad view that ignorant men have taken. Blake would candidly confess that his visions were not literal matters of fact, but phenomena seen by his imagination: *realities* nonetheless for that, but transacted within the realm of the mind. He makes a distinction which widely separates such visions from hallucinations of madness, and indicates that Blake's aberrant habits of talk and of writing which startled outsiders was the fruit of an excessive culture of the imagination combined with daring license of expressions.

The suggestion, made earlier, that Blake was in close contact with the collective unconscious and had an ongoing dialogue with its figures, seems to be borne out in the comments of William Hazlitt, one of the earliest Blake scholars, preceding even Gilchrist and quoted by him: ". . . Blake was, in spirit, a denizen of other and earlier ages of the world than the present mechanical one to which chance had so rudely transplanted him. It is within the last century or so, that the heavens have gone further off. The supernatural world has during that period removed itself further from civilized, cultivated humanity than it ever was before—in all time, heathen or Christian. There is, at this moment, infinitely less practical belief in an invisible world, or even apprehension of it, than at any previous historical era. . . . It is *only* within the last century and a half, the faculty of seeing visions could have been one to bring a man's sanity into question. Ever before, by simple believing Romanist, by reverent awe-struck pagan, or in the fervent East, the exceptional power had been accepted as a matter of course in gifted men, and had been turned to serious account in the cause of religion." [7]

Is there a difference in the vision which is seen by the devout Christian saint and the hallucination of the schizophrenic? Why beatification for the one and confinement in jail for the other? The Catholic church accepts the doctrine of the bodily assumption of the Virgin into heaven. I saw a young girl patient in a psychiatric hospital stop before a holy picture and listen attentively as the Virgin "spoke" to her. In churches and synagogues every day of every year, sane people in complete sincerity articulate ideas and direct messages to Mary, to the saints, to Jesus, to Yahweh, to God. What is the difference?

It seems to me that we must regard all visions, whether those of the insane or those of the highly imaginative and creative person as being made of the same arcane stuff. They are a sudden flooding of consciousness with heretofore unconscious material. Dreams, also, fall into this description and have the same components, especially where they are apparently unrelated to the life or current activity of the dreamer. The differentiating factor is the conscious ego, which stands at the threshold of consciousness and judges the material which comes by, forms an opinion about it, and makes a decision as to what is to be thought about it or done about it. How the visionary perception is dealt with is determined by the state of psychological equilibrium in the perceiver. Thus, if one "hears voices" and replies to them in the hearing of his friends, he may be thought at the very least to be eccentric. If the "voices" command him to do something heinous, to commit a crime of passion, for example, and he obeys, he will be incarcerated. But which of us has never had an impulse which directed him to lust or to murder? In the quiet of a lonely night such a person might verbally confront the impulse and speak to it in an agony of trying to muster control, or he might recite the old formula: "Get thee behind me Satan." But he would probably be somewhat circumspect in reporting the incident at the breakfast table.

It is quite clear that Blake had his visions, and that he was able to express them without being unduly controlled by them. The very process of engraving each single word on the copper plate acted as a mediating influence, bringing the affect engendered by the experience under the conscious control of the ego. The emotion experienced, however, was not repressed. It was preserved in the magnificently articulated words with which Blake expressed the visions. This is a typical procedure of the creative genius. Blake wrote, "One thought fills immensity." Rene Magritte, in his technically perfect manner, painted a small room in accurate perspective in which there was a rose of a size so great as to be just barely contained between the floor and the ceiling and the walls on either side and in the rear. The vision is the same. Each man expressed it according to his skill, and there it was, objectified. Reader or viewer could ponder its significance. The creative person could then go on to writing the next line of prose or painting another picture. But a monomaniac would have been held spellbound by the idea, repeating it over and over again without anything ever coming of it.

If the charge against Blake of being an emotionally unbalanced person has been recognized as having been based on a wrong premise, there is still another allegation relating to the visionary experiences of Blake that is not so easily dismissed. Blake has been understood by many scholars as being a mystic, and the religious element in his prophetic work is cited as evidence for this conclusion. To evaluate this possibility we ought to consider what mysticism really is, and whether it brings about the kind of creative productivity that accounts for the fantastic scenes and events related by Blake. Mark Schorer in his book *William Blake—The Politics of Vision* asserts that mysticism is active, only secondarily speculative.[8] If we accept his contention that mysticism is basically a technique, and its attempts to formulate even casual reports of what it has discovered are incidental to the act of discovery, then we can hardly say that the man who makes writing or painting his career can be properly considered a mystic. The technique of the mystic is primarily a technique of meditation. The meditation may have as its *effect* a contribution to philosophical thought, but the mystic does not engage in the process for the *purpose* of producing a philosophical doctrine. His basic impulse is to establish relations with a supernatural reality that is not accessible to reason or to sense, but to what he calls "love." This requires a rudimentary theory of knowledge. The fact that "love" works not in any diffusive way but through a strictly concentrated discipline that is intended to release the mystic from all natural claims implies a sharp dualism. The dichotomy between supernatural and natural is unassailable—these two can never be joined, for by definition they involve the sphere of nature and another sphere above or beyond which does not touch the natural one.

With reason and unreason it is quite different, for both are propensities of man, and there is valid ground for arguing about which is which. What appears to be indicated by the dicta of reason to one man may seem irrational to another. Reason is only one way of approaching a problem—it is the way of thinking, of attempting to find meaning in it. Reason may also enter into another approach to a problem, the feeling-into or the judgmental approach, which is less a logical than an evaluative way of dealing with it. The same problem may be seen as being dependent for solution upon perceptions obtained through the senses. Sensation is simply accepting data as it is perceived in the objective world. The reasoning function need not be present here. Nor is reasoning a part of the intuitive approach to the problem, for when the synthesis of perceptions has already taken place in the unconscious the intuitive hunch emerges fullblown and does not need to be reasoned out. So the four functions, which Jung elucidates at length in *Psychological Types,* include elements of the rational and the irrational, and all four operate in varying degrees of intensity within each individual. Thus reason is far from incompatible with the irrational—they exist side by side. Similarly, observes Schorer, religion and poetry exist if not to protest against reason and science, then at least to supplement them.[9]

Blake's paradoxical situations in which reason and unreason as personified by Angel and Devil are able to meet and discourse about their differences seem to be at odds with what has been described as the dualistic attitude of the mystic. Angel and

Devil are not above and below, they are differing aspects of the same thing. They struggle together as equals within natural man, each hoping to convince the other of the rightness of his point of view. They meet symbolically in fire, and then the Angel is able to become a Devil. In the mystic, the tensions are not seen so much within nature, but as existing between the supernatural reality and nature. In order to move in the direction of the longed-for union with the Other, the mystic takes his stand against the mundane pleasures. He must express "love" in a double discipline, one physical, the other mental—first through a renunciation of the expression of the warm, human sexual feelings and second through ascetic practices and contemplation of the Divine. Renunciation, seen psychologically, is repression of the spontaneous thoughts and impulses that arise in man. It inhibits the free flow of source material which can give impetus to creative work. Limitation of expression is necessary for the mystic, whose eternal goal is fixed. But for the man who is searching for a system of his own, and who refuses "to be enslaved by any man's," the need is to preserve whatever primitive emotions and responses may exist, and to channel them through the process of transformation into art.

The parallel for these differing points of view can be seen in the two trends existing within the Church in the early Christian centuries. There were the devout followers of the dogma with all its strictures for personal sacrifice and submission to the will of a supernatural force, and there were also the alchemists. We must realize that some of these were spiritual alchemists who did not intend the transmutation of metals alone, or even at all, but the transmutation of man's material consciousness to spiritual consciousness, his lower to his higher self. The central tenet of alchemy—that all things possess a hidden quality opposite to their particular apparent quality, which fire can reveal—has a strong apocalyptic flavor.[10] The fire brings out the mystery; it is the catalytic force, and through it all things change in form, although in essence they remain the same.

The visionary experience, which belongs neither to madness nor to mystical communion with the supernatural, seems to be a necessary ingredient of the creative process. For creativity is more than rearrangement or synthesis of what is already known.

It depends upon a revelation of that which is not yet known, but which exists beyond consciousness. The creative impulse, which is an urge in man to come into a productive relationship with this Other, is much more common in man than is its adequate expression.

Whenever man confronts the mysterious Other, he undergoes an experience of the collective unconscious. This is always dangerous and potentially destructive. It is for this reason that the fine line between genius and insanity has often been remarked. The difference seems to be in the strength of the ego and its ability to maintain its sense of cohesiveness and continuity in the face of powerful forces which do not belong to the ego sphere. That a man be open to a confrontation between ego and unconscious is a necessary element for psychic growth and the expansion of consciousness. It is of greatest importance, however, for the ego to exercise controls in dealing with unconscious material. If too much becomes ·suddenly available the ego is unable to absorb it, and then there is the possibility of consciousness being overwhelmed. At such times the individual has the feeling that it is impossible to cope with his experience. On the other hand, the suffusion of unconscious material gradually into consciousness makes for its assimilation into a wider view and a fuller appreciation of the dimensions of experience. This then can be translated into philosophy or art.

The current widespread interest in and use of the psychedelic drugs is a manifestation of the desire to see the natural world in a new and more meaningful way. Often these drugs are used as a shortcut to the unconscious, and without adequate preparation on the part of the user. While sensual impressions are intensified so that reality is distorted beyond recognition, the way is open for archetypal images to appear in all their frightful shapes. The effect of the drug may be to diminish the capacity for judgment, and accidents may then occur, or panic set in. This is, of course, a possibility in any encounter with the unconscious, but the risk is increased when the position of the ego vis-à-vis the unconscious is deliberately weakened.

The creative act, the concentration upon the production of something of value which can be communicated to other people, requires entrée to the unconscious; it also requires ego participation. The fear of being taken over by the unconscious may be countered by the act of objectification. Blake performed this by writing down what he heard and drawing pictures of what he saw. The visions then became manageable creations of his own mind. He never became completely overwhelmed by the terrors of the unconscious, although he was certainly endangered at times. Before he leaned over to look into the Abyss, he made sure that his foot was securely fixed in the root of an oak. The oak may be interpreted as the standpoint of the observing ego, supporting the visionary experience which is brought about by the concentration of "The Mental Traveller." Blake retained his perspective of the material world while also participating in the experience of the inner vision. With a steady hand, he was able to commit what he saw to the copper plate, so that it could be communicated in all its rich tracery and vibrant design. It is only by setting the inner world against the world of substance that visions can come into a fruitful relationship with values. If either one is forsaken for the other, the inevitable result will be sterility.

6
The Symbol

———————————

THE MULTITUDE OF VARIED SYMBOLS WHICH BLAKE EMPLOYS throughout his work are, for him, the sources of his creative activity. They span the hiatus between the known and the unknown—the small center of consciousness presided over by the ego and the all-embracing Other. The transcendent function of the symbol has a deep significance not alone for Blake, but for all who permit themselves to follow in the directions where it leads. According to the interest and capacity of the individual, much or little may be transmitted through the symbol. The space on the farther side is limitless: it contains the chaos out of which our world was created—and it contains the chaos out of which each man must fashion his own creation.

That the symbol is the foundation of all art should be self evident. It is not the representation of what we already know in a painting or a poem or the nobly arching vault of a Gothic cathedral which makes the heart sing with praise or the brain faint with wonder. It is the evocative nature of the symbol embedded in the art form that transports the viewer beyond himself—into sacred rites he has never experienced, the beauty of landscapes he has never seen, and the vivid emotions of ancestors whose names are forever lost but whose patterns of thought and feeling and expression are as integral a part of man's heritage as the blood in his veins.

The symbol is the slender filament which reaches from our world to the Infinite. Only the man who can lay hold of the symbol and make it part of his being, standing the tension of the opposites in his own soul, can participate in the creative process.

Notes to the Text

All references to the works of William Blake, unless otherwise stated, are from *The Complete Writings of William Blake, with all the variant readings,* edited by Geoffrey Keynes, the Nonesuch Press edition, 1957, and will be designated in the footnotes by the letter *K,* followed by the page number.

References to the works of C. G. Jung, unless otherwise indicated, are from the *Collected Works,* Bollingen Series XX, Princeton University Press, and will be designated (CW), followed by paragraph numbers.

I INTRODUCTION

1. Herbert Jenkins, *William Blake: Studies of His Life and Personality,* p. 86.
2. Alexander Gilchrist, *The Life of William Blake,* Vol. I, p. 2.
3. *The Marriage of Heaven and Hell, K,* p. 154.
4. G. E. Bentley Jr., and Martin K. Nurmi, *A Blake Bibliography,* p. 13.
5. H. H. Gilchrist, ed., *Anne Gilchrist: Her Life and Writings,* p. 258.
6. *Songs of Innocence, K,* p. 214.
7. Sigmund Freud, *A General Introduction to Psychoanalysis,* p. 228.

II THE FIRST HALF OF LIFE

1. *Gates of Paradise, K,* p. 760.
2. A. Gilchrist, p. 6.
3. *Ibid.*
4. *Jerusalem, K,* p. 730.
5. *Poetical Sketches, K,* p. 3.
6. *Op. cit.,* p. 11.
7. *Op. cit.,* p. 6.
8. *Op. cit.,* pp. 9-10.
9. *Songs of Innocence, K,* p. 120.
10. A. Gilchrist, p. 59.
11. *Ibid.*
12. *Songs of Innocence, K,* p. 120.
13. Harold Bloom, *Blake's Apocalypse, A Study in Poetic Argument,* p. 17.
14. S. Foster Damon, *A Blake Dictionary,* pp. 100-101.
15. *There Is No Natural Religion, K,* p. 97.
16. Bloom, p. 16.
17. Damon, *Dictionary,* p. 101.
18. Max Plowman, *Introduction to the Study of Blake,* p. 127.
19. *To John Flaxman,* 12, Sept. 1800; *K,* p. 799.
20. Damon, *Dictionary,* p. 39.
21. *The French Revolution, K,* pp. 135-136.
22. *Ibid.*
23. *Op. cit.,* pp. 140-141.
24. Mona Wilson, *The Life of William Blake,* pp. 55-56.
25. A. Gilchrist, p. 258.
26. *Poetical Sketches, K,* pp. 10-11.
27. Northrop Frye, *Fearful Symmetry,* p. 201.
28. Jolande Jacobi, *Complex / Archetype / Symbol in the Psychology of C. G. Jung,* p. 78, quoting F. Creuzer, *Symbolik und Mythologie der alten Völker,* I, 1810, pp. 63, 64.
29. *The Book of Urizen, K,* p. 222.

III THE MARRIAGE OF HEAVEN AND HELL
The Twenty-four Plates

1. Blake, *A Collection of Critical Essays,* ed. Northrop Frye.
2. In "Physica Trismegisti," pp. 405-437, an alchemical treatise quoted in Jung, *Psychology and Alchemy* (CW), par. 377.

3. In Khunrath, *Von hylealischen, das ist, pri-materialischen, catholischen, oder algemeinem natürlichen Chaos* (Magdeburg, 1597), quoted in Jung, *Psychology and Alchemy* (CW), par. 422, note 48.

4. Anthony Blunt, *The Art of William Blake*, p. 45.

5. These experiments are recorded by Hayter in *New Ways of Gravure*, London, 1949, pp. 85ff., and by Todd in *Print Collectors Quarterly*, XXIX, 1948, pp. 25ff.

6. A. Gilchrist, pp. 69-70.

7. A. Gilchrist, p. 88.

PLATE 1
The Marriage of Heaven and Hell

1. C. G. Jung, "Concerning Mandala Symbolism" in *Archetypes and the Collective Unconscious* (CW), par. 633.

2. *Ibid.*

PLATE 2
The Argument

1. Bloom, p. 73.

2. *The Four Zoas, K,* p. 273.

3. Bloom, *loc. cit.*

4. Algernon Charles Swinburne, *William Blake,* p. 206.

5. Damon, *William Blake: His Philosophy and Symbols,* p. 90.

6. Thomas Wright, *The Life of William Blake,* p. 39.

7. Emily Hamblen, *On the Minor Prophecies of William Blake,* p. 162.

PLATE 3

1. Mark Schorer, *William Blake: The Politics of Vision,* p. 216.

2. Jung, *Structure and Dynamics of the Psyche* (CW), par. 749ff.

3. *Ibid.*

4. Damon, *William Blake: His Philosophy and Symbols,* p. 316, quoting Emanuel Swedenborg, *Last Judgment,* 45.

5. Swinburne, p. 211.

6. Alan W. Watts, *The Two Hands of God,* pp. 49-50.

7. Swinburne, *loc. cit.*

8. Damon, *Dictionary,* pp. 40-41.

9. *Ibid.*

10. *Ibid.*

PLATE 4
The Voice of the Devil

1. The definition of *enantiodromia* is taken from Erich Neumann, *The Archetypal World of Henry Moore*, p. 4.
2. Damon, *Dictionary*, p. 11.
3. Damon, *William Blake: His Philosophy and Symbols*, p. 317.
4. From notes taken at a lecture on C. G. Jung's *Aion* (CW), delivered by Miss Barbara Hannah at the C. G. Jung Institute, Zurich, Apr. 24, 1963.

PLATES 5-6

1. Bloom, pp. 80-81.
2. Percy B. Shelley, *Poetry and Prose*, p. 147.
3. Bloom, *loc. cit.*
4. Jung, "The Relations between the Ego and the Unconscious," in *Two Essays*, par. 254.
5. Jung, "Foreword to Werblowsky's 'Lucifer and Prometheus,'" in *Psychology and Religion: West and East* (CW), par. 470.

PLATES 6-7
A Memorable Fancy

1. In Jung, *Structure and Dynamics of the Psyche* (CW).
2. Jung, *op. cit.*, pars. 183-85.
3. This title is an obvious reference to Swedenborg, who called his visions "Memorable Relations."
4. Edith Hamilton, *Mythology*, p. 35.
5. Jung, *Symbols of Transformation* (CW), par. 237.
6. Revised Standard Version.
7. Jung, *op. cit.*, par. 245.
8. *Milton, K*, p. 495.
9. Wright, *The Life of William Blake*, Preface, pp. xii-xiii.
10. Jacob Boehme, *The Confessions*, pp. 1-2.
11. Watts, *op. cit.*, pp. 81-82.

PLATES 7-10.
Proverbs of Hell

1. Jung, *Psychology and Religion: West and East* (CW), par. 100.
2. *Ibid.*
3. Jung, *Psychology and Religion: West and East* (CW), par. 103.

quoting Koepgen, *Die Gnosis des Christentums*, pp. 185, 189-190.

4. Jung, *op. cit.*, par. 103.
5. *Op. cit.*, pars. 106-07.
6. Jung, *Archetypes and the Collective Unconscious* (CW), par. 42.
7. *Op. cit.*, par. 685.
8. Jung, *Psychology and Alchemy* (CW), par 498.
9. Lion symbolism from notes on a lecture delivered by Dr. M.-L. von Franz, Apr. 30, 1963, in her series on "The Individuation Process in Fairy Tales," Jung Institute, Zurich.
10. Jung, *Psychology and Alchemy* (CW), par. 220, quoting *Rosarium philosophorum*, an alchemical text.
11. *Psychology and Alchemy* (CW), par. 433.
12. Hamilton, p. 36.
13. Neumann, *Amor and Psyche*, p. 103.
14. *Op. cit.*, p. 46.
15. *Visions of the Daughters of Albion, K*, pp. 190-191.
16. A. Gilchrist, p. 53.
17. *Jonah* 1:4. King James Version.
18. *Jonah* 1:11-12.
19. "The Hound of Heaven," in *Victorian and Later English Poets*, ed. Stephens, Beck and Snow, p. 1073.
20. Hamilton, p. 162.
21. Brehmes, *Tierleben*, p. 413.
22. Neumann, *Amor and Psyche*, p. 104.
23. *Ibid.*
24. Jung, *Psychological Types*, p. 472.
25. *The Letters, K*, p. 793.
26. *Gates of Paradise, K*, p. 760.
27. Damon, *William Blake: His Philosophy and Symbols*, p. 321.

PLATE 11

1. Hamblen, p. 167.
2. Jung, *Psychology and Religion* (CW), par. 140.
3. Paul Radin, *Primitive Religion*, pp. 21ff.
4. *Op. cit.*, p. 171.
5. For a fuller discussion of this problem from a psychological point of view, see John Layard's article, "The Incest Taboo and the Virgin Archetype," in *Eranos Yearbook*, V. XII, pp. 253ff.

6. W. P. Witcutt, *Blake, A Psychological Study*, p. 115.

7. Margaret Rudd, *Organiz'd Innocence*, pp. 21-22.

8. Jung, *Archetypes and the Collective Unconscious* (CW), par. 8.

PLATES 12-13
A Memorable Fancy

1. Irene Langridge, *William Blake: A Study of his Life and Art*, p. 101.

2. *Annotations to Bacon, K*, p. 399.

3. *Annotations to Watson's Apology for the Bible, K*, p. 392.

4. *Annotations to Lavater, K*, p. 77.

5. Hamblen, p. 168.

6. Jung, *Mysterium Coniunctionis* (CW), par. 697.

7. *Ibid.*

8. *Isaiah* 20:2-4, King James Version.

9. *Ezekiel* 4:4-6, King James Version.

10. Jung, *Mysterium Coniunctionis* (CW), par. 705.

11. *Ibid.*

12. *Ibid.*

PLATES 14-15

1. Damon, *William Blake: His Philosophy and Symbols*, p. 327.

2. *Tiriel, K*, p. 36.

3. *The French Revolution, K*, pp. 140, 142.

4. *The Marriage of Heaven and Hell, K*, p. 149.

5. Damon, *William Blake: His Philosophy and Symbols*, p. 323.

6. *Exodus* 20:11.

7. *Genesis* 2:2-3.

8. *2 Peter* 3:8.

9. L. A. Duncan Johnstone, in his analysis, *A Psychological Study of William Blake*, p. 11, identifies Los as follows: "Los is the power symbolized by the loins. Los indicates the natural sun . . . he is the Logos, the Illumination of the mortal world which has fallen into darkness through the Fall. The Logos alone keeps alive the recollection of Man's eternal primal state."

10. *Milton, K*, p. 516.

11. Damon, *William Blake: His Philosophy and Symbols*, p. 323.

12. *Genesis* 3:22-24.

13. The cavern as symbol of the body as established by Plato in the

famous passage of his *Republic, Book VII:* "And now, I said, let me show in a figure how far our nature is enlightened or unenlightened. Behold! human beings living in an underground den, which has a mouth opening toward the light and reaching all along the den; here they have been from their childhood, and have their legs and necks chained so they cannot move, and can only see before them, being prevented by chains from turning round their heads." In *The Dialogues of Plato,* translated by Benjamin Jowett, p. 388.

14. Frye, *Fearful Symmetry,* pp. 199-200.
15. Frye, *op. cit.,* p. 200.
16. Jung, *Archetypes and the Collective Unconscious* (CW), par. 379.
17. Translated and retold by Edith Hamilton in *Mythology,* p. 269.
18. *Jerusalem, K,* p. 636.
19. Hamblen, p. 172.
20. Cf. Jung, "The Psychology of the Unconscious," in *Two Essays* (CW), par. 106.
21. *Ibid.*
22. *Ibid.*

PLATES 16-17

1. Quoted from Hesiod in Hamilton, p. 66.
2. Hamilton, p. 312.
3. *Genesis* 6:4.
4. *Jewish Encyclopedia,* V. 5, article on "Giants," pp. 657ff.
5. Neumann, *The Great Mother,* p. 18.
6. *Matthew* 25:35-36.
7. *Matthew* 25:41.
8. *Leonardo da Vinci* (ed. Reynal & Company), p. 60.

PLATES 17-20
A Memorable Fancy

1. Bloom, pp. 92-93.
2. *Ibid.*
3. *On Lavater, K,* p. 88.
4. *Songs of Innocence,* "A Dream," *K,* p. 111.
5. *Fragments from the Note-Book 1808–1811, K,* p. 541.
6. Notably Hamblen, pp. 72ff.

7. For a complete account of Blake's arraignment on charges of sedition, cf. J. Bronowski, *William Blake*, chapter 2, "The Sedition Writings," pp. 33-85, and A. Gilchrist, *The Life of William Blake*, chapter 19, "Trial for Sedition," pp. 166-175.

8. Warren and Martin, *New Groundwork of British History*, p. 716.

9. *America, K*, p. 203.

10. Bloom, p. 93.

11. Rudd, pp. 132-133.

12. *The Marriage of Heaven and Hell, K*, p. 154.

13. *Judges* 6:11ff.

14. Hamilton, p. 27.

15. *The Marriage of Heaven and Hell, K*, p. 155.

16. *Jerusalem, K*, p. 649.

17. Jung, *Psychology and Alchemy* (CW), par. 140.

18. *Op. cit.*, p. 95.

19. Jung, *Psychology and Religion: West and East* (CW), par. 597.

20. Damon, *Dictionary*, p. 239.

21. Hobbes, *Leviathan*, quoted in Damon, *Dictionary*, p. 239.

22. *Ibid.*

23. *Encyclopedia Britannica*, article on "Harps," V. 11, p. 213.

24. *World Book Encyclopedia*, article on "Harps," V. 8, p. 3283.

25. *Encyclopedia Britannica, loc cit.*

26. From notes on Dr. von Franz' lecture on "The Individuation Process in Fairy Tales," delivered at the Jung Institute, Zurich, June 25, 1963.

27. Cf. "Proverbs of Hell."

28. Damon, *William Blake: His Philosophy and Symbols*, p. 95.

29. Swinburne, *William Blake*, p. 251 (Bonchurch ed.).

30. Bloom, p. 95.

31. *On Watson, K*, p. 388.

32. March and Freeman, *The New World of Physics*, pp. 21ff.

33. Jacobi, *Complex / Archetype / Symbol in the Psychology of C. G. Jung*, p. 96.

PLATES 21-22

1. Damon, *William Blake: His Philosophy and Symbols*, p. 328.

2. *A Vision of the last Judgment, K*, p. 609.

3. *Poems from the Note-Book, 1793, K*, p. 176.

4. *Songs of Innocence, K,* p. 212.
5. Bloom, p. 96.
6. *Matthew* 5:17.
7. *I Kings,* 19:11-12.
8. *I Kings,* 18:38.
9. *II Kings,* 2:11-12.
10. Jung, *Psychological Types,* p. 605.
11. Jung's "Commentary" in Richard Wilhelm, *The Secret of the Golden Flower,* p. 96.
12. Jung, "The Soul and Death," in *Structure and Dynamics of the Psyche* (CW), par. 806.
13. *Tiriel, K,* pp. 109-110.
14. Bloom, p. 97.
15. *Ibid.*
16. *Op. cit.,* p. 98.
17. *Daniel* 4:24-25.

PLATES 25-27
A Song of Liberty

1. Plowman, *Introduction to the Study of Blake,* p. 136.
2. Hamblen, p. 178.
3. In the concluding plate of *The Marriage of Heaven and Hell.*
4. *Isaiah* 11:6.
5. *Isaiah* 11:7.
6. Jung, *Psychological Types,* p. 328.

IV THE UNHOLY BIBLE

The Later Prophetic Writings

1. *Auguries of Innocence, K,* p. 431.
2. Damon, *Dictionary,* p. 46.
3. *Op. cit.,* p. 142.
4. *The Four Zoas, K,* p. 263.
5. *To Flaxman, 12 Sept. 1800, K,* p. 799.
6. Arthur Symons, *William Blake,* p. 265.
7. Damon, *Dictionary,* p. 277.
8. *Jerusalem, K,* p. 716.
9. Jacobi, *The Psychology of C. G. Jung,* p. 92.

Visions of the Daughters of Albion

1. *Visions of the Daughters of Albion, K,* p. 189.
2. Damon, *Dictionary,* p. 237.
3. *The Marriage of Heaven and Hell, K,* p. 152.
4. *Visions of the Daughters of Albion, K,* p. 189.
5. *Op. cit.,* p. 190.
6. *Ibid.*
7. *Ibid.*
8. *The Marriage of Heaven and Hell, K,* p. 152.
9. *Visions of the Daughters of Albion, K,* p. 191.
10. *Ibid.*
11. *Ibid.*
12. *The Marriage of Heaven and Hell, K,* p. 158.
13. *Visions of the Daughters of Albion, K,* p. 192.
14. *A Song of Liberty, K,* p. 159.
15. *Visions of the Daughters of Albion, K,* p. 192.
16. *The Marriage of Heaven and Hell, K,* p. 153.
17. *Visions of the Daughters of Albion, K,* p. 193.
18. *Op. cit.,* p. 194.
19. *Op. cit.,* p. 195.
20. *The Marriage of Heaven and Hell, K,* p. 155.
21. John Middleton Murry, *Essay on Visions of the Daughters of Albion,* pp. 23-24.

The Book of Urizen

1. *Book of Urizen, K,* p. 222.
2. *Op. cit.,* p. 223.
3. *Ibid.*
4. *Op. cit.,* p. 224.
5. *Ibid.*
6. *Ibid.*
7. *Op. cit.,* p. 226.
8. *Op. cit.,* p. 229.
9. *Op. cit.,* p. 230.
10. *Ibid.*
11. *Op. cit.,* p. 231.
12. *Op. cit.,* pp. 231-232.

13. *Op. cit.*, pp. 232-233.
14. *Op. cit.*, p. 233.
15. *Ibid.*
16. *Op. cit.*, pp. 233-234.
17. Murry, *William Blake*, p. 134.
18. *Book of Urizen, K*, p. 235.
19. *Ibid.*

The Song of Los and the Book of Los

1. *Song of Los, K*, p. 245.
2. *Ibid.*
3. *Op. cit.*, p. 246.
4. *Ibid.*

Europe, A Prophecy

1. *Europe, K*, p. 239.
2. *Op. cit.*, p. 240.
3. *Ibid.*
4. *Ibid.*
5. *Op. cit.*, p. 242.
6. *Op. cit.*, p. 243.
7. *Op. cit.*, p. 245.

America, A Prophecy

1. *The Marriage of Heaven and Hell, K*, p. 149.
2. *America, K*, p. 198.
3. *Ibid.*
4. *Ibid.*
5. *Ibid.*
6. *Ibid.*
7. *The Marriage of Heaven and Hell, K*, p. 172.
8. *Visions of the Daughters of Albion, K*, p. 191.
9. *America, K*, p. 199.

The Four Zoas

1. *The Marriage of Heaven and Hell, K*, p. 162.
2. Murry, *William Blake*, p. 185.
3. *To Thomas Butts, 22 November, 1802, K*, p. 818.
4. Murry, *William Blake*, p. 193.

5. *Milton, K,* p. 518.
6. *Isaiah,* 62:4.
7. Murry, *William Blake,* p. 191.
8. *Revelations* 4:6.
9. *Ezekiel* 1:5ff.
10. *The Four Zoas, K,* p. 264.
11. Murry, *William Blake,* p. 195.
12. *The Four Zoas, K,* p. 264.
13. *Op cit.,* p. 265.
14. *Ibid.*
15. *Op. cit.,* p. 379.
16. *The Marriage of Heaven and Hell, K,* p. 151.
17. Murry, *William Blake,* p. 210.

Milton

1. Damon, *Dictionary,* pp. 274-275.
2. *Paradise Lost,* i:16.
3. Damon, *Dictionary,* p. 275.
4. *The Marriage of Heaven and Hell, K,* p. 150.
5. *Ibid.*
6. *Ibid.*
7. *Milton, K,* p. 485.
8. *Op. cit.,* p. 522.
9. *Op. cit.,* p. 485.
10. *Op. cit.,* p. 513.
11. *Op. cit.,* p. 481.
12. *Op. cit.,* p. 489.
13. *Op. cit.,* p. 492.
14. *Op. cit.,* p. 495.
15. *Op. cit.,* p. 499.
16. *Op. cit.,* p. 496.
17. Murry, *William Blake,* p. 215.
18. *Milton, K,* p. 502.
19. *Op. cit.,* p. 505.

Jerusalem

1. Murry, *William Blake,* pp. 255-256.
2. *Ibid.*
3. Frye, *Fearful Symmetry,* p. 355.

4. *Jerusalem, K*, p. 622.
5. *Ibid.*
6. Frye, *op. cit.*, p. 357.
7. *Jerusalem, K*, p. 622.
8. *Ibid.*
9. *Op. cit.*, p. 632.
10. *Ibid.*
11. *Op. cit.*, p. 639.
12. *The Marriage of Heaven and Hell, K*, p. 158.
13. *Ibid.*
14. *Jerusalem, K*, p. 693.
15. *Op. cit.*, p. 694.
16. *Op. cit.*, pp. 694-695.
17. *The Marriage of Heaven and Hell, K*, p. 158.
18. *Jerusalem, K*, p. 738.
19. By Harold Bloom, author of the book, *Blake's Apocalypse.*
20. *Jerusalem, K*, p. 745.
21. Jung, *Aion* (CW) par. 42.

V   sources of creative activity

1. Jacobi, *Complex / Archetype / Symbol in the Psychology of C. G. Jung*, p. 109.
2. Jung, *Memories, Dreams, Reflections*, p. 254.
3. *Op. cit.*, pp. 252-253.
4. Pierre Teilhard de Chardin, *The Phenomenon of Man*, p. 112.
5. A. Gilchrist, *Life of William Blake*, p. 327.
6. *Op. cit.*, p. 320.
7. *Op. cit.*, pp. 326-327.
8. Schorer, *William Blake, The Politics of Vision*, p. 44.
9. *Op. cit.*, p. 45.
10. *Op. cit.*, p. 48.

Bibliography

For the serious student of Blake, the following two books are indispensable:

Bentley, G. E. Jr., and Nurmi, Martin K. *A Blake Bibliography. Annotated Lists of Works, Studies, and Blakeana.* Minneapolis: University of Minnesota Press, 1964. The aim of this book is to list every reference to William Blake published between 1757 and 1863 and every criticism and edition of his works from the beginning to the present. Partly because of the deluge of scholarship in the last forty years, it includes perhaps twice as many titles as Sir Geoffrey Keynes's great bibliography of 1921.
S. Foster Damon. *A Blake Dictionary. The Ideas and Symbols of William Blake.* Providence, R.I.: Brown University Press, 1965. A momentous event in Blake scholarship, this *Dictionary* assembles, synthesizes, and interprets the clues to Blake's meaning that are scattered throughout the whole body of his work, literary and graphic.

A. GENERAL REFERENCES

The Holy Bible. King James Version. London: Oxford University Press.

Bryan's *Dictionary of Painters and Engravers,* Vol. I. London: George Bell & Sons, 1909.

Kunitz, Stanley J. and Haycraft, Howard. *British Authors of the 19th Century.* New York: H. W. Wilson Company, 1936.

Legouis, Emile and Cazamian, Louis. *A History of English Literature.* London: J. M. Dent and Sons Ltd., 1961.

Warner, George Townsend; Marten, Sir Henry K. and Muir, D. Erskine. *The New Groundwork of British History.* London and Glasgow: Blackie & Sons, Ltd., 1961.

Encyclopedia Britannica. Chicago, London, Toronto: Encyclopedia Britannica Ltd., 1960.

Jewish Encyclopedia. New York and London: Funk and Wagnalls Co., 1903.

World Book Encyclopedia. Chicago: Field Enterprises, Inc., 1953.

B. BOOKS

Adams, Hazard. *Blake and Yeats: The Contrary Vision.* Ithaca, N.Y.: Cornell University Press, 1955.

Blake, with an introduction and notes by Geoffrey Keynes. The Pitman Gallery. New York, London: Pitman Publishing Co., 1949.

Blake, William. *The Complete Writings of William Blake, with all the variant readings.* Geoffrey Keynes ed. London: The Nonesuch Press, 1947.

————. *The Marriage of Heaven and Hell.* Reproduced in facsimile from an original copy of the work printed and illuminated by the author between the years 1825-1827 and now in the Fitzwilliam Museum, Cambridge. With a note by Max Plowman. London & Toronto: J. M. Dent and Sons Ltd., 1927.

————. *Visions of the Daughters of Albion.* With an essay by John Middleton Murry. London: J. M. Dent and Sons Ltd., 1932.

Bloom, Harold. *Blake's Apocalypse.* New York: Doubleday-Anchor, 1963.

Blunt, Anthony. *The Art of William Blake.* New York: Columbia University Press, 1959.

Boehme, Jacob. *The Confessions*. London: Methuen and Co., Ltd., 1954.

———. *Six Theosophic Points*. Ann Arbor: University of Michigan Press (Ann Arbor Paperbacks), 1958.

Brehms. *Tierleben*. Bebilderte Volksaugabe in einem Band. Berlin: Safari-Verlag, 1961.

Bronowski, J. *William Blake, A Man Without a Mask*. Harmondsworth, Middlesex: Penguin Books Ltd., 1944.

Butterworth, Adeline M. *William Blake, Mystic*. Liverpool: The Liverpool Booksellers Company Ltd., 1911.

Damon, S. Foster. *William Blake: His Philosophy and Symbols*. New York: Peter Smith, 1947.

Freud, Sigmund. *A General Introduction to Psychoanalysis*. Garden City, N.Y.: Garden City Publishing Co., 1943.

Frye, Northrop, ed. *Blake, A Collection of Critical Essays*. New York, Prentice Hall, 1966.

———. *Fearful Symmetry*. Boston: Beacon Press, 1947.

Gilchrist, Alexander. *The Life of William Blake*. London: J. M. Dent and Sons, Ltd., 1945. Also in the first edition, London and Cambridge: MacMillan and Co., 1863.

Gilchrist, H. H. ed. *Anne Gilchrist, Her Life and Writings*. London, 1881.

Hamblen, Emily S. *On the Minor Prophecies of William Blake*. London and Toronto: J. M. Dent and Sons Ltd., 1930.

Hamilton, Edith. *Mythology*. Boston: Little Brown & Co., 1942.

Harding, M. Esther. *Psychic Energy*. Princeton: The Bollingen Series, Princeton Univ. Press, 1948.

Jacobi, Jolande. *Complex/Archetype/Symbol in the Psychology of C. G. Jung*. Princeton: The Bollingen Series, Princeton Univ. Press, 1959.

———. *The Psychology of C. G. Jung*. New Haven and London: Yale University Press, 1962.

Jenkins, Herbert. *William Blake: Studies of his Life and Personality*. London: Herbert Jenkins Ltd., 1911.

Jung, Carl G. *Answer to Job* (translated by R. F. C. Hull). New York: Meridian Books, 1960.

———. *Memories, Dreams, Reflections*. New York: Vintage Books, 1965.

――――. *Psychological Types*. London: Routledge & Kegan Paul Ltd., 1959.

――――. The following works are from the Bollingen Series XX; Princeton Univ. Press. The volume number in the Collected Works and the date of publication in parentheses follow the title in each case.

Aion. (CW 9, ii. 1959)

Archetypes and the Collective Unconscious. (CW 9, i. 1959)

Mysterium Coniunctionis. (CW 14. 1963)

Psychology and Alchemy. (CW 12. 1953)

Psychology and Religion: West and East (CW 11. 1958)

Structure and Dynamics of the Psyche. (CW 8. 1960)

Symbols of Transformation. (CW 5. 1956)

Two Essays on Analytical Psychology. (CW 7. 1953)

Langridge, Irene. *William Blake: A Study of his Life and Art Work*. London: George Bell & Sons, 1904.

Leonardo da Vinci. Reynal & Co., New York, 1956.

March, Arthur and Freeman, Ira. *The New World of Physics*. New York: Randon House, 1962.

Neumann, Erich. *Amor and Psyche*. (Translated from the German by Ralph Manheim.) Princeton: The Bollingen Series, Princeton Univ. Press, 1956.

――――. *The Archetypal World of Henry Moore*. (Translated from the German by R. F. C. Hull.) Princeton: The Bollingen Series, Princeton Univ. Press, 1955.

――――. *The Great Mother*. (Translated by Ralph Manheim.) Princeton: The Bollingen Series, Princeton Univ. Press, 1954.

Plato. *The Dialogues*. (Translated by Benjamin Jowett in *Great Books of the Western World*, Vol. 7.) Chicago: Encyclopedia Britannica, 1952.

Plowman, Max. *An Introduction to the Study of Blake*. London and Toronto: J. M. Dent and Sons Ltd., 1927.

Radin, Paul. *Primitive Religion*. New York: Dover Publications Inc., 1957.

Read, Herbert. *Education Through Art*. London: Faber and Faber, 1958.

Rudd, Margaret. *Organiz'd Innocence: The Story of Blake's Prophetic Books*. London: Routledge & Kegan Paul, 1956.

Schorer, Mark. *The Politics of Vision*. New York: Vintage (K-89), 1959.

Shelley, Percy Bysshe. *Poetry and Prose*. Oxford: The Clarendon Press, 1952.

Stephen, Beck and Snow, ed. *Victorian and Later English Poets*. New York: American Book Company, 1937.

Swedenborg, Emanuel. *Conjugal Love*. New York: Swedenborg Foundation, 1928.

————. *The Apocalypse Revealed*. London: The Swedenborg Society, 1851.

Swinburne, Algernon Charles. *William Blake*. London: William Heineman, Ltd., 1925.

Symons, Arthur. *William Blake*. London: Archibald Constable & Co., 1907.

Teilhard de Chardin, Pierre. *The Phenomenon of Man*. New York: Harper, 1959.

Watts, Alan W. *The Two Hands of God: The Myths of Polarity* New York: George Braziller, 1963.

Wicksteed, Joseph H. *Blake's Innocence and Experience*. London and Toronto: J. M. Dent and Sons Ltd., 1923.

Wilhelm, Richard (trans.). *The Secret of the Golden Flower: A Chinese Book of Life*. With a European commentary by C. G. Jung. London: Kegan Paul, Trench, Trubner & Co. Ltd., 1931.

Wilson, Mona. *The Life of William Blake*. London: Peter Davies Ltd., 1932.

Witcutt, W. P. *Blake: A Psychological Study*. London: Hollis & Carter, 1946.

Wright, Thomas. *The Life of William Blake*. 2 Vols. Olney, Bucks Thomas Wright, 1929.

C. MISCELLANEOUS

Duncan-Johnstone, L. A. "A Psychological Study of William Blake. Lecture No. 40, delivered December, 1945. London: *The Guild of Pastoral Psychology*, 1958.

Garnett, Richard. "William Blake." (A monograph in *The Port folio*, No. 22, October, 1895 (a monthly publication). London: Seeley and Co., Ltd.

Layard, John. "The Incest Taboo and the Virgin Archetype." In
    the *Eranos Yearbook,* Vol. VII. Zurich: Rhein Varlag, 1945.
Nurmi, Martin K. "Blake's Marriage of Heaven and Hell: A Criti-
    cal Study." *Kent State University Bulletin.* Kent, Ohio,
    April, 1957. (a monograph.)
Raine, Kathleen. "William Blake." A pamphlet supplement to
    British Book News, published for the British Council and
    the National Book League. London, New York, Toronto:
    Longmans Green & Co., 1951.

D.   UNPUBLISHED

von Franz, Marie-Louise. Lectures on *The Individuation Process
    in Fairy Tales,* delivered at the C. G. Jung Institute, Zurich,
    June, 1963.
Hannah, Barbara. Lectures on *Aion,* delivered at the C. G. Jung
    Institute, Zurich, April, 1963.

Acknowledgements

I want to thank Liliane Frey, H. K. Fierz, Barbara Hannah and William Willeford who encouraged me during the Zurich studies of *The Marriage of Heaven and Hell,* William H. Kennedy and M. Esther Harding who suggested that I expand the original thesis into a book, Vernon Brooks and Patricia Spindler for the editing, my daughter Judith Singer Sharp who had to remind me when to turn the light off at night during the writing and who read and criticized the manuscript, and the dear friend who helped me wait out the period from completion until publication.

I am also grateful to the following American and English publishers for permission to include quotations from copyrighted material in *The Unholy Bible:*

Princeton University Press for the many passages from *The Collected Works of C. G. Jung,* as well as the quotations from *Amor and Psyche* and *The Great Mother* by Erich Neumann, and from *Complex/Archtype/Symbol* by Jolande Jacobi;

Beacon Press for material from Northrop Frey's *Fearful Symmetry;*

267

George Braziller for the passages from *The Two Hands of God* by Alan Watts;

Brown University Press for quoted matter from S. Foster Damon's *A Blake Dictionary;*

Doubleday & Company for material from *Blake's Apocalypse* by Harold Bloom;

Harper & Row for a paragraph from Teilard de Chardin's *The Phenomenon of Man;*

Little Brown & Company for passages from Edith Hamilton's *Mythology;*

Random House for *The New World of Physics* by March and Freeman, and *Memories, Dreams, Reflections* by C. G. Jung;

Reynal & Company for the quotation from *Leonardo da Vinci;*

Peter Smith for passages from S. Foster Damon's *William Blake;*

Yale University Press for a quotation from *The Psychology of C. G. Jung* by Jolande Jacobi;

J. M. Dent & Sons for material from Max Plowman's *Introduction to the Study of Blake* and Emily S. Hamblen's *On the Minor Prophecies of William Blake;*

Herbert Jenkins, Ltd., for material from *William Blake* by Herbert Jenkins;

Hollis & Carter for the passage from W. P. Witcutt's *Blake;*

and Routledge and Kegan Paul for the quotation from *Organiz'd Innocence* by Margaret Rudd.

The Pierpont Morgan Library of New York City has kindly provided photographs of the twenty-four plates of Blake's *Marriage of Heaven and Hell* for use in this volume, and I am grateful to them for this courtesy.

Index

Other Titles from Sigo Press

The Unholy Bible *by June Singer*
$32.00 cloth, $14.95 paper

Emotional Child Abuse *by Joel Covitz*
$24.95 cloth, $13.95 paper

Dreams of a Woman *by Shelia Moon*
$27.50 cloth, $12.95 paper

Androgyny *by June Singer*
$24.95 cloth, $13.95 paper

The Dream-The Vision of the Night *by Max Zeller*
$21.95 cloth, $13.95 paper

Sandplay Studies *by Bradway et al.*
$27.50 cloth, $16.95 paper

Symbols Come Alive in the Sand *by Evelyn Dundas*
$12.95 paper

Inner World of Childhood *by Frances G. Wickes*
$27.50 cloth, $14.95 paper

Inner World of Man *by Frances G. Wickes*
$27.50 cloth, $14.95 paper

Inner World of Choice *by Frances G. Wickes*
$27.50 cloth, $14.95 paper

*Available from SIGO PRESS, 25 New Chardon Street, #8748A,
Boston, Massachusetts, 02114. tel. (617) 526-7064*

*In England: Element Books, Ltd., Longmead, Shaftesbury, Dorset,
SP7 8PL. tel. (0747) 51339, Shaftesbury.*